Phillip K. Trocki

Modern Curriculum Press
Parsippany

EXECUTIVE EDITOR   Wendy Whitnah

PROJECT EDITOR   Diane Dzamtovski

EDITORIAL DEVELOPMENT
DESIGN AND PRODUCTION   The Hampton-Brown Company

ILLUSTRATORS   Anthony Accardo, Joe Boddy, Roberta Collier-Morales, Mark Farina,
Sandra Forrest, Carlos Freire, Meryl Henderson, Jane McCreary,
Masami Miyamoto, Deborah Morse, Rik Olson, Doug Roy, John Sandford,
Rosalind Solomon.

PHOTO CREDITS   5, Boyd Norton/Comstock; 6, Uniphoto/Pictor; 9, Uniphoto/Pictor;
17, Prenzel/Animals Animals; 29, Curt Anderson/Courtesy of Schmitt Music Co.;
33, Nancy Brown/Image Bank; 41, Lynn M. Stone/Image Bank;
43, David de Lossy/Image Bank; 45, Andy Caulfield/Image Bank;
50, Lawrence Migdale; 61, Michael S. Thompson/Comstock; 64, Photo Researchers;
65, Archive Photos; 69, David Ryan/Uniphoto; 72, Comstock;
77, Michael P. Gadomski/Photo Researchers; 85, Mary Kate Denny/Photo Edit;
101, Michael Skott/Image Bank; 103, Grant Huntington;
105, Deborah Gilbert/Image Bank; 113, Todd Eberle;
116, Michael S. Thompson/Comstock; 129, Chris Alan Wilton/Image Bank;
133, Rafael Macia/Photo Researchers; 136, Paul Shambroom/Photo Researchers;
137, Boyd Norton/Comstock.

COVER DESIGN   The Hampton-Brown Company
COVER PHOTO   Romilly Lockyer/Image Bank

Typefaces for the manuscript and cursive type in this book were provided
by Zaner-Bloser, Inc., Columbus, Ohio, copyright, 1993.

Copyright © 1994 by Modern Curriculum Press, Inc.

MODERN CURRICULUM PRESS
299 Jefferson Road, Parsippany, NJ 07054

ISBN 0-8136-2842-3

3 4 5 6 7 8 9 10 PO OO 99 98 97

Table of Contents

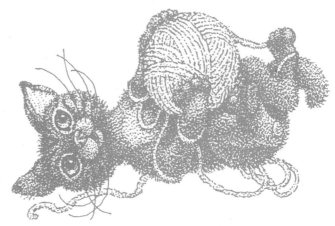

Spelling Workout—Our Philosophy

Integration of Spelling with Reading and Writing

In each core lesson for *Spelling Workout,* students read spelling words in context in a variety of expository selections and genre, including poetry, riddles, and stories. The reading selections provide opportunities for reading across the curriculum, focusing on the subject areas of science, social studies, health, language arts, music, and art.

After students read the selection and practice writing their spelling words, they use List Words to help them write about a related topic in a variety of forms and innovations such as poems, letters, descriptive writings, newspaper articles, advertisements, jokes, and posters. A proofreading exercise is also provided for each lesson to help students apply the writing process to their own writings and reinforce the use of spelling words in context.

The study of spelling should not be limited to a specific time in the school day. Use opportunities throughout the day to reinforce and maintain spelling skills by integrating spelling with other curriculum areas. Point out spelling words in books, texts, and the student's own writing. Encourage students to write, as they practice spelling through writing. Provide opportunities for writing with a purpose.

Phonics-Based Instructional Design

Spelling Workout takes a solid phonic and structural analysis approach to encoding. The close tie between spelling and phonics allows each to reinforce the other. *Spelling Workout* correlates closely to *MCP Phonics, MCP Discovery Phonics I* and *II,* and other phonics material published by Modern Curriculum Press, although these programs are complete within themselves and can be used independently. In addition, lessons are correlated to the phonics strategies in Silver Burdett Ginn *New Dimensions in the World of Reading* Teacher's Editions.

Research-Based Teaching Strategies

Spelling Workout utilizes a test-study-test method of teaching spelling. The student first takes a pretest of words that have not yet been introduced. Under the direction of the teacher, the student then self-corrects the test, rewriting correctly any word that has been missed. This approach not only provides an opportunity to determine how many words a student can already spell but also allows students to analyze spelling mistakes. In the process students also discover patterns that make it easier to spell List Words. Students study the words as they work through practice exercises, and then reassess their spelling by taking a final test.

High-Utility List Words

The words used in *Spelling Workout* have been chosen for their frequency in students' written and oral vocabularies, their relationships to subject areas, and for structural as well as phonetic generalizations. Each List Word has been cross-referenced with one or more of the following:

Carroll, Davies, and Richman. *The American Heritage Word Frequency Book*

Dale and O'Rourke. *The Living Word Vocabulary*

Dolch. *220 Basic Sight Words*

Fry, Polk, and Fountoukidis. "Spelling Demons—197 Words Frequently Misspelled by Elementary Students"

Green and Loomer. *The New Iowa Spelling Scale*

Harris and Jacobson. *Basic Elementary Reading Vocabularies*

Hanna. *Phoneme Grapheme Correspondences as Cues to Spelling Improvement*

Hillerich. *A Written Vocabulary of Elementary Children*

Kucera and Francis. *Computational Analysis of Present-Day American English*

Rinsland. *A Basic Vocabulary of Elementary Children*

Sakiey and Fry. *3000 Instant Words*

Thomas. "3000 Words Most Frequently Written"

Thomas. "200 Words Most Frequently Misspelled"

A Format That Results in Success

Spelling Workout treats spelling as a developmental process. Students progress in stages, much as they learn to speak and read. In *Spelling Workout,* they move gradually from simple sound/letter relationships to strategies involving more complex word-structure patterns. The use of a sports format motivates and maintains student interest.

Sample Core Lesson

- A **Warm Up** reading selection in each lesson uses spelling words in context.

- **On Your Mark** guides students to take the pretest and self-assess their spelling.

- The "Coach" explains spelling patterns in **Pep Talk,** providing a lesson focus.

- The **List Words** box contains high-frequency spelling words.

- **Game Plan** gives students an opportunity to practice new words.

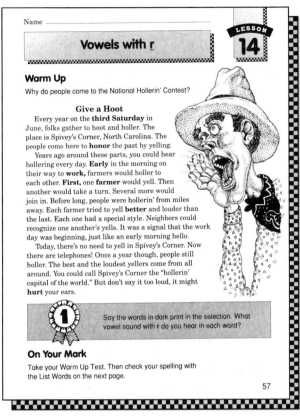

Name _____

Vowels with r

LESSON 14

Warm Up

Why do people come to the National Hollerin' Contest?

Give a Hoot

Every year on the **third Saturday** in June, folks gather to hoot and holler. The place is Spivey's Corner, North Carolina. The people come here to **honor** the past by yelling.

Years ago around these parts, you could hear hollering every day. **Early** in the morning on their way to **work,** farmers would holler to each other. **First,** one **farmer** would yell. Then another would take a turn. Several more would join in. Before long, people were hollerin' from miles away. Each farmer tried to yell **better** and louder than the last. Each one had a special style. Neighbors could recognize one another's yells. It was a signal that the work day was beginning, just like an early morning hello.

Today, there's no need to yell in Spivey's Corner. Now there are telephones! Once a year though, people still holler. The best and the loudest yellers come from all around. You could call Spivey's Corner the "hollerin' capital of the world." But don't say it too loud, it might **hurt** your ears.

1 Say the words in dark print in the selection. What vowel sound with r do you hear in each word?

On Your Mark

Take your Warm Up Test. Then check your spelling with the List Words on the next page.

57

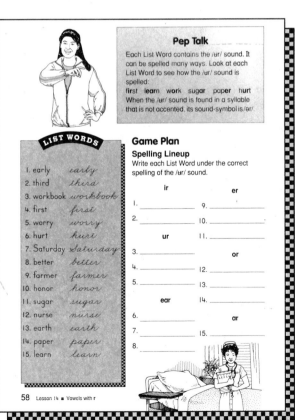

Pep Talk

Each List Word contains the /ʉr/ sound. It can be spelled many ways. Look at each List Word to see how the /ʉr/ sound is spelled:

first learn work sugar paper hurt

When the /ʉr/ sound is found in a syllable that is not accented, its sound-symbol is/ər/.

LIST WORDS

1. early — *early*
2. third — *third*
3. workbook — *workbook*
4. first — *first*
5. worry — *worry*
6. hurt — *hurt*
7. Saturday — *Saturday*
8. better — *better*
9. farmer — *farmer*
10. honor — *honor*
11. sugar — *sugar*
12. nurse — *nurse*
13. earth — *earth*
14. paper — *paper*
15. learn — *learn*

Game Plan

Spelling Lineup

Write each List Word under the correct spelling of the /ʉr/ sound.

ir		er
1. _____		9. _____
2. _____		10. _____
ur		11. _____
3. _____		or
4. _____		12. _____
5. _____		13. _____
ear		14. _____
6. _____		ar
7. _____		15. _____
8. _____		

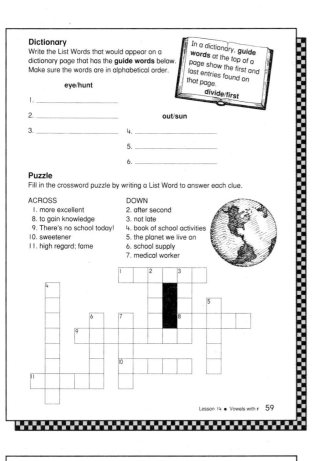

Dictionary

Write the List Words that would appear on a dictionary page that has the **guide words** below. Make sure the words are in alphabetical order.

In a dictionary, **guide words** at the top of a page show the first and last entries found on that page.

divide/first

eye/hunt

1. _____

2. _____

out/sun

3. _____   4. _____

5. _____

6. _____

Puzzle

Fill in the crossword puzzle by writing a List Word to answer each clue.

ACROSS
1. more excellent
8. to gain knowledge
9. There's no school today!
10. sweetener
11. high regard; fame

DOWN
2. after second
3. not late
4. book of school activities
5. the planet we live on
6. school supply
7. medical worker

Lesson 14 ■ Vowels with r   59

Flex Your Spelling Muscles

Writing

Use the List Words to create a poster to advertise a contest you know about or would like to have. Remember to include important information such as what kind of contest it is, and when and where it will take place.

Proofreading

Each sentence below has two mistakes. Use the proofreading marks to fix each mistake. Write the misspelled List Words on the lines.

Proofreading Marks
⌒ spelling mistake
⊙ add period

1. Many years ago, people in Africa used drums instead of papir to communicate

1. _____

2. They could lurn about other people bettur and faster with drums.

2. _____
_____

3. The drums could tell if someone was hert and if a doctor was needed

3. _____

4. The drums held a special place of honar among the people

4. _____

Now proofread your poster. Fix any mistakes.

Go for the Goal

Take your Final Test. Then fill in your Scoreboard. Send your mistakes to the Word Locker.

SCOREBOARD
number correct   number wrong

★ ★ ★ ★ ★ ★ ★ ★ **All-Star Words** ★ ★ ★ ★ ★ ★ ★ ★

churn   earn   dessert   squirm   afford

Write a sentence for each word, then erase the All-Star Word. Trade papers with a partner. Write the word that belongs in each blank.

60   Lesson 14 ■ Vowels with r

• *A variety of activities that emphasize word meaning provide many opportunities to practice List Words.*

• *Students use dictionary skills.*

• *Word puzzles and games help to motivate students.*

• ***Flex Your Spelling Muscles*** *encourages students to practice and apply the List Words in different contexts.*

• ***Writing*** *activities provide opportunities for students to write their spelling words in a variety of writing forms and genres.*

• ***Proofreading*** *practice builds proofreading proficiency and encourages students to check their own writing.*

• ***Go for the Goal*** *encourages self-assessment of students' final test by encouraging students to record their scores in the Scoreboard. Students keep track of words they are having difficulty with by writing them in a Word Locker provided in the Teacher's Edition as a reproducible sheet.*

• ***All-Star Words*** *offer more challenging words with similar spelling patterns. Students are given opportunities to practice the words with a partner.*

Sample Review Lesson

- The **Instant Replay** lesson allows students to review what they've learned.

- **Time Out,** signaled by the "Coach," briefly reviews the spelling patterns used in the previous five lessons.

- **Check Your Word Locker** suggests that students evaluate words they are having trouble with by reviewing the words they've written in their Word Locker. A partner activity provides practice for those words in a variety of learning modalities — kinesthetic, visual, and auditory.

- A variety of activities provide practice and review of selected List Words from the previous lessons.

- **Go for the Goal** encourages self-assessment of students' **Final Replay Test** by encouraging students to record their scores in the Scoreboard.

- **Clean Out Your Word Locker** provides further practice for students' troublesome words by suggesting that students write the words in a **Spelling Notebook,** a student-created word book that students can refer to whenever they need to check their spelling, or when they need a resource for writing.

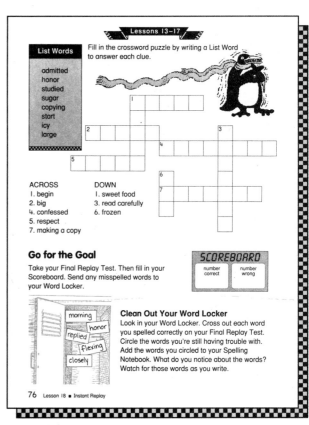

Spelling Workout in the Classroom

Classroom Management

Spelling Workout is designed as a flexible instructional program. The following plans are two ways the program can be taught.

The 5–day Plan
Day 1 – Warm Up and Warm Up Test
Day 2 and 3 – Game Plan
Day 4 – Flex Your Spelling Muscles
Day 5 – Final Test

The 3–day Plan
Day 1 – Warm Up and Warm Up Test/Game Plan
Day 2 – Game Plan/Flex Your Spelling Muscles
Day 3 – Final Test

Testing

Testing is accomplished in several ways. A pretest is administered after reading the Warm Up selection and a final test at the end of each lesson. Dictation sentences for each pretest and final test are provided.

Research suggests that students benefit from correcting their own pretests. After the pretest has been administered, have students self-correct their tests by checking the words against the List Words. You may also want to guide students by reading each letter of the word, asking students to point to each letter and circle any incorrect letters. Then have students rewrite each word correctly.

Tests for Instant Replay lessons are provided in the Teacher's Edition as reproducibles following each lesson. These tests provide not only an evaluation tool for teachers, but also added practice in taking standardized tests for students.

Individualizing Instruction

All-Star Words are included in every core lesson as a challenge for better spellers and to provide extension and enrichment for all students.

Review pages called Instant Replay lessons reinforce correct spelling of difficult words from previous lessons.

A reproducible sheet called Word Locker allows each student to analyze spelling errors and practice writing troublesome words independently.

A reproducible individual Student Record Chart provided in the Teacher's Edition allows students to record their test scores.

Ideas for meeting the needs of ESL students are provided.

Dictionary

In the back of each student book is a comprehensive dictionary with definitions of all List Words and All-Star Words. Students will have this resource at their fingertips for any assignment.

The Teacher's Edition —Everything You Need!

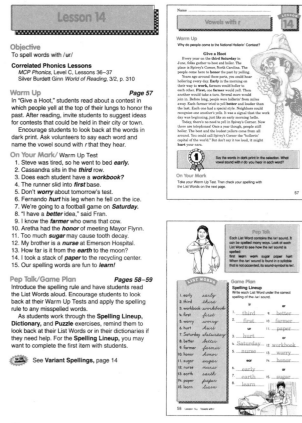

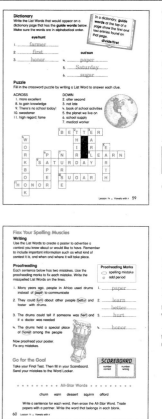

- *The goals of each core lesson are clearly stated.*

- *Spelling lessons are correlated to MCP Phonics, MCP Discovery Phonics I and II, and Silver Burdett Ginn New Dimensions in the World of Reading. Page references refer to Teacher's Edition pages.*

- *Ideas for introducing and setting a purpose for reading are given for each reading selection.*

- *A **Warm Up Test,** or pretest, is administered before the start of each lesson. Dictation sentences are provided.*

- *Concise teaching notes give guidance for working through the lesson.*

- *Ideas for meeting the needs of **ESL** students are given.*

- ***Spelling Strategy** activities provide additional support for reinforcing and analyzing spelling patterns.*

- *Suggestions for ways students can publish their writing complete the writing process.*

- *A **Writer's Corner** extends the content of each reading selection by suggesting ways in which students can explore real-world writing.*

- *A **Final Test** is administered at the end of the lesson. Dictation sentences are provided.*

Instant Replay Test

Side A

Read each sentence and set of words. Fill in the circle next to the word that is spelled correctly to complete the sentence.

1. Mark makes his bed every _____.
   - (a) morening
   - (b) mornin
   - (c) mornning
   - (d) morning

2. It is an _____ to receive this award.
   - (a) honor
   - (b) awner
   - (c) honer
   - (d) onar

3. The shy boy _____ quietly.
   - (a) replied
   - (b) repliede
   - (c) repelied
   - (d) replide

4. My bike _____ on the wet road.
   - (a) sliped
   - (b) slipt
   - (c) slippt
   - (d) slipped

5. The baby will _____ to walk soon.
   - (a) learn
   - (b) lernn
   - (c) lern
   - (d) lurn

6. Carmen planted a seed in the _____.
   - (a) erth
   - (b) erthe
   - (c) urth
   - (d) earth

7. An elephant is a _____ jungle animal.
   - (a) larej
   - (b) larg
   - (c) large
   - (d) larje

8. Tanya _____ for the spelling test.
   - (a) studyed
   - (b) studied
   - (c) studdied
   - (d) studeed

LESSON 18

- *Instant Replay lessons review spelling objectives, give guidance for further practice of List Words, and provide dictation sentences for a **Final Replay Test**. Reproducible two-page standardized tests to help prepare students for test-taking are supplied for assessment purposes after each Instant Replay lesson.*

3

TAKE IT HOME

Your child has learned to spell many new words and would like to share them with you and your family. Here are some great ways to turn your child's spelling review of Lessons 13–17 into family fun!

Happily Ever After!

With a little help from family members, your child can use the spelling words to write a story. You can make up a story of your own, or retell an old favorite. Your child will be spelling "happily ever after!"

One lovely morning before the sun was up, the first swimmer slipped into the icy water. A noisy

large   morning   start
clear   before   appear   early
sugar   first   earth   honor
learn   rained   copying
studied   hurried   worried
replied   swimmer   slipped
biggest   beginning   winner
admitted   living   nicely
noisy   lovely   icy   hoped

64 Take It Home Master ■ Lessons 13–17

Spelling Enrichment

Bulletin-Board Suggestion

Slices of Spelling Success Display uncovered pizza slices made of brown construction paper for each member of the class. The names of students should appear on the slices. Using brightly colored construction paper, prepare circles, triangles, and squiggles that represent toppings for a pizza. Each time a student seeks help spelling a word, have the student use a dictionary to write the correct spelling of the word onto a shape. Then allow students to add each topping to their own slice of pizza. The slices will form personal spelling lists.

Group Practice

Fill-In Write spelling words on the board. Omit some of the letters and replace them with dashes. Have the first student in Row One come to the board to fill in any of the missing letters in any of the words. Then have the first student in Row Two continue the procedure. Continue having students in each row take turns coming up to the board to fill in letters until all the words are completed. Any student who is able to correctly fill in a word earns a point for his or her row. The row with the most points at the end of the game wins.

Erase Write List Words on the board. Then ask the class to put their heads down while you call on a student to come to the board and erase one of the words. This student then calls on a class member to identify the erased word. The identified word is then restored and the student who correctly identified the erasure can be the person who erases next.

Crossword Relay First draw a large grid on the board. Then, divide the class into several teams. Teams compete against each other to form separate crossword puzzles on the board. Individuals on each team take turns racing against members of the other teams to join List Words until all possibilities have been exhausted. A List Word may appear on each crossword puzzle only once. The winning team is the team whose crossword puzzle contains the greatest number of correctly spelled List Words or the team who finishes first.

Scramble Prepare letter cards sufficient to spell all the List Words. Distribute letter cards to all students. Some students may be given more than one letter card. The teacher then calls out a List Word. Students holding the letters contained in the word race to the front of the class to form the word by standing in the appropriate sequence with their letter cards.

Proofreading Relay Write two columns of misspelled List Words on the board. Although the errors can differ, be sure that each list has the same number of errors. Divide the class into two teams and assign each team to a different column. Teams then compete against each other to correct their assigned lists by team members taking turns erasing and replacing an appropriate letter. Each member may correct only one letter per turn. The team that corrects its entire word list first wins.

Detective Call on a student to be a detective. The detective must choose a spelling word from the list and think of a structural clue, definition, or synonym that will help classmates identify it. The detective then states the clue using the format, "I spy a word that . . . ." Students are called on to guess and spell the mystery word. Whoever answers correctly gets to take a turn being the detective.

Spelling Tic-Tac-Toe Draw a tic-tac-toe square on the board. Divide the class into X and O teams. Take turns dictating spelling words to members of each team. If the word is spelled correctly, allow the team member to place an X or O on the square. The first team to place three X's or O's in a row wins.

Words of Fortune Have students put their heads down while you write a spelling word on the board in large letters. Then cover each letter with a sheet of sturdy paper. The paper can be fastened to the board with magnets. Call on a student to guess any letter of the alphabet they think may be hidden. If that particular letter is hidden, then reveal the letter in every place where it appears in the word by removing the paper.

The student continues to guess letters until an incorrect guess is made or the word is revealed. In the event that an incorrect guess is made, a different student continues the game. Continue the game until every List Word has been hidden and then revealed.

Dictionary Activities

Around the World Designate the first person in the first row to be the traveler. The traveler must stand next to the student seated behind him or her. Then dictate any letter of the alphabet at random. Instruct the two students to quickly name the letter of the alphabet that precedes the given letter. The student who is first to respond with the correct answer

- *Reproducible **Take It Home Masters** that also follow each Instant Replay lesson strengthen the school-home connection by providing ideas for parents and students for additional practice at home.*

- *Suggested games and group activities make spelling more fun.*

Spelling Strategies for Your ESL Students

You may want to try some of these suggestions to help you promote successful language learning for ESL students.

- Prompt use of spelling words by showing pictures or objects that relate to the topic of each selection. Invite students to discuss the picture or object.
- Demonstrate actions or act out words. Encourage students to do the same.
- Read each selection aloud before asking students to read it independently.
- Define words in context and allow students to offer their own meanings of words.
- Make the meanings of words concrete by naming objects or pictures, role-playing, or pantomiming.

Spelling is the relationship between sounds and letters. Learning to spell words in English is an interesting challenge for English First Language speakers as well as English as a Second Language speakers. You may want to adapt some of the following activities to accommodate the needs of your students—both native and non-English speakers.

Rhymes and Songs

Use rhymes, songs, poems, or chants to introduce new letter sounds and spelling words. Repeat the rhyme or song several times during the day or week, having students listen to you first, then repeat back to you line by line. To enhance learning for visual learners in your classroom and provide opportunities for pointing out letter combinations and their sounds, you may want to write the rhyme, song, poem, or chant on the board. As you examine the words, students can easily see similarities and differences among them. Encourage volunteers to select and recite a rhyme or sing a song for the class. Students may enjoy some of the selections in *Miss Mary Mack and Other Children's Street Rhymes* by Joanna Cole and Stephanie Calmenson or *And the Green Grass Grew All Around* by Alvin Schwartz.

Student Dictation

To take advantage of individual students' known vocabulary, suggest that students build their own sentences incorporating the List Words. For example:
> *Mary ran.*
> *Mary ran away.*
> *Mary ran away quickly.*

Sentence building can expand students' knowledge of how to spell words and of how to notice language patterns, learn descriptive words, and so on.

Words in Context

Using words in context sentences will aid students' mastery of new vocabulary.

- Say several sentences using the List Words in context and have students repeat after you. Encourage more proficient students to make up sentences using List Words that you suggest.
- Write cloze sentences on the board and have students help you complete them with the List Words.

Point out the spelling patterns in the words, using colored chalk to underline or circle the elements.

Oral Drills

Use oral drills to help students make associations among sounds and the letters that represent them. You might use oral drills at listening stations to reinforce the language, allowing ESL students to listen to the drills at their own pace.

Spelling Aloud Say each List Word and have students repeat the word. Next, write it on the board as you name each letter, then say the word again as you track the letters and sound by sweeping your hand under the word. Call attention to spelling changes for words to which endings or suffixes were added. For words with more than one syllable, emphasize each syllable as you write, encouraging students to clap out the syllables. Ask volunteers to repeat the procedure.

Variant Spellings For a group of words that contain the same vowel sound, but variant spellings, write an example on the board, say the word, and then present other words in that word family *(cake: rake, bake, lake)*. Point out the sound and the letter(s) that stand for the sound. Then add words to the list that have the same vowel sound *(play, say, day)*. Say pairs of words *(cake, play)* as you point to them, and identify the vowel sound and the different letters that represent the sound *(long a: a_e, ay)*. Ask volunteers to select a different pair of words and repeat the procedure.

Vary this activity by drawing a chart on the board that shows the variant spellings for a sound. Invite students to add words under the correct spelling pattern. Provide a list of words for students to choose from to help those ESL students with limited vocabularies.

Categorizing   To help students discriminate among consonant sounds and spellings, have them help you categorize words with single consonant sounds and consonant blends or digraphs. For example, ask students to close their eyes so that they may focus solely on the sounds in the words, and then pronounce *smart, smile, spend,* and *special.* Next, pronounce the words as you write them on the board. After spelling each word, create two columns—one for *sm,* one for *sp.* Have volunteers pronounce each word, decide which column it fits under, and write the word in the correct column. Encourage students to add to the columns any other words they know that have those consonant blends.

To focus on initial, medial, or final consonant sounds, point out the position of the consonant blends or digraphs in the List Words. Have students find and list the words under columns labeled *Beginning, Middle, End.*

Tape Recording   Encourage students to work with a partner or their group to practice their spelling words. If a tape recorder is available, students can practice at their own pace by taking turns recording the words, playing back the tape, and writing each word they hear. Students can then help each other check their spelling against their *Spelling Workout* books. Observe as needed to be sure students are spelling the words correctly.

Comparing/Contrasting   To help students focus on word parts, write List Words with prefixes or suffixes on the board and have volunteers circle, underline, or draw a line between the prefix or suffix and its root word. Review the meaning of each root word, then invite students to work with their group to write two sentences: one using just the root word; the other using the root word with its prefix or suffix. For example: *My favorite mystery was* due *at the library Monday afternoon. By Tuesday afternoon the book was* overdue! Or, *You can* depend *on Jen to arrive for softball practice on time. She is* dependable. Have students contrast the two sentences, encouraging them to tell how the prefix or suffix changed the meaning of the root word.

Questions/Answers   Write List Words on the board and ask pairs of students to brainstorm questions or answers about the words, such as "Which word names more than one? How do you know?" (foxes, *an* es *was added at the end)* or, "Which word tells that something belongs to the children? How do you know?" *(children's is spelled with an 's)*

Games

You may want to invite students to participate in these activities.

Picture Clues   Students can work with a partner to draw pictures or cut pictures out of magazines that represent the List Words, then trade papers and label each other's pictures. Encourage students to check each other's spelling against their *Spelling Workout* books.

Or, you can present magazine cutouts or items that picture the List Words. As you display each picture or item, say the word clearly and then write it on the board as you spell it aloud. Non-English speakers may wish to know the translation of the word in their native language so that they can mentally connect the new word with a familiar one. Students may also find similarities in the spellings of the words.

Letter Cards   Have students create letter cards for vowels, vowel digraphs, consonants, consonant blends and digraphs, and so on. Then say a List Word and have students show the card that has the letters representing the sound for the vowels or consonants in that word as they repeat and spell the word after you. Students can use their cards independently as they work with their group.

Charades/Pantomime   Students can use gestures and actions to act out the List Words. To receive credit for a correctly guessed word, players must spell the word correctly. Such activities can be played in pairs so that beginning English speakers will not feel pressured. If necessary, translate the words into students' native languages so that they understand the meanings of the words before attempting to act them out.

Change or No Change   Have students make flash cards for root words and endings. One student holds up a root word; another holds up an ending. The class says "Change" or "No Change" to describe what happens when the root word and ending are combined. Encourage students to spell the word with its ending added.

Scope and Sequence for MCP Spelling Workout

Skills	Level A	Level B	Level C	Level D	Level E	Level F	Level G	Level H
Consonants	1–12	1–2	1–2	1	1	1, 7, 9	RC	RC
Short Vowels	14–18	3–5	4	2	RC	RC	RC	RC
Long Vowels	20–23	7–11	5, 7	3	RC	RC	RC	RC
Consonant Blends/Clusters	26–28	13–14	8–9 29	5, 7	RC	RC	RC	RC
y as a Vowel	29–30	15–16	10–11	RC	RC	RC	RC	RC
Consonant Digraphs—**th, ch, sh, wh, ck**	32–33	28–29 32	27–28 31	9	RC	RC	RC	RC
Vowel Digraphs		25–26 33	21–22 25	19–22	7–10	11 13–16 19	25	RC
R–Controlled Vowels		19–20	13–14	8	RC	RC	RC	RC
Diphthongs	24	27	26	22–23	11	16–17	RC	RC
Silent Consonants			23	10	4	4–5	RC	RC
Hard and Soft **c** and **g**		32	3	4	2	2	RC	RC
Plurals			19–20	25–27 29	33–34	33	RC	RC
Prefixes		34	32–33	31–32	13–17	20–23 25	7–8	7–11 19–20
Suffixes	34–35	21–23	15–17	13–17	25–29 31–32	26–29 31–32	9 13–14 16, 26	5, 25–27
Contractions		17	34	28	23	RC	RC	RC
Possessives				28–29	23	RC	RC	RC
Compound Words				33	19	RC	RC	RC
Synonyms/Antonyms				34	RC	RC	RC	RC
Homonyms		35	35	35	RC	RC	RC	RC
Spellings of /f/ **f, ff, ph, gh**				11	3	3	RC	RC
Syllables					20–23	RC	RC	RC
Commonly Misspelled Words					35	34	17, 35	17, 29 35
Abbreviations						35	RC	RC
Latin Roots							11, 15 31	13–16

Skills	Level A	Level B	Level C	Level D	Level E	Level F	Level G	Level H
Words with French or Spanish Derivations							10, 29	RC
Words of Latin/French/Greek Origin								21–23 28
Latin Prefixes							33	RC
List Words Related to Specific Curriculum Areas							19–23 28, 32	31–34
Vocabulary Development	●	●	●	●	●	●	●	●
Dictionary	●	●	●	●	●	●	●	●
Writing	●	●	●	●	●	●	●	●
Proofreading	●	●	●	●	●	●	●	●
Literature Selections	●	●	●	●	●	●	●	●
All-Star Words	●	●	●	●	●	●	●	●
Review Tests in Standardized Format	●	●	●	●	●	●	●	●

Spelling Through Writing

	Level A	Level B	Level C	Level D	Level E	Level F	Level G	Level H
Poetry	●	●	●	●	●	●	●	●
Narrative Writings	●	●	●	●	●	●	●	●
Descriptive Writings	●	●	●	●	●	●	●	●
Expository Writings	●	●	●	●	●	●	●	●
Persuasive Writings				●	●	●		
Notes/Letters	●	●	●		●	●		●
Riddles/Jokes	●		●					
Recipes	●	●	●			●	●	
Newspaper Articles		●	●	●	●	●		●
Conversations/Dialogues				●	●	●		●
Menus						●	●	
Questionnaires		●			●	●	●	●
Logs/Journals			●	●	●	●	●	
Advertisements		●	●	●	●	●	●	●
Reports					●	●	●	●
Literary Devices							●	●
Scripts							●	●
Speeches						●		●

Numbers in chart indicate lesson numbers
RC = reinforced in other contexts
● = found throughout

Lesson 1

Objective

To spell words with single and double consonants

Correlated Phonics Lessons

MCP Phonics, Level C, Lessons 2–4

Silver Burdett Ginn *World of Reading,* 3/1, p. 188

Warm Up   *Page 5*

In this selection, students read to find out about the world's biggest bird. After reading, ask them to compare ostriches with other large birds they may be familiar with, such as turkeys and eagles.

Ask volunteers to say the words in dark print and identify the consonant sounds they hear.

On Your Mark/Warm Up Test

1. Jim is a very *fast* runner.
2. The robin is a beautiful *bird.*
3. There are *nine* players on a baseball team.
4. What an interesting *life* your uncle has had!
5. It has been a long time *since* we had a picnic.
6. Did too much watering *kill* that plant?
7. Danielle *cannot* come to my party.
8. Father had a boiled *egg* for breakfast.
9. The *water* in the pond is very cold.
10. How did the pencil *mark* get on your shirt?
11. Each *person* brought a sandwich for lunch.
12. That building is *quite* large.
13. There is a playground *beside* our school.
14. Did your *sister* design the costumes for the play?
15. A large *forest* covered the mountain.

Pep Talk/Game Plan   *Pages 6–7*

You may want to name each new coach for students. Knowing their names will add interest to the lessons.

Introduce the spelling rule and have students read the List Words aloud. Encourage students to look back at their Warm Up Tests and apply the spelling rule to any misspelled words.

As students work through the **Spelling Lineup, Missing Letters, Word Parts,** and **Rhyming** exercises, remind them to look back at their List Words or in their dictionaries if they need help.

Point out to students that each syllable in a two-syllable word has its own vowel sound, and contrast the number of vowel sounds in pairs of words such as *quite* and *sister.* For the **Spelling Lineup,** remind students to listen for one or more vowel sounds to determine how many syllables a word has.

 See **Student Dictation,** page 14

18

A Big Bird!

What has feathers, runs **fast**, and is taller than the tallest basketball player? It's the biggest **bird** in the world, the ostrich. This giant bird can grow to be almost **nine** feet tall. The largest ones live in North Africa. Some people think that ostriches bury their heads in the sand. They say that the ostriches are hiding from their enemies.

Just think about these facts. An ostrich can weigh as much as 350 pounds. One kick from an ostrich foot can **kill** a **person**. As you can see, the ostrich has no reason to hide from anything. It can run faster than its enemies anyway. The ostrich does have one problem. It **cannot** fly!

Ostrich hens lay their eggs in holes in the sand. One **egg** is often larger than a softball. The shell of the egg is very strong. It won't break even if a person stands on it. If you wanted to hard-boil one egg, you'd need plenty of **water**. When it was done, you could use it to make as much egg salad as two dozen chicken eggs would make. That's **quite** a meal!

 Say the words in dark print in the selection. What consonant sounds do you hear?

On Your Mark

Take your Warm Up Test. Then check your spelling with the List Words on the next page.

5

Pep Talk

The alphabet has two kinds of letters. The **vowels** are **a, e, i, o, u,** and sometimes **y** and **w.** All the other letters are **consonants.** Read the List Words. Some words have more than one syllable, as in <u>forest</u>. Notice that each syllable has its own vowel sound.

LIST WORDS

1. fast   *fast*
2. bird   *bird*
3. nine   *nine*
4. life   *life*
5. since   *since*
6. kill   *kill*
7. cannot *cannot*
8. egg   *egg*
9. water   *water*
10. mark   *mark*
11. person *person*
12. quite *quite*
13. beside *beside*
14. sister *sister*
15. forest *forest*

Game Plan

Spelling Lineup

Write the List Words that have one syllable.

1. __fast__   6. __kill__
2. __bird__   7. __egg__
3. __nine__   8. __mark__
4. __life__   9. __quite__
5. __since__

Write the List Words that have two syllables.

10. __cannot__
11. __water__
12. __person__
13. __beside__
14. __sister__
15. __forest__

Missing Letters

Write letters to finish the List Words in the sentences. Then write the List Words.

1. The ostrich is a large b i r d . _____bird_____
2. Some ostriches are n i n e feet tall. _____nine_____
3. That's taller than a very tall p e r s o n . _____person_____
4. An ostrich e g g weighs about three pounds! _____egg_____
5. An ostrich can k i l l an enemy with one kick. _____kill_____

Word Parts

A compound word is a word made by joining two or more words. Find the compound word in each sentence. Circle the part of the compound word that spells a List Word. Then write the List Word.

1. (Break)fast is a morning meal. _____fast_____
2. A (life)guard keeps swimmers safe. _____life_____
3. A book(mark) keeps my place in a book. _____mark_____
4. A robin might wash in a (bird)bath. _____bird_____
5. My new coat is (water)proof. _____water_____
6. An (egg)shell is a bird's first home. _____egg_____

Rhyming

Write the List Words that rhyme with the words given.

1. florist _____forest_____   4. twister _____sister_____
2. decide _____beside_____   5. prince _____since_____
3. wife _____life_____   6. white _____quite_____

Flex Your Spelling Muscles

Writing

Birds come in many colors, shapes, and sizes. Write a description of one or more birds you have seen or heard about. Include details, such as what they look and sound like. Use as many List Words as you can.

Proofreading

Each sentence below has two mistakes. Use the proofreading marks to fix the mistakes. Then write the misspelled List Words on the lines.

Proofreading Marks
◯ spelling mistake
≡ capital letter

1. The hummingbird is the (berd) with the smallest (eeg).   1. _____bird_____ _____egg_____
2. a duck has feet shaped like paddles so it can swim in the (watter).   2. _____water_____
3. Penguins (canot) fly, but they can swim (faste).   3. _____cannot_____ _____fast_____
4. An eagle lives in the african rain (forrest).   4. _____forest_____

Now proofread your description of birds. Fix any mistakes.

Go for the Goal

Take your Final Test. Then fill in your Scoreboard. Send your mistakes to the Word Locker.

SCOREBOARD
number correct / number wrong

★ ★ ★ ★ ★ ★ ★ **All-Star Words** ★ ★ ★ ★ ★ ★ ★

carpet   shirt   sidewalk   mile   canvas

Write a sentence for each word. Read each sentence aloud to a partner, leaving out the All-Star Word. Have your partner say the word that goes in the sentence.

◎ Spelling Strategy

Call on volunteers to identify the consonants in each List Word. Then invite students to get together with a partner and each write five different List Words, leaving blanks for the consonants. Have the partners
• exchange papers and fill in each other's missing letters
• check the spellings of all the words in their *Spelling Workout* books.

Flex Your Spelling Muscles   *Page 8*

As students complete the **Writing** activity, encourage them to brainstorm ideas, write a first draft, revise, and proofread their work. The **Proofreading** exercise will help them prepare to proofread their descriptions. To publish their writing, students may want to
• illustrate their descriptions and create a display
• make illustrated cards to trade or share.

✍ Writer's Corner

To learn how to attract birds to their area for bird-watching all year round, students can write for a bird-feeding pamphlet. Have the class write a request on a postcard and mail it to the Consumer Information Center, Department 582Y, Pueblo, CO 81009.

Go for the Goal/Final Test

1. Where does your **sister** go to school?
2. We ran **quite** a long race yesterday.
3. The leaking pen left a **mark** on my hand.
4. The ostrich **egg** was very large.
5. Will frost **kill** the flowers in my garden?
6. The author's **life** was filled with adventure.
7. The ostrich is a very big **bird**.
8. Don't ride your bike so **fast!**
9. She invited **nine** friends to her birthday party.
10. It has been a week **since** I got Chen's letter.
11. I need a flashlight because I **cannot** see.
12. Mix the flour with **water** to make paste.
13. You are a very smart **person.**
14. Please sit **beside** me and read me a story.
15. What wild animals live in this **forest?**

Remind students to complete the Scoreboard and write any misspelled words in their Word Locker.

★ ★ All-Star Words

You may want to point out that the All-Star Words follow the spelling rule. Ask two volunteers to demonstrate how to do the activity, using a List Word.

Lesson 2

Objective

To spell words with single consonants, double consonants, and consonant blends

Correlated Phonics Lessons

MCP Phonics, Level C, Lessons 25–28
Silver Burdett Ginn *World of Reading,* 3/1, p. 188

Warm Up — Page 9

In this selection, students learn fascinating facts about cats, including who won the prize for "fat cat." Afterward, invite students to talk about any special cats they know of.

Ask volunteers to say *prize* and *left* and tell how many consonants they hear in each word. Ask other volunteers to identify the different sounds that *s* stands for in *was* and *perhaps.*

On Your Mark/ Warm Up Test

1. **Some** of the guests came late.
2. In the summer, we live **mostly** at the beach.
3. The path around the lake is **four** miles long.
4. I **wore** my new shoes to school.
5. **Was** I supposed to empty the wastebasket?
6. The **ground** was frozen during the winter.
7. Three slices of pizza are **left.**
8. The principal came **into** our classroom.
9. The store had shoes in my **size.**
10. Don't **yell** so loud!
11. Who won first **prize** in the essay contest?
12. **Perhaps** I'll get a postcard from my friend today.
13. Put the dough in a warm place so that it will **rise.**
14. My sister **kept** me waiting for an hour.
15. We would like something **else** to eat.

Pep Talk/Game Plan — Pages 10–11

Introduce the spelling rule and have students read the List Words aloud. Encourage students to look back at their Warm Up Tests and apply the spelling rule to any misspelled words.

As students work through the **Spelling Lineup, Vocabulary,** and **Alphabetical Order** exercises, remind them to look back at their List Words or in their dictionaries if they need help. For the **Spelling Lineup,** ask a volunteer to read the first set of directions aloud and help students complete the first item. You may wish to repeat this procedure for the remaining parts of the exercise.

 See **Charades/Pantomime,** page 15

Consonants

Warm Up

How much does the heaviest cat weigh?

Cat Tales

There are about 40 million cats in North America. A few are famous. You may have seen them on TV or in cartoons. Here are **some** not-so-famous cats who could have been prize winners.

The **prize** for "fat cat" goes to a cat in Connecticut. Most cats weigh about ten pounds. This cat weighed in at 43 pounds. That's heavier than **four** bowling balls! "Fat cat" should have watched what it ate.

Speaking of eating, most cats like to catch a mouse or two. The prize for "mouser" goes to Mickey. He caught more than 22 thousand mice. It took him a long time to make this record. For 23 years he **was** the "house" cat for a company in England. It is not known what this company made. **Perhaps** it was cheese.

Two other "house" cats owned their own house. They share the prize for "richest cats." The cats belonged to a doctor in California. When he died, he **left** them everything. It all came to $415, 000. That's a lot of cat chow!

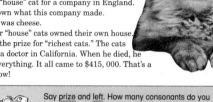

Say prize and left. How many consonants do you hear? Say was and perhaps. How are the sounds at the end of each word different?

On Your Mark

Take your Warm Up Test. Then check your spelling with the List Words on the next page.

9

Pep Talk

A **consonant blend** is two or more consonants that come together in a word. Their sounds blend together, but each sound is heard, as in prize and left. The /z/ sound can be spelled with the letter **z**, as in size, or the letter **s**, as in was.

LIST WORDS

1. some	*some*
2. mostly	*mostly*
3. four	*four*
4. wore	*wore*
5. was	*was*
6. ground	*ground*
7. left	*left*
8. into	*into*
9. size	*size*
10. yell	*yell*
11. prize	*prize*
12. perhaps	*perhaps*
13. rise	*rise*
14. kept	*kept*
15. else	*else*

Game Plan

Spelling Lineup

Write each List Word under the correct heading. One word will be written twice.

/z/ sound spelled s	/z/ sound spelled z
1. __was__	3. __size__
2. __rise__	4. __prize__

Write the two List Words that rhyme with pour.

5. __four__   6. __wore__

Write the missing blends to finish List Words.

7. __gr__ound   10. __pr__ize
8. __ke__pt   11. __mo__stly
9. __left__

Write the missing consonants to finish List Words.

12. per__h__a__p__s   15. __y__e__ll__
13. __into__   16. __some__
14. el__s__e

Vocabulary

Write the List Word that matches each clue.

1. You do this when you want someone to hear you. _yell_

2. You win this in a contest. _prize_

3. You do this as you get up from your chair. _rise_

4. Two plus two equals this number. _four_

5. This is the soil or land you walk on. _ground_

6. This is another word for *maybe*. _perhaps_

Alphabetical Order

Write the List Words from the box in alphabetical order. When you write words in alphabetical order, use these rules:

1. If the first letter of two words is the same, use the second letter.

2. If the first two letters are the same, use the third letter.

All words in a dictionary are listed in alphabetical order.

kept	yell	else	size	into
left	was	wore	mostly	some

1. _else_   6. _size_
2. _into_   7. _some_
3. _kept_   8. _was_
4. _left_   9. _wore_
5. _mostly_   10. _yell_

Flex Your Spelling Muscles

Writing

Think of a cat you have seen in real life or on television that did something silly. Use the List Words to write a description about it.

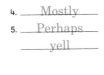

Proofreading

Each sentence has two mistakes. Use the proofreading marks to fix the mistakes. Write the misspelled List Words on the lines.

Proofreading Marks
◯ spelling mistake
⊙ add period

1. My cat wins the (prise) for high jumping⊙

2. He lands on all (foer) feet when he hits the (grownd)⊙

3. Sometimes he jumps (intoo) a tree⊙

4. (Mostley) he jumps on tables and chairs⊙

5. (Perrhaps) that is why he makes me (yeel)⊙

1. _prize_
2. _four_
   ground
3. _into_
4. _Mostly_
5. _Perhaps_
   yell

Now proofread your description. Fix any mistakes.

Go for the Goal

Take your Final Test. Then fill in your Scoreboard. Send your mistakes to the Word Locker.

SCOREBOARD

number correct	number wrong

★ ★ ★ ★ ★ ★ ★ **All-Star Words** ★ ★ ★ ★ ★ ★ ★

promise   honest   gaze   grind   ashes

Write a sentence for each All-Star Word, but leave a blank in place of the word. Trade papers with a partner. Write the word that belongs in each blank.

◉ **Spelling Strategy** Ask volunteers to help you write all the List Words on the board. Then invite the class to say each word aloud and to tell you whether or not it has a consonant blend. If there is a blend, have students tell if it is at the beginning or end of a word. Then have students circle the pair of letters and pronounce the blend, emphasizing the sounds of both consonants. You may need to explain that the root of *mostly* is *most* and that it ends with the consonant blend *st*.

Flex Your Spelling Muscles   *Page 12*

As students complete the **Writing** activity, encourage them to brainstorm ideas, write a first draft, revise, and proofread their work. The **Proofreading** exercise will help them prepare to proofread their descriptions. To publish their writing, students may want to

• read their descriptions aloud to the class

• use their descriptions to create skits.

✍ Writer's Corner

Students might enjoy watching an entertaining video about cats such as *Just Call Me Kitty,* which can be purchased from Unicorn Video Inc. (818-407-4336). Afterward, encourage students to create a class book that contains interesting cat facts.

Go for the Goal/Final Test

1. The traffic **kept** us from arriving on time.
2. **Perhaps** I should come back tomorrow.
3. Please don't **yell** in my ear.
4. Mom walked **into** the room.
5. The **ground** is wet from the rain.
6. Is that costume the one you **wore** to the party?
7. Joey eats **mostly** fruits and vegetables.
8. You will have to buy your shoes somewhere **else.**
9. The temperature did not **rise** above freezing.
10. Carrie won first **prize** in the art contest.
11. These shoes are the wrong **size.**
12. Isn't there anything **left** to eat?
13. That **was** the funniest movie I ever saw!
14. We would like **four** theater tickets.
15. **Some** of the apples are not ripe.

Remind students to complete the Scoreboard and write any misspelled words in their Word Locker.

★★ **All-Star Words** You may want to point out that the All-Star Words follow the spelling rule and review how to write a cloze sentence.

Lesson 3

Objective

To spell words with hard and soft *c* and *g*

Correlated Phonics Lessons

MCP Phonics, Level C, Lesson 6
Silver Burdett Ginn *World of Reading,* 3/1, p. 206

Warm Up   **Page 13**

In "Ladybug, Ladybug," students learn how to perform a clever trick. Afterward, invite them to try the trick in class or at home. Ask them to describe or perform other magic tricks they know how to do.

Encourage students to look back at the words in dark print. Ask volunteers to say the words and identify the sounds that *c* and *g* stand for.

On Your Mark/Warm Up Test

1. How thick is the **ice** on the pond?
2. Let's **pick** some apples and make a pie.
3. Tam has **gone** to the grocery store.
4. Please help me unpack this **case** of new books.
5. The clowns wore paint on their **faces.**
6. The lion growled when we passed its **cage.**
7. The **magic** show was amazing!
8. I went fishing for the first time at **age** ten.
9. The horse pulled the big **wagon** up the hill.
10. Please **give** me another glass of milk.
11. Did you enjoy the story about the gentle **giant?**
12. **Once,** long ago, this city was a small town.
13. Beware of **danger** when you cross the street.
14. The guide showed us many interesting **places.**
15. Let's **climb** up the hill and look at the view.

Pep Talk/Game Plan   **Pages 14–15**

Introduce the spelling rule and ask students to read the List Words aloud, having them tell whether *c* or *g* is hard or soft in each word. Then encourage students to look back at their Warm Up Tests and apply the spelling rule to any misspelled words.

As students work through the **Spelling Lineup,** **Vocabulary,** and **Puzzle** exercises, remind them to look back at their List Words or in their dictionaries if they need help.

 See **Rhymes and Songs,** page 14

Hard and Soft <u>c</u> and <u>g</u>

Warm Up

How does Juan make a paper ladybug move?

Ladybug, Ladybug

Juan held a plain piece of paper up in front of his friends. He showed them that it was just an ordinary everyday piece of paper. Next he picked up a cut out drawing of a **giant** ladybug and placed it on the paper. Then he said, "Ladybug, ladybug, turn around." And like **magic**, the paper bug began to turn and move. Then he held up the sheet, and made the ladybug **climb** up. You should have seen his friends' **faces**.

How did he do it? Simple. Juan taped a paper clip to the underside of the bug. He held the sheet of paper with one hand, and in his other hand, he hid a small magnet. He moved the magnet around behind the sheet of paper. Now that you know how the trick is done, why not **give** it a try. Presto! You'll drive your friends buggy!

 Look back at the words in dark print. Say each word. What two sounds does the **c** make? What two sounds does the **g** make?

On Your Mark

Take your Warm Up Test. Then check your spelling with the List Words on the next page.

13

Pep Talk

The letter **c** can make a hard sound, as in <u>case</u> and a soft sound, as in <u>ice</u>.
The letter **g** can make a hard sound, as in <u>gone</u> and a soft sound, as in <u>cage</u>.

LIST WORDS

1. ice — *ice*
2. pick — *pick*
3. gone — *gone*
4. case — *case*
5. faces — *faces*
6. cage — *cage*
7. magic — *magic*
8. age — *age*
9. wagon — *wagon*
10. give — *give*
11. giant — *giant*
12. once — *once*
13. danger — *danger*
14. places — *places*
15. climb — *climb*

Game Plan

Spelling Lineup

Write each List Word under the correct heading. Some words may be written twice.

hard c as in <u>car</u>		soft c as in <u>city</u>
1. pick	9.	ice
2. case	10.	faces
3. cage	11.	once
4. magic	12.	places
5. climb		

hard g as in <u>game</u>		soft g as in <u>page</u>
6. gone	13.	cage
7. wagon	14.	magic
8. give	15.	age
	16.	giant
	17.	danger

22

Vocabulary

Write the List Word that matches each clue.

1. It can carry a heavy load. _____ wagon _____
2. A pet bird may live in this. _____ cage _____
3. It will make your drink cold. _____ ice _____
4. Tales may start, "___ upon a time." _____ Once _____
5. This means the opposite of here. _____ gone _____
6. These have eyes and mouths. _____ faces _____
7. This is the opposite of take. _____ give _____
8. This means to choose. _____ pick _____
9. This means how old a person is. _____ age _____
10. Presto! A rabbit's in my hat! _____ magic _____

Puzzle

Write a List Word to complete each sentence. Then read down the shaded boxes to answer the riddle.

1. It takes strong legs to ___ a mountain. `C L I M B`
2. Tom went to many ___ on his trip. `P L A C E S`
3. The sign said, "___ ! Ice on Road!" `D A N G E R`
4. Jack climbed the beanstalk and met a ___ . `G I A N T`
5. The bottles of juice came in a cardboard ___ . `C A S E`

Riddle: What would you need to take an elephant for a ride on your bike?

Answer: M A G I C

Flex Your Spelling Muscles

Writing

What magic tricks have you seen? Maybe you know how to do a magic trick yourself. Use the List Words to write directions telling how it's done.

Proofreading

Each sentence below has two mistakes. Use the proofreading marks to fix the mistakes. Write the misspelled List Words on the lines.

Proofreading Marks
◯ spelling mistake
≡ capital letter

1. the magician asked Roy to pik a card.   1. _____ pick _____
2. he put Roy's card in a hat and waved a majic wand. 2. _____ magic _____
3. now he will giv the hat a tap.   3. _____ give _____
4. suddenly, the card is gon!   4. _____ gone _____
5. did you see the surprise on all the people's fases? 5. _____ faces _____

Now proofread your directions. Fix any mistakes.

Go for the Goal

Take your Final Test. Then fill in your Scoreboard. Send your mistakes to the Word Locker.

SCOREBOARD	
number correct	number wrong

★ ★ ★ ★ ★ ★ All-Star Words ★ ★ ★ ★ ★ ★

cargo   garage   glisten   pack   exercise

Write what you think each All-Star Word means. Then check the definitions in your dictionary. Trade papers with a partner. Write the All-Star Word that goes with each meaning.

◎ **Spelling Strategy**   To help students figure out whether *c* or *g* is hard or soft, write List Words containing *c* on the board and call on a volunteer to
• underline the letter that follows the *c*
• name the letter
• say the word and tell whether the *c* is hard or soft.
Follow the same procedure with List Words that contain *g*. Remind students that when they see *c* or *g* followed by *e* or *i*, they should try a soft sound when pronouncing *c* or *g*. Then ask the class which List Word does not follow this rule (*give*).

Flex Your Spelling Muscles   *Page 16*

As students complete the **Writing** activity, encourage them to brainstorm ideas, write a first draft, revise, and proofread their work. The **Proofreading** exercise will help them prepare to proofread their directions. To publish their writing, students may want to perform their magic tricks for the class.

✎ Writer's Corner

The class might enjoy writing away for a magic tricks catalog. Enclose $1.25 and a long, self-addressed stamped envelope along with a letter of request. Mail the package to Abracadabra Magic and Fun Shop, Department C-606, 125 Lincoln Boulevard, Middlesex, NJ 08846.

Go for the Goal/Final Test

1. What a fantastic *magic* trick that was!
2. Does your little brother have a red *wagon?*
3. The children have *gone* outside to play.
4. The *giant* lived in a castle on a cloud.
5. Africa and Asia are faraway *places.*
6. I went canoeing with my cousin *once.*
7. *Ice* hockey is a fast-moving sport.
8. At the *age* of six, he learned to ride a bike.
9. Let's *pick* some flowers and make a bouquet.
10. My cats always *climb* the trees in the yard.
11. Please help me carry this heavy *case* of supplies.
12. Tomorrow I will clean my parakeet's *cage.*
13. If you are careful, you will avoid *danger.*
14. Their *faces* were reflected in the store window.
15. *Give* the bus driver your ticket.

Remind students to complete the Scoreboard and write any misspelled words in their Word Locker.

★ ★ **All-Star Words**   You may want to point out that the All-Star Words follow the spelling rule and review how to use guide words to look up dictionary entries.

Lesson 4

Objective
To spell words with short-vowel sounds

Correlated Phonics Lesson
MCP Phonics, Level C, Lessons 8–10, 12, 14

Warm Up   *Page 17*
In this selection, students find out about a fish that catches its meals with its own fishing line. Invite students to talk about other animals they may know of that have unusual hunting or eating habits.

Encourage students to look back at the words in dark print. Ask volunteers to say the words and identify the vowel sounds they hear.

On Your Mark/Warm Up Test
1. I have one **little** sister and one big sister.
2. The book has lost **its** paper jacket.
3. Go over the fence, not **under** it.
4. The waves made our boat **rock.**
5. The **dead** leaves fell to the ground.
6. Do you like stories that are set in the **past?**
7. Show it to **them,** please.
8. The **collar** on this shirt is a little tight.
9. The dog **dug** up an old bone.
10. Your dog **does** so many tricks!
11. Don't **gobble** up your lunch!
12. The diver went to the **bottom** of the lake.
13. A ball field should be **level** and smooth.
14. On Thursday morning, I **felt** sick.
15. Who sits **next** to you in that class?

Pep Talk/Game Plan   *Pages 18–19*
Introduce the spelling rule and have students read the List Words aloud. Encourage students to look back at their Warm Up Tests and apply the spelling rule to any misspelled words.

As students work through the **Spelling Lineup, Dictionary,** and **Scrambled Letters Puzzle** exercises, remind them to look back at their List Words or in their dictionaries if they need help. Before beginning the **Spelling Lineup,** review the concept of syllables, asking students to tap out the syllables in one or two List Words that you read.

 See **Tape Recording,** page 15

Name _____

Short-Vowel Sounds

Warm Up
Where does the anglerfish keep its fishing line?

Something Fishy

Have you ever heard of an "anglerfish"? An "angler" is a person who fishes with a line and hook. If you think an anglerfish is a fish that goes fishing, you're close. It **does** go fishing—with its own line and bait.

This strange fish does not "fish" in the usual way. It does not hang its line down into the water. It does its fishing from the **bottom** of the ocean. The anglerfish stays deep **under** the water. Like a **rock** on the ocean floor, it doesn't move. It does look up. **Its** eyes are on top of its head. Its fishing lines are on its head, too! These float up through the water. When fish swimming **past** think they see worms, they come closer. The anglerfish doesn't need a hook to catch **them.** It has a very large jaw. When the fish swim by to eat the "worms," the anglerfish will just **gobble** them up.

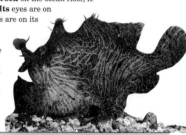

 Say each word in dark print. What vowel sounds do you hear?

On Your Mark
Take your Warm Up Test. Then check your spelling with the List Words on the next page.

17

Pep Talk
The vowels are **a, e, i, o, u,** and sometimes **y** and **w.** Every syllable in a word has a vowel sound. <u>Rock</u> has one vowel sound. <u>Bottom</u> has two. Short-vowel sounds are often spelled with just the vowel sound itself, but: short **e** in <u>dead</u> is spelled **ea,** and short **u** in <u>does</u> is spelled **oe.**

LIST WORDS

1. little *little*
2. its *its*
3. under *under*
4. rock *rock*
5. dead *dead*
6. past *past*
7. them *them*
8. collar *collar*
9. dug *dug*
10. does *does*
11. gobble *gobble*
12. bottom *bottom*
13. level *level*
14. felt *felt*
15. next *next*

Game Plan
Spelling Lineup
Write the List Words that have one syllable.

1. __its__   6. __dug__
2. __rock__   7. __does__
3. __dead__   8. __felt__
4. __past__   9. __next__
5. __them__

Write the List Words that have two syllables.

10. __little__   13. __gobble__
11. __under__   14. __bottom__
12. __collar__   15. __level__

18   Lesson 4 ■ Short-Vowel Sounds

Dictionary

Each List Word below has been divided into syllables. Say each word. Put an accent mark (´) after the syllable with the strong sound. Then write the List Word.

> In a dictionary, an **accent mark** appears after the syllable with the strong sound.
> lit´ tle

1. col ´lar   collar
2. un ´der   under
3. bot ´tom   bottom
4. gob ´ble   gobble
5. lev ´el   level

Scrambled Letters Puzzle

Unscramble the letters to spell List Words. Print one letter in each box. Then read down the shaded boxes to answer the riddle.

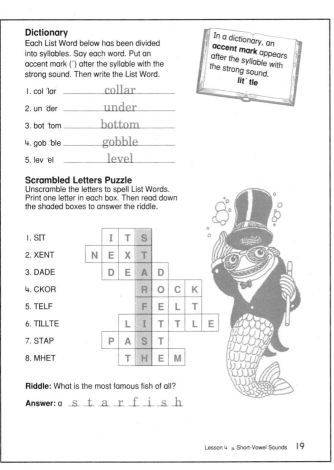

1. SIT   I T S
2. XENT   N E X T
3. DADE   D E A D
4. CKOR   R O C K
5. TELF   F E L T
6. TILLTE   L I T T L E
7. STAP   P A S T
8. MHET   T H E M

Riddle: What is the most famous fish of all?

Answer: a s t a r f i s h

Lesson 4 ■ Short-Vowel Sounds   19

Flex Your Spelling Muscles

Writing

Have you ever seen a strange fish, bug, or other animal? Write a poem telling about a real animal or a made up one. Use as many List Words as you can.

Proofreading

Each sentence below has two mistakes. Use the proofreading marks to fix the mistakes. Write the misspelled List Words on the lines.

Proofreading Marks
⬭ spelling mistake
⊙ add period

1. A flounder fish lives on the ocean (bottom)⊙   1. bottom
2. It (dus) look strange because both (itz) eyes are on the same side of its head.   2. does   its
3. The flat flounder lies (levil) with the sand ⊙   3. level
4. It lies (uhnder) sand that it has (duge) up.   4. under   dug
5. Flounders can be colored like a (rok) on top ⊙   5. rock
6. People like (thim) because they are tasty ⊙   6. them

Now proofread your animal poem. Fix any mistakes.

Go for the Goal

Take your Final Test. Then fill in your Scoreboard. Send your mistakes to the Word Locker.

SCOREBOARD
number correct   number wrong

* * * * * * * **All-Star Words** * * * * * * * *

tender   lack   humble   chop   instead

Write a sentence for each word, then scramble the letters in the All-Star Words. Trade papers with a partner. Unscramble each other's words.

20   Lesson 4 ■ Short-Vowel Sounds

◉ **Spelling Strategy**   Remind students that *ea* spells short *e* in *dead* and that *oe* spells short *u* in *does*. Then write *had, men, bit, stop,* and *run* on the board as separate column headings. Invite students to say each word aloud and

• name the vowel sound they hear
• name the letter that stands for that sound
• tell which List Word or List Words contain the same short-vowel sound.

Call on a volunteer to write each List Word on the board in the appropriate column.

Flex Your Spelling Muscles   *Page 20*

As students complete the **Writing** activity, encourage them to brainstorm ideas, write a first draft, revise, and proofread their work. The **Proofreading** exercise will help them prepare to proofread their poems. To publish their writing, students may want to

• record their poems and play them for another class
• compile an anthology titled "Creepy Creatures."

✍ Writer's Corner

> Students might enjoy finding out about sea creatures by reading a book such as *The Mysterious Undersea World* by Jan L. Cook. Encourage students to draw a picture of their favorite creature and to write a caption under it.

Go for the Goal/Final Test

1. I went to bed early because I *felt* sleepy.
2. The library needed *its* carpets cleaned.
3. My pilgrim costume has a big white *collar.*
4. My old bicycle is too *little* for me now.
5. Does this plant look *dead* to you?
6. A ball can roll far on a *level* floor.
7. When does the *next* bus leave?
8. A marble just rolled *under* the dresser.
9. My mother *dug* a hole so she could plant a tree.
10. Call your cousins and ask *them* to come with us.
11. Abe likes to sit in a chair and *rock.*
12. I've been to two movies in the *past* week.
13. The crab is at the *bottom* of the tide pool.
14. She *does* her homework every night.
15. Don't *gobble* those sweets before dinner!

Remind students to complete the Scoreboard and write any misspelled words in their Word Locker.

★★ **All-Star Words**   You may want to point out that the All-Star Words follow the spelling rule and model writing a sentence with a scrambled List Word.

Lesson 5

Objective
To spell words with long-vowel sounds

Correlated Phonics Lessons
MCP Phonics, Level C, Lessons 16–20
Silver Burdett Ginn *World of Reading,* 3/1, p. 144

Warm Up   **Page 21**
In "A Squiggly Tale," students read about a traffic jam caused by a pig. After reading, discuss the puns "a squiggly tale" (like a pig's tail) and "road hog."

Encourage students to look back at the words in dark print. Ask volunteers to say each word and identify the vowel sound they hear.

On Your Mark/Warm Up Test
1. Jim picked up the phone and said, "***Hello.***"
2. Please ***raise*** the window shade.
3. Father will ***drive*** us to school today.
4. I ate a ***huge*** sandwich for lunch.
5. How long are the ***lines*** outside the theater?
6. Don't ***blame*** me if you are late for the meeting.
7. There is a park at the end of my ***street.***
8. Please take the ***seat*** next to me.
9. A cloud of exhaust ***fumes*** hung above the traffic.
10. Do you ***know*** who planned the surprise party?
11. We have ***only*** one more lap to run!
12. Many ***people*** enjoy playing soccer.
13. They carried ***steel*** beams to the building site.
14. I must remember to ***mail*** this postcard.
15. Mom ***used*** a wrench to open the drain pipe.

Pep Talk/Game Plan   **Pages 22–23**
Introduce the spelling rule and have the class read the List Words aloud, helping students name each long-vowel sound and the spelling of that sound. Then encourage students to look back at their Warm Up Tests and apply the spelling rule to any misspelled words.

As students work through the **Spelling Lineup, Missing Words,** and **Puzzle** exercises, remind them to look back at their List Words or in their dictionaries if they need help.

 See **Picture Clues,** page 15

Long-Vowel Sounds

Warm Up
What kind of jam won't spread on bread?

A Squiggly Tale

You can believe it or not, but last week the Landview Police Department got a call from a Mrs. Sadie Rose, who was very upset. Mrs. Sadie Rose said that there was a pig causing a **huge** traffic jam on the main road through town. Traffic was blocked for miles.

A police unit, with siren wailing, drove to the scene. When they arrived, they found a pig standing in the middle of the **street**. An officer neared the pig carefully. "What are you doing here?" asked the officer. "I'm on my way to the market," answered the pig.

"Sir, roads are for cars to **drive** on," said the officer.

"I **know**," answered the pig.

"Sir, only people in cars are allowed on the highway," said the officer.

The pig looked very insulted. "I have every right to be here," replied the pig. "After all, I am a road hog."

Personally, I don't believe it!

 Say each word in dark print in the selection. What vowel sound do you hear in each word?

On Your Mark
Take your Warm Up Test. Then check your spelling with the List Words on the next page.

21

Pep Talk
A **long-vowel sound** often has the same sound as its letter name, but long-vowel sounds can be spelled many ways.
For example:
long a in <u>raise</u> is spelled **ai**
long e in <u>seat</u> is spelled **ea.**
The sound-symbols for long-vowels are:
a = /ā/ e = /ē/ i = /ī/ o = /ō/ u = /yoō/

LIST WORDS
1. hello *hello*
2. raise *raise*
3. drive *drive*
4. huge *huge*
5. lines *lines*
6. blame *blame*
7. street *street*
8. seat *seat*
9. fumes *fumes*
10. know *know*
11. only *only*
12. people *people*
13. steel *steel*
14. mail *mail*
15. used *used*

Game Plan
Spelling Lineup
Write each List Word under the correct heading. One word will be used twice.

/ā/
1. raise
2. blame
3. mail

/ī/
4. drive
5. lines

/ō/
6. know
7. only
8. hello

/ē/
9. street
10. seat
11. people
12. only
13. steel

/yoō/
14. huge
15. fumes
16. used

Missing Words

Write a List Word to finish each sentence.

1. Our teacher will __know__ the answer to this question.
2. The smell of the paint __fumes__ is strong.
3. Look both ways before you cross the __street__ .
4. The bus driver will __drive__ you to school.
5. Most bridges today are made of strong __steel__ .
6. Students __raise__ their hands to ask a question.
7. Hannah __used__ a rubber patch to fix my tire.
8. Please put a stamp on this letter before you __mail__ it.

Puzzle

Fill in the crossword puzzle by writing a List Word to answer each clue.

ACROSS
3. a road
4. very, very big
5. to say someone did something bad
6. rows of persons or things
7. another word for just

DOWN
1. to lift up
2. men, women, and children
3. a chair or bench
4. a greeting

```
                              ¹R
              ²P               A
        ³S T R E E T           I
        E     O               S
        A     P         ⁴H U G E
        ⁵B L A M E      E
        E            ⁶L I N E S
                      L
                     ⁷O N L Y
```

Flex Your Spelling Muscles

Writing
Use the List Words to write a joke or riddle you know. For example: Why did the chicken cross the street? Answer: To get to the other side. Then try out your joke on a friend.

Proofreading
Each sentence below has two mistakes. Use the proofreading marks to fix the mistakes. Write the misspelled List Words on the lines.

Proofreading Marks
◯ spelling mistake
≡ capital letter

1. have you heard the joke that peeple tell about an elephant?

2. i've onley heard it once, so tell me again.

3. how do you knoe when an elephant has been in the refrigerator?

4. there will be a huje footprint in the butter.

1. __people__
2. __only__
3. __know__
4. __huge__

Now proofread your joke or riddle. Fix any mistakes.

Go for the Goal

Take your Final Test. Then fill in your Scoreboard. Send your mistakes to the Word Locker.

SCOREBOARD	
number correct	number wrong

 All-Star Words

weak   drain   device   fold   usually

Write a sentence for each All-Star Word. Trade papers with a partner. Circle the letters that stand for the long-vowel sounds in the All-Star Words.

◉ **Spelling Strategy** Say *make, seal, sky, cold,* and *few* to illustrate the five long-vowel sounds. Then write these List Words on the board to illustrate different spellings of the sounds: /ā/ = blame, mail; /ē/ = only, steel, seat, people; /ī/ = drive; /ō/ = hello, know; /yōō/ = huge. Circle the letter or letters in each word that spell the long-vowel sound. Ask students if they can name the List Word that contains both the long *o* and the long *e* sounds (*only*).

Flex Your Spelling Muscles   *Page 24*

As students complete the **Writing** activity, encourage them to brainstorm ideas, write a first draft, revise, and proofread their work. The **Proofreading** exercise will help them prepare to proofread their jokes or riddles. To publish their writing, students may want to
• orally present their jokes in a talent-show format
• create a joke book titled "A Laugh a Minute!"

✐ **Writer's Corner**

Students might enjoy reading a joke or riddle book such as *Remember Betsy Floss, and Other Colonial American Riddles* by David A. Adler. Invite students to write and illustrate some of the jokes in the book, as well as others they know, to create a display in a school corridor.

Go for the Goal/Final Test

1. Can your older sister *drive* yet?
2. I don't *blame* you for feeling sad.
3. I called to say "*hello.*"
4. The *lines* to get into this movie are so long!
5. A whale is a *huge* animal.
6. What are they building at the end of your *street?*
7. Let's *raise* the flag on the flagpole.
8. My *mail* is delivered around noon every day.
9. Dad *used* three eggs in the pancake batter.
10. Many *people* have cocker spaniels as pets.
11. This *seat* is very comfortable.
12. We *know* you can win the game!
13. Forks made of stainless *steel* will not rust.
14. Try to avoid breathing those *fumes.*
15. I have *only* ten cents in my pocket.

Remind students to complete the Scoreboard and write any misspelled words in their Word Locker.

★★ **All-Star Words** You may want to point out that the All-Star Words follow the spelling rule and remind students that one or more letters can stand for a long-vowel sound.

Lesson 6 • Instant Replay

Objective

To review consonants and spelling words with hard and soft *c* and *g,* short-vowel sounds, and long-vowel sounds

Time Out   *Pages 25–28*

Check Your Word Locker Based on your observations, note which words are giving students the most difficulty and offer assistance for spelling them correctly. Here are some frequently misspelled words to watch for: *quite, once, does, know, people,* and *raise.*

To give students extra help and practice in taking standardized tests, you may want to have them take the Review Test for this lesson on pages 30–31. After scoring the tests, return them to students so that they can record their misspelled words in their Word Locker.

After practicing their troublesome words, students can work through the exercises for **Lessons 1–5.** Before they begin each exercise, you may want to go over the spelling rule.

Take It Home Invite students to cut out magazine or newspaper pictures at home and to write captions for them, using as many List Words in **Lessons 1–5** as possible. For a complete list of the words, encourage students to take their *Spelling Workout* books home. Students can also use Take It Home Master 1 on pages 32–33 to help them do the activity. Encourage students to bring their pictures and captions to school to share with the class.

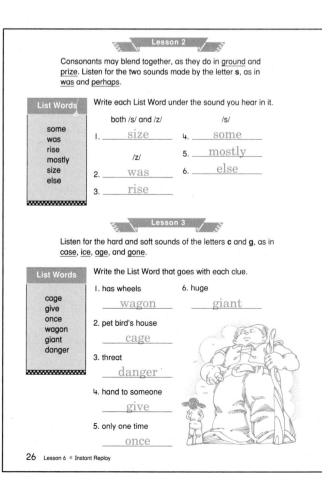

Name _____

Instant Replay • Lessons 1–5

LESSON 6

Time Out

Take another look at consonant sounds and blends, the hard and soft sounds of **c** and **g**, and words with short- and long-vowel sounds.

Check Your Word Locker
Look at the words in your Word Locker. Write the troublesome words for Lessons 1 through 5.

_____

Practice writing your troublesome words with a partner. Take turns writing each word as the other slowly spells it aloud.

Lesson 1

The **vowels** in the alphabet are **a**, **e**, **i**, **o**, **u**, and sometimes **y** and **w**. All the other letters are **consonants**.

| List Words | Each riddle has an answer with rhyming words in it. Write a List Word to finish each answer. |

List Words
bird
sister
quite
nine
mark
fast

1. What color is paper?
   quite white

2. What is an ink blot?
   a dark _mark_

3. What is next to the second hen?
   a third _bird_

4. Where is that name?
   on line _nine_

5. What is a quick boom?
   a _fast_ blast

6. How did Mom greet a family member?
   kissed her _sister_

25

Lesson 2

Consonants may blend together, as they do in <u>ground</u> and <u>prize</u>. Listen for the two sounds made by the letter **s**, as in <u>was</u> and <u>perhaps</u>.

List Words
some
was
rise
mostly
size
else

Write each List Word under the sound you hear in it.

both /s/ and /z/
1. _size_
2. _was_
3. _rise_

/z/

/s/
4. _some_
5. _mostly_
6. _else_

Lesson 3

Listen for the hard and soft sounds of the letters **c** and **g**, as in <u>case</u>, <u>ice</u>, <u>age</u>, and <u>gone</u>.

List Words
cage
give
once
wagon
giant
danger

Write the List Word that goes with each clue.

1. has wheels
   wagon

2. pet bird's house
   cage

3. threat
   danger

4. hand to someone
   give

5. only one time
   once

6. huge
   giant

26   Lesson 6 ■ Instant Replay

Short-vowel sounds are often spelled with just the vowel itself, as in dug. Notice the different spellings of the short-vowel sounds in does and dead.

List Words

under
collar
does
dead
bottom
level

Write the List Words in alphabetical order.

1. bottom   6. under
2. collar
3. dead
4. does
5. level

Lesson 5

Long-vowel sounds have the same sound as their letter names, but long-vowel sounds can be spelled many ways, as in street, seat, know, and mail.

List Words

raise
know
people
huge
mail
only

Circle each List Word that is misspelled. Then write it on the line correctly.

1. You know all the (poeple) in this room. ___people___

2. We have a (huje) dog named Dinosaur. ___huge___

3. Please (raize) your hand before you speak. ___raise___

4. I can stay (onlly) a few days. ___only___

5. Everyone will (knoe) the words to this song. ___know___

6. I see a huge pile of (mial) on the table. ___mail___

List Words

only
mostly
giant
huge
bird
danger
people
raise
once
under

Lessons 1–5

Circle the word that does not make sense in each sentence. Then choose the List Word that makes better sense in the sentence and write it on the line.

1. There is a (board) in the tree. ___bird___

2. The bear is (hug). ___huge___

3. I saw a giraffe mountain. ___giant___

4. I am the (onion) child in my family. ___only___

5. (Worm) upon a time, a frog met a prince. ___Once___

6. I will (raisin) the blinds. ___raise___

7. Many (peaches) live in the city. ___people___

8. The (daisy) passed, so I felt safer. ___danger___

9. A river flows (uncle) the bridge. ___under___

10. I (moose) like to read mysteries. ___mostly___

Go for the Goal

Take your Final Replay Test. Then fill in your Scoreboard. Send any misspelled words to your Word Locker.

SCOREBOARD

number correct	number wrong

ground
cannot
gobble
climb
fumes

Clean Out Your Word Locker
Look in your Word Locker. Cross out each word you spelled correctly on your Final Replay Test. Circle the words you're still having trouble with. Add the words you circled to your Spelling Notebook. What do you notice about the words? Watch for those words as you write.

Go for the Goal/Final Replay Test   *Page 28*

1. This room is *quite* hot.
2. My *sister* is named Rosa.
3. In science, we learned about an extinct *bird.*
4. You may invite someone *else* to go with you.
5. Make sure you buy those shoes a *size* larger.
6. What kinds of books do you read *mostly?*
7. We need to buy a *cage* for our hamsters.
8. Did Saul *give* you a package to bring home?
9. If you try hiking *once,* you will probably enjoy it.
10. First you cut away all the *dead* branches.
11. Leave a little water in the *bottom* of the sink.
12. An egg won't roll off a *level* counter.
13. Your job will be to *raise* the flag each morning.
14. Does anyone *know* how to make soup?
15. Those *people* are waiting to buy tickets.
16. What *does* she want us to bring to the picnic?
17. The costume had a high, stiff *collar* on it.
18. I put the book *under* the chair.
19. We have room for *only* one more person.
20. Make sure you *mail* those letters for me.
21. A hurricane can blow over even *huge* trees.
22. No, there is no *danger* that Lin will be late.
23. What a *giant* pumpkin that is!
24. Yolanda painted the *wagon* yellow and black.
25. Here are *some* magazines you may cut up.
26. The new playground *was* opened last week.
27. From this window, you can watch the sun *rise.*
28. I have *nine* pencils, but I need ten.
29. Stand with your toes up against the red *mark.*
30. Can a racehorse run as *fast* as a cheetah?

Clean Out Your Word Locker   Before writing the words, students can pronounce them and identify the consonant sounds, short- or long-vowel sounds, and any sounds spelled with *c* or *g.*

Instant Replay Test

Side A

Read each set of words. Fill in the circle next to the word that is spelled correctly.

1. ⓐ wagon ⓒ wagen
   ⓑ wagone ⓓ waggen

2. ⓐ wass ⓒ waz
   ⓑ was ⓓ whas

3. ⓐ levvel ⓒ level
   ⓑ levle ⓓ levell

4. ⓐ kwite ⓒ quiete
   ⓑ kwuite ⓓ quite

5. ⓐ peeple ⓒ peopple
   ⓑ peopel ⓓ people

6. ⓐ giant ⓒ jient
   ⓑ jiant ⓓ gient

7. ⓐ mosely ⓒ mostely
   ⓑ mostly ⓓ mostley

8. ⓐ daea ⓒ dead
   ⓑ dede ⓓ ded

9. ⓐ sister ⓒ sista
   ⓑ sisster ⓓ sistur

10. ⓐ nien ⓒ nine
    ⓑ ninne ⓓ neine

Name _____

Instant Replay Test

Side B

Read each set of words. Fill in the circle next to the word that
is spelled correctly.

11. ⓐ bottom   ⓒ botom
     ⓑ boddom   ⓓ bodum

12. ⓐ elts   ⓒ ellse
     ⓑ elze   ⓓ else

13. ⓐ hooj   ⓒ huge
     ⓑ huje   ⓓ uge

14. ⓐ coller   ⓒ coler
     ⓑ colar   ⓓ collar

15. ⓐ burd   ⓒ birde
     ⓑ bird   ⓓ berd

16. ⓐ once   ⓒ onec
     ⓑ wuns   ⓓ wonce

17. ⓐ raz   ⓒ raize
     ⓑ rase   ⓓ raise

18. ⓐ rise   ⓒ risse
     ⓑ ries   ⓓ rize

19. ⓐ daneger   ⓒ dangir
     ⓑ dainger   ⓓ danger

20. ⓐ ownly   ⓒ onely
     ⓑ only   ⓓ oneley

TAKE IT HOME

Your child has learned to spell many new words and would like to share them with you and your family. Below you'll find some enjoyable activities that will help your child review the words from Lessons 1–5.

Pictures Worth a Thousand Words

How many spelling words are your pictures worth? Have your child cut out magazine and newspaper photos. Remember, the photos can come from articles, stories, ads, or anything else you can find. Then try some "Caption action"! With your child, write captions for the pictures, using spelling words.

Mail $20 <u>fast</u> to get a super-duper dog <u>collar</u>! <u>State</u> color and <u>size</u>.

Last week's rainfall predicted to <u>raise</u> water <u>level</u>!

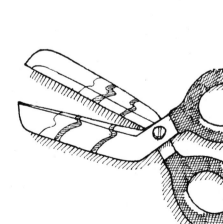

Show and Spell

Here's a new twist on an old game—Charades! With your child, take turns acting out the spelling word that each picture below represents. Remember, you can't just guess a word—you have to spell it, too!

Picture names: egg, bird or cage,
mail, climb or rock, ice, prize, magic

Lesson 7

Objective
To spell words with long-vowel sounds

Correlated Phonics Lessons
MCP Phonics, Level C, Lessons 16–20
Silver Burdett Ginn *World of Reading,* 3/2, p. 403

Warm Up   *Page 29*
In this selection, students find out about a huge mural painted on the side of a Minneapolis music store. Afterward, invite students to discuss what musical instruments they play or what their favorite instruments are.

Ask volunteers to say the words in dark print and name the letters that spell the long-vowel sounds.

On Your Mark/Warm Up Test
1. The rescue team found the man *alive.*
2. The museum has a *human* skeleton on display.
3. The lesson begins on *page* 25.
4. That was a really funny *joke* she told!
5. I *grind* the herbs to bring out their flavor.
6. I wonder what is *inside* the locked chest.
7. Let's *read* the story together.
8. Have you *seen* your cousin since last week?
9. The donkey carried a heavy *load* on its back.
10. Fast *music* makes me want to dance.
11. Stripes and polka dots are a *crazy* combination.
12. I hope the dish didn't *break* when it dropped.
13. Our *team* didn't lose a game all season.
14. Does the sun rise in the *east* and set in the west?
15. My grandfather built a *stone* fireplace.

Pep Talk/Game Plan   *Pages 30–31*
Introduce the spelling rule and have students read the List Words aloud. Point out the two pronunciations for the word *read,* using these sentences:

> *I will read the story tonight.*
> *I read that story yesterday.*

Explain that in the first sentence *read* has the sound of long *e*. In the second sentence *read* is used in the past tense and has the sound of short *e* as in *head*. Then encourage students to look back at their Warm Up Tests and apply the spelling rule to any misspelled words.

As students work through the **Spelling Lineup, Alphabetical Order,** and **Missing Words** exercises, remind them to look back at their List Words or in their dictionaries if they need help.

 See **Spelling Aloud,** page 14

Long-Vowel Sounds

Warm Up
What kind of store is in this building?

Musical Art
This wall is **alive** with the sight of **music!** Music is a tune that you can hear, isn't it? Yes, but you can see music, too. You can see the notes that a music writer puts on paper for other people to sing or play.

The tune on this wall has to be one of the world's largest. It's like a giant **page** of music. Is it the work of a songwriter who likes to paint? Is it the **crazy joke** of some singing sign painter? No, it is a mural, which is a special kind of painting done on a wall. This mural is five stories high! Why would anyone put so much music on the side of a building? Can you guess? **Inside** the building is a music store.

You can see this song on a building in the city of Minneapolis. If you can **read** music, you may even like to sing or play the song.

 Say each word in dark print in the selection. Listen for the long-vowel sounds. What do you notice about the ways the long-vowel sounds are spelled?

On Your Mark
Take your Warm Up Test. Then check your spelling with the List Words on the next page.

29

Pep Talk
Words with long-vowel sounds can have different spelling patterns. The **ea** in break spells /ā/. The **ea** in team spells /ē/. The **ea** in read can spell /ē/ or /e/. Look at how the long-vowel sound is spelled in each List Word.

LIST WORDS
1. alive   *alive*
2. human   *human*
3. page   *page*
4. joke   *joke*
5. grind   *grind*
6. inside   *inside*
7. read   *read*
8. seen   *seen*
9. load   *load*
10. music   *music*
11. crazy   *crazy*
12. break   *break*
13. team   *team*
14. east   *east*
15. stone   *stone*

Game Plan
Spelling Lineup
Write each List Word under the correct heading.

/ā/ as in <u>day</u>	/ō/ as in <u>glow</u>
1. page	11. joke
2. crazy	12. load
3. break	13. stone

/ē/ as in <u>free</u>	/yo͞o/ as in <u>huge</u>
4. read	14. human
5. seen	15. music
6. team	
7. east	

/ī/ as in <u>side</u>
8. alive
9. grind
10. inside

30   Lesson 7 ▪ Long-Vowel Sounds

Alphabetical Order

Circle the List Words that are hiding in the puzzle. Look across and down. Write the List Words in alphabetical order.

S	H	U	M	A	N	O	T
G	L	E	U	C	N	L	E
R	X	A	S	E	E	N	A
I	N	S	I	D	E	C	M
N	S	T	C	R	A	Z	Y
D	P	A	B	R	E	A	K

1. break
2. crazy
3. east
4. grind
5. human
6. inside
7. music
8. seen
9. team

Missing Words

Write a List Word from the box to finish each answer.

alive page load stone read joke

1. Why are you laughing? She told a joke.
2. Where is the name of this book's publisher? It is on the title page.
3. Why do you water your plants? It keeps them alive.
4. How will you move the furniture? I will load it into a truck.
5. What will you use to build that wall? I'll use a special kind of hard stone.
6. What will you do with that magazine? I think I'll read it.

Flex Your Spelling Muscles

Writing

How do you feel about music? Do you find yourself humming tunes or singing songs? Use the List Words to write a paragraph telling what kind of music you like and why.

Proofreading

Each sentence below has two mistakes. Use the proofreading marks to fix each mistake. Write the misspelled List Words on the lines.

Proofreading Marks
- ⬭ spelling mistake
- ^ add something

1. Have you sean the dancers on stage? — 1. seen
2. They are the best dance teem alliv. — 2. team, alive
3. The musik they use sounds wild and crazee. — 3. music, crazy
4. Did you rede about them in the newspaper? — 4. read
5. There is a story about the dancers inscid on the second paje. — 5. inside, page

Now proofread your paragraph about music. Fix any mistakes.

Go for the Goal

Take your Final Test. Then fill in your Scoreboard. Send your mistakes to the Word Locker.

SCOREBOARD	
number correct	number wrong

★ ★ ★ ★ ★ ★ ★ ★ ★ All-Star Words ★ ★ ★ ★ ★ ★ ★ ★ ★

erase pirate ruler coach release

Write a sentence for each word. Read the sentences to your partner, but say *blank* in place of the All-Star Words. Have your partner write the missing words.

Spelling Strategy To give students practice recognizing long-vowel sounds, invite them to get together with a partner and take turns pronouncing each List Word. As students say the words, they can emphasize the long-vowel sounds (j**o**ke, t**ea**m) and name the letters that stand for the sounds they hear.

Flex Your Spelling Muscles *Page 32*

As students complete the **Writing** activity, encourage them to brainstorm ideas, write a first draft, revise, and proofread their work. The **Proofreading** exercise will help them prepare to proofread their paragraphs. Before they begin the exercise, remind students that the proofreading mark ^ is used to add something. It could be a space, a comma, a question mark, or an exclamation mark. To publish their writing, students may want to read their paragraphs aloud, accompanied by their favorite music.

Writer's Corner

Students might enjoy watching a video about music, such as *All About Music,* distributed through Pyramid Film and Video (800-421-2304). Afterward, students can make posters advertising a second showing of the video, which can be arranged for another class.

Go for the Goal/Final Test

1. The truck removed the ***load*** of soil.
2. Few people are ***alive*** who remember that event.
3. I have never heard that ***joke*** before.
4. Have you ever ***seen*** a double rainbow?
5. Don't ***break*** the glass!
6. The final clue was hidden under a large ***stone.***
7. Mr. Leary will coach our ***team*** in the spring.
8. You're ***crazy*** to climb such a tall tree!
9. I like to fall asleep to the sounds of soft ***music.***
10. ***Human*** beings walk on two legs.
11. Whose picture is on the front ***page*** of the paper?
12. ***Grind*** the peanuts into peanut butter.
13. We live on the ***east*** end of town.
14. You may ***read*** quietly for the next half hour.
15. We found a kitten ***inside*** the cardboard box.

Remind students to complete the Scoreboard and write any misspelled words in their Word Locker.

★★ **All-Star Words** You may want to point out that the All-Star Words follow the spelling rule. Write a sentence using a List Word and call on a volunteer to read it, saying *blank* in place of the word.

Lesson 8

Objective
To spell words with *s*, *r*, and *l* consonant blends

Correlated Phonics Lessons
MCP Phonics, Level C, Lessons 25–28
Silver Burdett Ginn *World of Reading*, 3/1, p. 28

Warm Up   **Page 33**
In "Put on a Happy Face," students discover why it's easier to smile than to frown. After reading, invite students to smile and then to frown. Ask how each expression makes them feel.

Encourage students to look back at the words in dark print. Call on volunteers to name the consonant sounds they hear at the beginning of the words. Ask another volunteer to name the consonant sounds at the end of *best*.

On Your Mark/Warm Up Test
1. What a beautiful *smile* you have!
2. There are many *smart* students in this school.
3. That was the *best* pizza I ever ate!
4. The books I received were *free.*
5. How will you *spend* your allowance?
6. *Blind* people sometimes use canes.
7. I know how to *float* on my back.
8. A green *plant* needs sunshine and water.
9. Most people dream while they *slumber.*
10. The bee will *sting* you if you aren't careful.
11. *Frowning* takes more energy than smiling.
12. I invited a few *friends* to stay for dinner.
13. There are many fish in that *creek.*
14. First, let the *glue* on the papers dry.
15. Did you *bring* your lunch to school today?

Pep Talk/Game Plan   **Pages 34–35**
Introduce the spelling rule and have students read the List Words aloud, telling the consonant blend or blends that each word contains. Also explain the meanings of words that may be unfamiliar, such as *slumber.* Then encourage students to look back at their Warm Up Tests and apply the spelling rule to any misspelled words.

As students work through the **Spelling Lineup, Rhyming,** and **Scrambled Letters Puzzle** exercises, remind them to look back at their List Words or in their dictionaries if they need help.

 for ESL students See **Charades/Pantomime,** page 15

Consonant Blends   LESSON 8

Warm Up
Is a smile or a frown easier for your face to make?

Put on a Happy Face
The more you crack it the more people will like it. That's what a **smile** is all about. Did you know that **frowning** is harder than smiling? A frown uses 43 of the muscles in your face. It takes only 17 muscles to smile. So it's easy. Put on a happy face, and make some new **friends**.

Smiling is good for your health, too. Doctors and many other **smart** people believe that laughing helps sick people feel better inside. The laughing makes their bodies get well, too! **Best** of all, a smile is **free!**

So don't be **blind** to the fact that it's easier to smile than to frown. It's the doctor's orders!

 Say each word in dark print in the selection. What consonant sounds do you hear at the beginning of the words. What consonant sounds do you hear at the end of <u>best</u>?

On Your Mark
Take your Warm Up Test. Then check your spelling with the List Words on the next page.

33

Pep Talk
A **consonant blend** is two or more consonants that come together in a word. Their sounds blend together, but each sound is heard. Each List Word has an **s, l,** or **r** blend at the beginning or at the end of the word, or at the beginning and at the end.

LIST WORDS

1. smile	*smile*
2. smart	*smart*
3. best	*best*
4. free	*free*
5. spend	*spend*
6. blind	*blind*
7. float	*float*
8. plant	*plant*
9. slumber	*slumber*
10. sting	*sting*
11. frowning	*frowning*
12. friends	*friends*
13. creek	*creek*
14. glue	*glue*
15. bring	*bring*

Game Plan
Spelling Lineup
Write the List Words that begin or end with **s** blends.

1. smile   4. spend
2. smart   5. slumber
3. best   6. sting

Write the List Words that begin with **r** blends.

7. free   10. creek
8. frowning   11. bring
9. friends

Write the List Words that begin with **l** blends.

12. blind
13. float
14. plant
15. slumber
16. glue

34 Lesson 8 ▪ Consonant Blends

36

Rhyming

Write the List Words that rhyme with the words given.

1. west _____ best _____   4. number _____ slumber _____
2. boat _____ float _____   5. part _____ smart _____
3. sneak _____ creek _____   6. clowning _____ frowning _____

Scrambled Letters Puzzle

Unscramble the letters to spell List Words. Print one letter in each box. Then read down the shaded boxes to answer the riddle.

1. DLNBI — B L I N D
2. EGUL — G L U E
3. TALNP — P L A N T
4. TISGN — S T I N G
5. DPENS — S P E N D
6. ERFE — F R E E
7. MILES — S M I L E

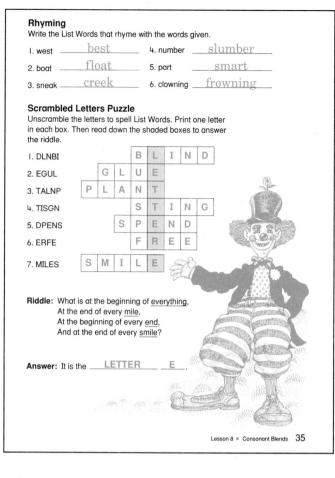

Riddle: What is at the beginning of everything,
At the end of every mile,
At the beginning of every end,
And at the end of every smile?

Answer: It is the _____ LETTER _____ E _____.

Lesson 8 ■ Consonant Blends 35

Flex Your Spelling Muscles

Writing

What makes you laugh? How does laughing make you feel? Write a brief paragraph that describes your feelings. Use as many List Words as you can.

Proofreading

Each sentence below has two mistakes. Use the proofreading marks to fix each mistake. Write the misspelled List Words on the lines.

Proofreading Marks
- ⬭ spelling mistake
- ≡ capital letter
- ⊙ add period

1. my family will spende Saturday at the circus.   1. _____ spend _____
2. I get to bering my freands with me.   2. _____ bring _____
                                          _____ friends _____
3. children get in frea that day.   3. _____ free _____
4. No frouning allowed when you see the clowns   4. _____ frowning _____
5. Those trained elephants are really snart   5. _____ smart _____
6. we all smyile when we see the lions.   6. _____ smile _____

Now proofread your paragraph. Fix any mistakes.

Go for the Goal

Take your Final Test. Then fill in your Scoreboard. Send your mistakes to the Word Locker.

SCOREBOARD
| number correct | number wrong |

★ ★ ★ ★ ★ ★ ★ ★ All-Star Words ★ ★ ★ ★ ★ ★ ★ ★

crack   stem   glide   blast   freeze

Write a sentence using each All-Star Word. Trade sentences with a partner. Circle the All-Star Words in the sentences.

36 Lesson 8 ■ Consonant Blends

◎ **Spelling Strategy**   Write the List Words *smile, free,* and *float* on the board and have students read them aloud. Then circle the consonant blend at the beginning of each word and explain that you can hear each letter in a consonant blend. Ask students to demonstrate this by repeating the words. Follow this procedure for the rest of the List Words. When you come to *smart* and *best,* point out that consonant blends may appear at the beginning or end of a word.

Flex Your Spelling Muscles   *Page 36*

As students complete the **Writing** activity, encourage them to brainstorm ideas, write a first draft, revise, and proofread their work. The **Proofreading** exercise will help them prepare to proofread their paragraphs. To publish their writing, students may want to create a mural of laughing faces, then match each face with one of their paragraphs.

✎ **Writer's Corner**

Students can receive a pamphlet of funny poetry by writing to Meadowbrook Press, Department FP, 18318 Minnetonka Boulevard, Deephaven, MN 55391. Enclose 25¢ and a long, self-addressed stamped envelope.

Go for the Goal/Final Test

1. You'll see a little bridge across the **creek.**
2. Don't **spend** all your money on the first day.
3. My dog is so **smart** it can do five tricks.
4. I will **bring** my swimming suit with me.
5. That story is the **best** one in the book.
6. My father gave me a big **smile.**
7. Now I have **glue** stuck to my fingers!
8. Who are your closest **friends?**
9. There are Braille books for **blind** people to read.
10. She was **frowning** as she cleaned the oven.
11. This soap will not **float** in the tub.
12. A wasp won't **sting** you if you leave it alone.
13. What disturbed the baby's **slumber?**
14. Put the **plant** on that sunny windowsill.
15. Let's go to the **free** movie in the gymnasium.

Remind students to complete the Scoreboard and write any misspelled words in their Word Locker.

★★ **All-Star Words**   You may want to point out that the All-Star Words follow the spelling rule and model writing a sentence using a List Word.

Lesson 9

Objective

To spell words with *r, l, s,* or *n* consonant blends

Correlated Phonics Lessons

MCP Phonics, Level C, Lessons 25–28
Silver Burdett Ginn *World of Reading,* 3/1, p. 28

Warm Up   *Page 37*

Invite students to read "Poetry Round Up" to find out what happens at the annual Cowboy Poetry Gathering. Afterward, have the class read the poem aloud and ask students what subjects they would write about if they were cowpokes.

Encourage students to look back at the words in dark print. Ask volunteers to say the words and identify the consonant blends.

On Your Mark/Warm Up Test

1. Where did you go on your *trip?*
2. My grandparents *drove* south last winter.
3. The teacher wrote a lesson *plan.*
4. The *kind* woman fixed the child's broken toy.
5. Our new school has four *floors.*
6. The snowman is *melting* in the sun.
7. The firefighters fought the *blaze.*
8. If you *spill* something, wipe it up.
9. What lovely *flowers* you brought!
10. *Friday* is the last day of the school week.
11. We cooked *frozen* vegetables for dinner.
12. *Please* pass the pepper.
13. Is the television set *broken?*
14. Don't buy bread that isn't *fresh.*
15. My birthday is a *special* day to me.

Pep Talk/Game Plan   *Pages 38–39*

Introduce the spelling rule and have students read the List Words aloud, identifying the *r, l, s,* or *n* blend in each word. Then encourage students to look back at their Warm Up Tests and apply the spelling rule to any misspelled words.

As students work through the **Spelling Lineup, Alphabetical Order,** and **Missing Words** exercises, remind them to look back at their List Words or in their dictionaries if they need help. For the **Spelling Lineup,** tell students that *sh* in *fresh* and *ng* in *melting* are not consonant blends.

 See **Letter Cards,** page 15

Consonant Blends   LESSON 9

Warm Up

What is the annual Cowboy Poetry Gathering?

Poetry Round Up

Every year, thousands of gals and guys **plan** a **trip** to a small Nevada town for a different **kind** of rodeo. It's a rodeo of rhyme called the annual Cowboy Poetry Gathering. This **special** event brings together cowpokes who not only enjoy poetry, but also enjoy life on the open range! They gather to recite the rhymes they've written during the year on the wild prairie. Here's a sample of their kind of poetic horseplay:

To My Horse, Whinny
There are other colts in my corral,
Among them you're the best.
You're faithful, loyal, my best pal,
And hooves beyond the rest!
  Of all the ponies in the race,
  I'm sure that you would beat 'em
  I'd really like to bring you **flowers,**
  But I know you'd only eat 'em.
    And I will love you for all time,
    I'm stating here and now.
    I'm writing you this round up rhyme,
    'Cause you're prettier than a cow.

 Look back at the words in dark print. Can you name the consonant blend in each word?

On Your Mark

Take your Warm Up Test. Then check your spelling with the List Words on the next page.

Pep Talk

In a **consonant blend,** you can hear the sounds of two or more letters together in a word. Listen for the blends in these words:

trip   melting   spill   kind

Find the **r, l, s,** or **n** blends in the List Words.

LIST WORDS

1. trip — *trip*
2. drove — *drove*
3. plan — *plan*
4. kind — *kind*
5. floors — *floors*
6. melting — *melting*
7. blaze — *blaze*
8. spill — *spill*
9. flowers — *flowers*
10. Friday — *Friday*
11. frozen — *frozen*
12. please — *please*
13. broken — *broken*
14. fresh — *fresh*
15. special — *special*

Game Plan

Spelling Lineup

Write the List Words under the headings. Circle the consonant blend in each word. Remember that **sh** and **ng** are not consonant blends.

one syllable

1. trip   6. blaze
2. drove   7. spill
3. plan   8. please
4. kind   9. fresh
5. floors

two syllables

10. melting   15. special
11. flowers
12. Friday
13. frozen
14. broken

Alphabetical Order

Write each group of List Words in alphabetical order.

please broken kind plan	1. broken 2. kind 3. plan 4. please	melting floors spill fresh	1. floors 2. fresh 3. melting 4. spill

Missing Words

Write List Words to finish the story. The word shapes will help you.

Friday was a special day. Dad drove us to the lake. The lake was frozen. Inside the cabin, Mom and I lit a fire. In the morning, the ice on the lake was melting. We even saw pretty purple flowers peeping through the snow.

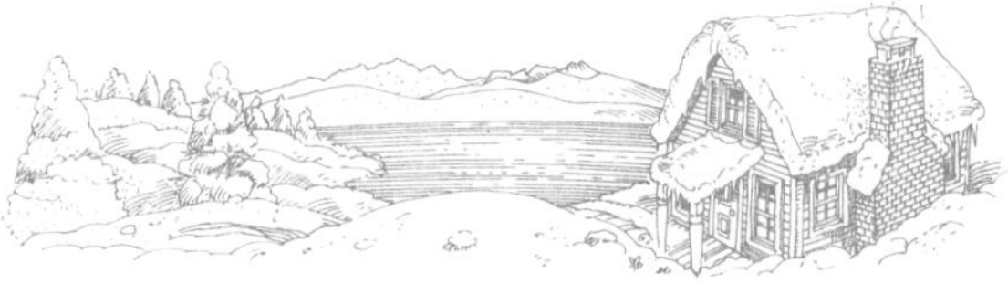

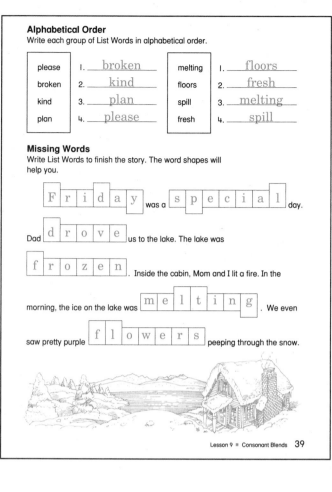

Lesson 9 ■ Consonant Blends 39

Flex Your Spelling Muscles

Writing

Poems can be serious or funny. They can rhyme or not rhyme. Poems can be just about anything you want them to be. Use the List Words to write a poem of your own.

Proofreading

Each sentence below has two mistakes. Use the proofreading marks to fix each mistake. Write the misspelled List Words on the lines.

Proofreading Marks
- ⬭ spelling mistake
- ∛ add apostrophe

1. We took a (tripp) west in Dads new car. — 1. trip
2. On (Fridae) we (droev) through the mountains. — 2. Friday, drove
3. It was so cold my sisters face felt (frosen). — 3. frozen
4. Our (plann) was to stop at my aunts ranch. — 4. plan
5. When we got there, there was a (freash) (blaiz) in the fireplace. — 5. fresh, blaze

Now proofread your poem. Fix any mistakes.

Go for the Goal

Take your Final Test. Then fill in your Scoreboard. Send your mistakes to the Word Locker.

SCOREBOARD	
number correct	number wrong

★ ★ ★ ★ ★ ★ ★ ★ ★ All-Star Words ★ ★ ★ ★ ★ ★ ★ ★ ★

treasure plane depend spare frost

Write a story using all the All-Star Words. Then erase two or three letters out of each All-Star Word. Trade papers with a partner. Fill in the missing letters.

40 Lesson 9 ■ Consonant Blends

Spelling Strategy You may want to divide the class into four groups and assign each one *r, l, s,* or *n.* Have the groups

- write the List Words in which their letter is part of a consonant blend
- underline the consonant blends
- get together with one another and share their work.

You may need to point out that the *n* group will have only one List Word *(kind).*

Flex Your Spelling Muscles **Page 40**

As students complete the **Writing** activity, encourage them to brainstorm ideas, write a first draft, revise, and proofread their work. The **Proofreading** exercise will help them prepare to proofread their poems. To publish their writing, students may want to

- invite another class to a poetry reading
- create and illustrate a class poetry book.

Writer's Corner

To learn more about the lives of cowpokes, students might enjoy reading a book such as *Cowboys of the Wild West* by Russell Freedman. Encourage students to pretend that they are cowpokes and to write a short poem about their life.

Go for the Goal/Final Test

1. The hotel we stayed in had twenty-five ***floors.***
2. Every ***Friday*** night my parents go to the movies.
3. What makes your pet so ***special*** to you?
4. ***Fresh*** bread is soft and delicious.
5. Those are such beautiful ***flowers!***
6. You are so ***kind*** to help me carry my groceries.
7. Can you fix the ***broken*** lamp?
8. Try not to ***spill*** any water on the rug.
9. We ***plan*** to go to the mountains on our vacation.
10. ***Please*** move to the front of the room.
11. The bag of ice cubes is ***melting*** in the hot car.
12. Who ***drove*** you home from the Scout meeting?
13. The surface of the lake was ***frozen*** solid.
14. We are going on a camping ***trip*** in July.
15. The ***blaze*** of the fire kept us warm.

Remind students to complete the Scoreboard and write any misspelled words in their Word Locker.

★★ **All-Star Words** You may want to point out that the All-Star Words follow the spelling rule and help students brainstorm ideas for their stories.

Lesson 10

Objective
To spell words in which *y* is used as a vowel

Correlated Phonics Lesson
MCP Phonics, Level C, Lesson 29

Warm Up   ***Page 41***
In this selection, students read to find out about an animal that's called a dog—but is really a ground squirrel. After reading, invite students to discuss how the prairie dog got its name.

Encourage students to look back at the words in dark print. Ask volunteers to say each word and name the sound *y* stands for.

On Your Mark/Warm Up Test
1. The *lady* who said "Hello" is my mother.
2. Puppies are so *playful!*
3. Louis *always* comes to school on time.
4. A giraffe uses its *very* long neck to reach food.
5. Is there an *empty* locker that I can use?
6. I get *angry* when you interrupt me.
7. You may borrow *any* book you like.
8. It rained, but we went to the park *anyway.*
9. *Maybe* we'll go to the movies on Saturday.
10. I will *carry* some of those packages for you.
11. Are there four people in your *family?*
12. Dad brought home some *pretty* tulips.
13. Make sure the horses have *plenty* of water.
14. This box is *heavy,* so let's lift it together.
15. I'm not *hungry,* because I just had lunch.

Pep Talk/Game Plan   ***Pages 42–43***
Introduce the spelling rule and have students read the List Words aloud. Encourage students to look back at their Warm Up Tests and apply the spelling rule to any misspelled words.

As students work through the **Spelling Lineup, Dictionary,** and **Word Shape Puzzle** exercises, remind them to look back at their List Words or in their dictionaries if they need help. For the **Word Shape Puzzle,** point out the literal meaning of the answer to the riddle at the bottom of page 43: a "hush puppy" is a small, deep-fried cornmeal cake.

 See **Tape Recording,** page 15

---

y as a Vowel   LESSON 10

Warm Up
When is a dog not really a dog?

Prairie Pups
They look like squirrels, but they bark like little dogs. They play in fields, but stay under the ground at night. They have grayish brown coats, and they're cute. What are they? They're prairie dogs!

It seems as if these **playful** little animals have **always** been around. They have been seen popping out of holes since the days when North America was being settled. Although we call them dogs, they are really ground squirrels. They live together in a large group called a village, deep under the ground. Digging room after room, they make space for their **very** large **family**. A village can have more than a thousand prairie dogs in it. There are prairie dog villages all through the plains of North America from Mexico to Canada.

Prairie dogs eat grass and roots and can cause **plenty** of trouble for farmers. In fact, these **hungry** animals eat so many plants, they hardly ever need water. They get enough water from the plants. **Maybe** you'll find this hard to believe, but think about it this way. Has a prairie dog ever asked you for a drink of water?

> Look back at the words in dark print. What do you notice about their spelling? Say each word. What vowel sound does the y stand for in each word?

On Your Mark
Take your Warm Up Test. Then check your spelling with the List Words on the next page.

41

Pep Talk
In some words **y** teams up with **a** to spell /ā/, as in **maybe**. At the end of a word with more than one syllable, **y** may spell /ē/, as in **pretty**. Listen for the sound that **y** makes in each List Word.

LIST WORDS
1. lady *lady*
2. playful *playful*
3. always *always*
4. very *very*
5. empty *empty*
6. angry *angry*
7. any *any*
8. anyway *anyway*
9. maybe *maybe*
10. carry *carry*
11. family *family*
12. pretty *pretty*
13. plenty *plenty*
14. heavy *heavy*
15. hungry *hungry*

Game Plan
Spelling Lineup
Write the List Words in which **y** spells the final sound /ē/.

1. _lady_   7. _family_
2. _very_   8. _pretty_
3. _empty_   9. _plenty_
4. _angry_   10. _heavy_
5. _any_   11. _hungry_
6. _carry_

Write the List Words in which **ay** spells /ā/.

12. _playful_   14. _anyway_
13. _always_   15. _maybe_

42   Lesson 10 ▪ y as a Vowel

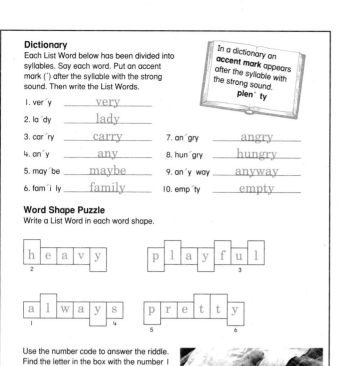

Dictionary

Each List Word below has been divided into syllables. Say each word. Put an accent mark (´) after the syllable with the strong sound. Then write the List Words.

> In a dictionary an **accent mark** appears after the syllable with the strong sound.
> plen´ ty

1. ver´y ___very___
2. la´dy ___lady___
3. car´ry ___carry___
4. an´y ___any___
5. may´be ___maybe___
6. fam´i ly ___family___
7. an´gry ___angry___
8. hun´gry ___hungry___
9. an´y way ___anyway___
10. emp´ty ___empty___

Word Shape Puzzle

Write a List Word in each word shape.

h e a v y (2)

p l a y f u l (3)

a l w a y s (1) (4)

p r e t t y (5) (6)

Use the number code to answer the riddle. Find the letter in the box with the number 1 under it. Print that letter on every line below that has the number 1 under it. Do the same for numbers 2 through 6.

Riddle: What do you call a quiet little dog?

Answer: a h u s h p u p p y
        1 2 4 2 5 3 5 5 6

Lesson 10 ■ y as a Vowel 43

Flex Your Spelling Muscles

Writing

The prairie dog villages and colorful flowers make the prairie a very interesting place. Write a description of where you live, a playground, or your favorite park. Tell what you would see, hear, or smell in that place. Try to use as many List Words as you can.

Proofreading

Each sentence has two mistakes. Use the proofreading marks to fix each mistake. Write the misspelled List Words on the lines.

> **Proofreading Marks**
> ◯ spelling mistake
> ﹏ take out something

1. Prairie dogs can be (playfulle), but they work (vary) hard, too.
2. A prairie dog (allwaes) starts its home by digging a a tunnel.
3. At the end of of the tunnel, (maybe) it'll make a sleeping room.
4. It puts (plente) of food in another room to keep for the the winter.

1. ___playful___
   ___very___
2. ___always___
3. ___maybe___
4. ___plenty___

Now proofread your description. Fix any mistakes.

Go for the Goal

Take your Final Test. Then fill in your Scoreboard. Send your mistakes to the Word Locker.

> **SCOREBOARD**
> number correct | number wrong

★ ★ ★ ★ ★ ★ ★ ★ **All-Star Words** ★ ★ ★ ★ ★ ★ ★

holiday   sixty   country   easy   Monday

Write a sentence for each word, but leave a blank for the All-Star Word that completes the sentence. Trade papers with a partner. See if you can write the correct word in each sentence.

44 Lesson 10 ■ y as a Vowel

◎ Spelling Strategy

To help students discriminate between the letter pair that spells /ā/ and the single letter y that spells /ē/, have them play "Look to the Left." With a partner, students can point to the y in each List Word and look at the letter to the left of the y.

- If the letter is a consonant, have them say the word with the /ē/ sound for y.
- If it is a vowel, have them name the vowel and say the word using the /ā/ sound for y.

Flex Your Spelling Muscles   Page 44

As students complete the **Writing** activity, encourage them to brainstorm ideas, write a first draft, revise, and proofread their work. The **Proofreading** exercise will help them prepare to proofread their descriptions. To publish their writing, students may want to
- create a class book of "Our Favorite Places"
- use their descriptions to make picture postcards.

✍ Writer's Corner

The class may enjoy finding out about Prairie Dog Town by writing to Stevan Villers, Living Desert State Park, P.O. Box 100, Carlsbad, NM 88220. Be sure students specifically request information about Prairie Dog Town.

Go for the Goal/Final Test

1. Do we have **any** more paper in the closet?
2. She is the **lady** who wrote that story.
3. That table is too **heavy** for you to lift!
4. You can keep your toys in this **empty** box.
5. My dog is **always** happy to see me.
6. If you are **hungry,** we can make sandwiches.
7. Tina plays a **very** good game of baseball.
8. My parents have **plenty** of time to read to me.
9. If it snows, **maybe** the school will close.
10. A strong mule can **carry** all our equipment.
11. Your new curtains are a **pretty** shade of blue.
12. Even if you are **angry,** don't slam the door!
13. My **family** hikes together on weekends.
14. The movie started, but let's go in **anyway.**
15. Kittens are more **playful** than older cats.

Remind students to complete the Scoreboard and write any misspelled words in their Word Locker.

★★ **All-Star Words** You may want to point out that the All-Star Words follow the spelling rule and review how to write a cloze sentence.

Lesson 11

Objective
To spell words in which *y* is used as a vowel

Correlated Phonics Lesson
MCP Phonics, Level C, Lesson 29

Warm Up   **Page 45**
In "Funny Money," students read about some of the items people used for money before there were coins and bills. Afterward, ask students to suggest what people might use for money in the future.

Encourage students to look back at the words in dark print. Ask volunteers to say each word and name the vowel sound that *y* spells or helps to spell.

On Your Mark/Warm Up Test
1. My mother is a sergeant in the *army.*
2. The manager will call me if *anyone* finds my cap.
3. We have *twenty* students in this class.
4. Is your little brother *shy* around strangers?
5. My sister always makes *candy* for birthdays.
6. Use the red towel, if it is *dry.*
7. A bee has stripes on its *body.*
8. I have enough *money* for a new mitt.
9. What did you *buy* your mother for a gift?
10. I like to put *honey* on biscuits.
11. I want *every* person to think of an animal.
12. There is something in my *eye.*
13. In stories, the fox is usually a *sly* animal.
14. I love *turkey* with dressing!
15. Is smoke coming out of their *chimney?*

Pep Talk/Game Plan   **Pages 46–47**
Introduce the spelling rule and have students read the List Words aloud. Then encourage students to look back at their Warm Up Tests and apply the spelling rule to any misspelled words.

As students work through the **Spelling Lineup, Scrambled Letters,** and **Definitions** exercises, remind them to look back at their List Words or in their dictionaries if they need help.

 See **Pictures Clues,** page 15

---

y as a Vowel

Warm Up
What kind of things have people used as money?

Funny Money
Money hasn't always been the coins and bills we have today. At one time or another, almost anything could be used for money. In fact, money can be anything people use to **buy** and sell things. Three hundred years ago, the Russians used leather for money. In China, tea was used. At one time, salt paid for things in parts of Africa. People have traded with gunpowder, cows, and even the jawbones of pigs! The island of Manhattan in New York City was bought by the Dutch from some Native Americans. The Native Americans were paid in glass beads. That was in 1626. Today, people use paper money printed by their governments.

Many board games use "play" money. Believe it or not, **every** year the play money printed for these games comes to more than all the real money printed in the world. Don't get any funny ideas or try to be **sly.** Can you guess what will happen if **anyone** tries to spend it?

 Look back at the words in dark print. Say each word. What vowel sound does the y spell or help to spell in each word?

On Your Mark
Take your Warm Up Test. Then check your spelling with the List Words on the next page.

45

Pep Talk
The letter **y** can spell or help spell the vowel sound /ī/ or /ē/. Look at how the /ī/ sound is spelled in <u>buy</u> and in <u>eye</u>. At the end of one-syllable words, **y** spells /ī/, as in <u>shy</u>. At the end of words with more syllables, **y** often spells /ē/, as in <u>army</u>.

LIST WORDS
1. army	*army*
2. anyone	*anyone*
3. twenty	*twenty*
4. shy	*shy*
5. candy	*candy*
6. dry	*dry*
7. body	*body*
8. money	*money*
9. buy	*buy*
10. honey	*honey*
11. every	*every*
12. eye	*eye*
13. sly	*sly*
14. turkey	*turkey*
15. chimney	*chimney*

Game Plan
Spelling Lineup
Write the List Words in which y spells or helps to spell /ē/.

1. army   6. money
2. anyone   7. honey
3. twenty   8. every
4. candy   9. turkey
5. body   10. chimney

Write the List Words in which y spells or helps to spell /ī/.

11. shy   14. eye
12. dry   15. sly
13. buy

46   Lesson 11 ■ y as a Vowel

Scrambled Letters
Unscramble the letters to make List Words.

1. HYS   shy   6. TNWYTE   twenty
2. YEOHN   honey   7. YUB   buy
3. YEE   eye   8. AENOYN   anyone
4. REVEY   every   9. HICEYNM   chimney
5. RYD   dry   10. BOYD   body

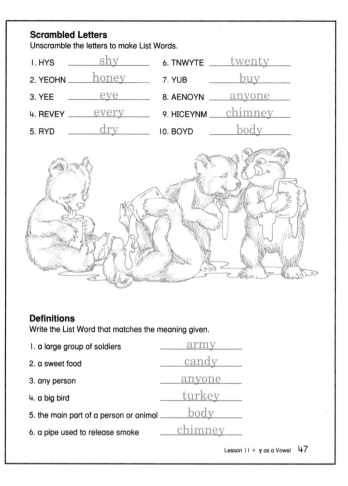

Definitions
Write the List Word that matches the meaning given.

1. a large group of soldiers   army
2. a sweet food   candy
3. any person   anyone
4. a big bird   turkey
5. the main part of a person or animal   body
6. a pipe used to release smoke   chimney

Lesson 11 = y as a Vowel   47

Flex Your Spelling Muscles

Writing
If you could choose one thing to use instead of money, what would it be? Write a paragraph to convince others that your form of money is the best. Use as many List Words as you can.

Proofreading
Each sentence below has two mistakes. Use the proofreading marks to fix each mistake. Write the misspelled List Words on the lines.

Proofreading Marks	
⌒	spelling mistake
⊙	add period
∧	add something

1. At one time, people used shells as monee⊙   1. money
2. Rare feathers and huney were used in trade⊙   2. honey
3. Who had the sliy idea to use paper?   3. sly
4. Would my turkee feather be worth something?   4. turkey

Now proofread your paragraph. Fix any mistakes.

Go for the Goal
Take your Final Test. Then fill in your Scoreboard. Send your mistakes to the Word Locker.

SCOREBOARD	
number correct	number wrong

★ ★ ★ ★ ★ ★ ★ All-Star Words ★ ★ ★ ★ ★ ★ ★

aye   spy   hockey   everybody   anyhow

Use the All-Star Words to create a crossword puzzle. Draw a grid and write a clue for each word. Swap papers with a partner. Can you fill in the puzzle with the correct All-Star Words?

48   Lesson 11 = y as a Vowel

⊙ **Spelling Strategy**   Remind students that at the end of one-syllable words, *y* spells /ī/, and at the end of a word with more syllables, *y* usually spells /ē/. Then write each List Word on the board and ask volunteers to
• tell how many syllables the word has
• name the long-vowel sound that *y* spells or helps to spell
• suggest a non-List Word with the same number of syllables in which *y* spells or helps to spell the same vowel sound.

Flex Your Spelling Muscles   *Page 48*
As students complete the **Writing** activity, encourage them to brainstorm ideas, write a first draft, revise, and proofread their work. The **Proofreading** exercise will help them prepare to proofread their paragraphs. To publish their writing, students may want to
• create a magazine titled "Money Mania"
• use their paragraphs to hold a class debate.

✍ Writer's Corner
Have students look at some dollar bills and coins and discuss what is printed on them. Students might also be interested in receiving the comic book *Once Upon a Dime*. The class can send a request on a postcard to the Federal Reserve Bank of New York, Public Information Department, 13th floor, 33 Liberty Street, New York, NY 10045.

Go for the Goal/Final Test
1. The male **turkey** is called a *tom.*
2. The store has several kinds of **candy** for sale.
3. Is Fort Riley an **army** base?
4. The magician is **sly,** so watch her hands closely.
5. Can you lend me **twenty** cents?
6. What a beautiful stone **chimney** this is!
7. I will wash the dishes if you will **dry** them.
8. Don't be **shy** about asking someone for help.
9. Does **anyone** here know how to speak Spanish?
10. That store sells several brands of **honey.**
11. Curl your **body** into a tight ball to do a somersault.
12. We must clean **every** room in the house.
13. Please cover your left **eye** and read the chart.
14. We have saved enough **money** for a field trip.
15. You can either **buy** skates or rent them.

Remind students to complete the Scoreboard and write any misspelled words in their Word Locker.

★★ **All-Star Words**   You may want to point out that the All-Star Words follow the spelling rule. Suggest that students begin their puzzles by first arranging the All-Star Words, then drawing a blank grid based on that arrangement.

43

Lesson 12 • Instant Replay

Objective
To review spelling words with long-vowel sounds, consonant blends, and *y* as a vowel

Time Out
Pages 49–52

Check Your Word Locker Based on your observations, note which words are giving students the most difficulty and offer assistance for spelling them correctly. Here are some frequently misspelled words to watch for: *read, break, friends, always, very, any, buy,* and *every.*

To give students extra help and practice in taking standardized tests, you may want to have them take the Review Test for this lesson on pages 46–47. After scoring the tests, return them to students so that they can record their misspelled words in their Word Locker.

After practicing their troublesome words, students can work through the exercises for **Lessons 7–11.** Before they begin each exercise, you may want to go over the spelling rule.

 **Take It Home** Invite students to locate the List Words in **Lessons 7–11** at home—on television, on the radio, in conversations, and in books and newspapers. For a complete list of the words, encourage students to take their *Spelling Workout* books home. Students can also use Take It Home Master 2 on pages 48–49 to help them do the activity. They can total the number of words they found and bring in their lists to share with the class.

44

Time Out
Take another look at words with long-vowel sounds, consonant blends, and **y** as a vowel.

Check Your Word Locker
Look at the words in your Word Locker. Which words for Lessons 7 through 11 did you have the most trouble with? Write them here.

_____

Practice writing your troublesome words with a partner. Try writing invisible letters for each word with your finger on your partner's back. Your partner can spell the word aloud as you write.

 **Lesson 7**

The vowels have long and short sounds. Long-vowel sounds can be spelled more than one way, as in <u>load</u> and <u>joke</u>.

List Words	Write a List Word that means the same or almost the same as each word given.
alive	1. crack ___break___
human	2. living ___alive___
music	3. group ___team___
crazy	4. person ___human___
break	5. foolish ___crazy___
team	6. tune ___music___

49

 **Lesson 8**

Consonants can be alone or come together in a word. In a **consonant blend,** you can hear the sound of each letter. Listen for the consonant blends in <u>smart,</u> <u>glue,</u> and <u>free.</u>

List Words	Write a List Word that means the opposite of each word or phrase given.
smile	1. sink ___float___ 4. frown ___smile___
best	2. worst ___best___ 5. save ___spend___
spend	3. take away ___bring___ 6. enemies ___friends___
float	
friends	
bring	

 **Lesson 9**

You can hear the sounds of two or more letters together in a **consonant blend.** Listen for the blends in <u>trip, plan, spill,</u> and <u>kind.</u>

List Words	Write a List Word that matches each clue.
kind	1. are walked on ___floors___
floors	2. not like all the rest ___special___
blaze	3. sweet and nice ___kind___
Friday	4. nice word when you ask ___please___
please	5. the last day of the school week ___Friday___
special	6. what a fire is ___blaze___

In some words, **y** helps to spell /ā/, as in <u>playful</u>. The letter **y** may also spell /ē/ at the end of a word with more than one syllable, as in <u>pretty</u>.

List Words

always			
anyway			
maybe			
family			
heavy			
hungry			

One word is misspelled in each set of List Words. Circle the word that is wrong. Then write it correctly on the line.

1. anyway   heavy   (famly)   family
2. (allways)   maybe   anyway   always
3. hungry   (haevy)   family   heavy
4. always   maybe   (aneyway)   anyway
5. family   (hungery)   always   hungry
6. heavy   (maybee)   hungry   maybe

The letter **y** can spell /ī/ at the end of one-syllable words, as in <u>shy</u>. At the end of a word with more than one syllable, **y** can spell /ē/, as in <u>body</u>.

List Words

anyone
twenty
candy
money
buy
turkey

Write a List Word that rhymes with each word given.

1. twenty-one   anyone
2. plenty   twenty
3. jerky   turkey
4. sandy   candy
5. my   buy
6. honey   money

List Words

human
anyone
maybe
special
buy
music
family
please
money
always
friends
heavy

Write the List Word that matches the meaning given.

1. not like others   special
2. a person   human
3. weighing very much   heavy
4. relatives   family
5. people you know and like   friends
6. any person   anyone
7. to get by paying money   buy
8. series of pleasing sounds   music
9. perhaps   maybe
10. satisfy   please
11. at all times   always
12. coins or paper bills   money

Go for the Goal

Take your Final Replay Test. Then fill in your Scoreboard. Send any misspelled words to your Word Locker.

SCOREBOARD

number correct	number wrong

Clean Out Your Word Locker
Look in your Word Locker. Cross out each word you spelled correctly on your Final Replay Test. Circle the words you're still having trouble with. Add the words you circled to your Spelling Notebook. What do you notice about the words? Watch for those words as you write.

Go for the Goal/Final Replay Test   *Page 52*

1. I am saving my ***money*** for a bicycle.
2. Did you ***buy*** your shoes at that store?
3. A ***turkey*** is larger than a goose.
4. My whole ***family*** liked that movie.
5. That chair is much too ***heavy*** for you to carry!
6. Have some fruit if you get ***hungry.***
7. On ***Friday*** you can spend the night at my house.
8. The poem you wrote will ***please*** your sister.
9. The singer made a ***special*** guest appearance.
10. I watched the leaf ***float*** on the lake.
11. Ask your ***friends*** to play soccer.
12. We may have to wait, so ***bring*** something to read.
13. My ***team*** won the tournament!
14. These dishes are easy to ***break,*** so be careful.
15. We learned this ***crazy*** song about frogs and mud.
16. Making ***candy*** is easy when you know how.
17. The eraser costs only ***twenty*** cents.
18. Does ***anyone*** know the capital of Australia?
19. The phone ***always*** rings when we're eating.
20. I'll ask Marty, and ***maybe*** he'll be able to come.
21. We're going ***anyway,*** so we'll give you a ride.
22. The ***kind*** police officer found my lost puppy.
23. The ***floors*** are covered with thick rugs.
24. Watch the fire ***blaze*** when he puts in pine cones.
25. That tree has been ***alive*** for hundreds of years.
26. A whale's voice sounds almost ***human.***
27. This ***music*** is difficult for a beginner to play.
28. The photographer asked us all to ***smile.***
29. This story is the ***best*** you have written.
30. I hope you can ***spend*** some time fishing.

Clean Out Your Word Locker   Before writing each word, students can say the word and name the vowel(s) that make a long-vowel sound or the consonants that make up the consonant blends.

Instant Replay Test

Side A

Read each set of phrases. Fill in the circle next to the phrase
with an underlined word that is spelled correctly.

1. ⓐ a kind <u>smille</u>　　ⓒ her joyful <u>smyle</u>
   ⓑ a bright <u>smile</u>　　ⓓ his happy <u>smiel</u>

2. ⓐ a <u>crazey</u> idea　　ⓒ a <u>craisy</u> word
   ⓑ the <u>crasy</u> clown　　ⓓ this <u>crazy</u> weather

3. ⓐ on <u>Friday</u>　　ⓒ last <u>Frieday</u>
   ⓑ next <u>Fryday</u>　　ⓓ by <u>Fridae</u>

4. ⓐ a <u>hevvy</u> elephant　　ⓒ the <u>heavy</u> piano
   ⓑ the <u>heavey</u> brick　　ⓓ a <u>hevey</u> refrigerator

5. ⓐ <u>allways</u> playing　　ⓒ <u>allwayz</u> joking
   ⓑ <u>alwayz</u> laughing　　ⓓ <u>always</u> finished

6. ⓐ a swim <u>team</u>　　ⓒ the football <u>teame</u>
   ⓑ the soccer <u>teme</u>　　ⓓ a baseball <u>teem</u>

7. ⓐ lunch <u>money</u>　　ⓒ milk <u>muney</u>
   ⓑ saved <u>monny</u>　　ⓓ play <u>muny</u>

8. ⓐ old <u>frends</u>　　ⓒ school <u>friends</u>
   ⓑ loyal <u>friendes</u>　　ⓓ good <u>freinds</u>

9. ⓐ a <u>speshle</u> plan　　ⓒ this <u>speshal</u> treat
   ⓑ a <u>special</u> menu　　ⓓ one <u>spechal</u> project

10. ⓐ the <u>kined</u> bus driver　　ⓒ the <u>kynd</u> artist
    ⓑ a <u>kind</u> teacher　　ⓓ my <u>kiend</u> aunt

Instant Replay Test

Side B

Read each set of phrases. Fill in the circle next to the phrase with an underlined word that is spelled correctly.

11. ⓐ drum <u>muzic</u>   ⓒ flute <u>musick</u>
    ⓑ piano <u>muzick</u>   ⓓ trumpet <u>music</u>

12. ⓐ a large <u>family</u>   ⓒ the young <u>famly</u>
    ⓑ the whole <u>familey</u>   ⓓ a happy <u>famely</u>

13. ⓐ to <u>spiend</u> energy   ⓒ to <u>spend</u> time
    ⓑ to <u>speand</u> our vacation   ⓓ to <u>spende</u> money

14. ⓐ to <u>anyone</u>   ⓒ for <u>anywon</u>
    ⓑ with <u>annyone</u>   ⓓ by <u>enyone</u>

15. ⓐ the <u>beste</u> worker   ⓒ your <u>beeste</u> effort
    ⓑ his <u>best</u> drawing   ⓓ my <u>besst</u> buddy

16. ⓐ <u>tweanty</u> stories   ⓒ <u>twenty</u> students
    ⓑ <u>twentey</u> balls   ⓓ <u>twennty</u> people

17. ⓐ the cement <u>floors</u>   ⓒ those wooden <u>floores</u>
    ⓑ some tile <u>flores</u>   ⓓ most schools' <u>floars</u>

18. ⓐ the leftover <u>turky</u>   ⓒ a <u>terkey</u> sandwich
    ⓑ the roast <u>turkey</u>   ⓓ some sliced <u>tirkey</u>

19. ⓐ a short <u>hueman</u>   ⓒ a tall <u>human</u>
    ⓑ a smart <u>uman</u>   ⓓ a thin <u>humen</u>

20. ⓐ the <u>hugry</u> baby   ⓒ some <u>hongry</u> children
    ⓑ those <u>hungrie</u> lions   ⓓ the <u>hungry</u> horse

TAKE IT HOME

Your child has learned to spell many new words and would like to share them with you and your family. Here are some ideas for helping your child review some of the words from Lessons 7–11, and have fun, too!

Post It!
Post a blank sheet of paper on the refrigerator door or keep a sheet handy on a counter or on a table. Encourage your child to listen for and locate their spelling words while you read together, watch television, listen to the radio, or have family conversations.

Word Search

How many words can you and your child find in this puzzle?
Hint: Be sure to read across and down.

plant	playful	lady	any
float	read	glue	trip

Z A F L W X O L C
Q H F A P P E Y W
U R K D J N G Z P
P L A Y F U L C M
L V Y Z L K U I O
A N Y R O R E A D
N T B C A F G K R
T F K Y T R I P Y

Lesson 13

Objective
To spell words with *r*-controlled vowels

Correlated Phonics Lessons
MCP Phonics, Level C, Lessons 36–37
Silver Burdett Ginn *World of Reading,* 3/2, p. 310

Warm Up   **Page 53**
In this selection, students discover why a town made
a salad that contained one thousand heads of
lettuce. Ask students what gigantic dish they would
enjoy making and what quantities of ingredients they
would need to make it.

Encourage students to look back at the words in
dark print. Ask volunteers to say each word and tell
how the letter *r* changes the vowel sound.

On Your Mark/Warm Up Test
1. How much did you weigh last **year?**
2. Tom takes good **care** of his little brother.
3. What a **large** van that is!
4. Don't **start** until you hear the whistle.
5. Wash your hands **before** you eat.
6. The words appear in alphabetical **order.**
7. That was the best birthday **party** ever!
8. Please put a knife and **fork** on the table.
9. Let's give the team a big **cheer.**
10. This **chair** has a leather seat.
11. Will you help weed the **garden?**
12. Aunt Maria wakes up early in the **morning.**
13. Let's **compare** the prices of those sneakers.
14. On a **clear** day, you can see the mountains.
15. A magician made a rabbit **appear** in the hat.

Pep Talk/Game Plan   **Pages 54–55**
Introduce the spelling rule and have students read
the List Words aloud, asking volunteers to name the
vowel-*r* sound and the spelling of that sound in each
word. Use List Word pairs, such as *year* and *cheer,* to
point out the different spellings of the same sound
(*before/fork, compare/chair*). Then encourage
students to look back at their Warm Up Tests and
apply the spelling rule to any misspelled words.

As students work through the **Spelling Lineup,**
Sound-Spellings, and **Classification** exercises,
remind them to look back at their List Words or in
their dictionaries if they need help. For the **Spelling
Lineup,** you may want to complete the first item
with students.

 See **Letter Cards,** page 15

50

Name _____

Vowels with r   LESSON 13

Warm Up
What has one thousand heads?

A Green Giant
What is red and green and has a thousand heads? Give
up? It's one of the world's biggest salads. At least the
people of Milford, Massachusetts, say it was the biggest.
They tossed their giant salad for Milford's bicentennial.
That was the **year** that Milford had its 200th birthday.
The people in Milford **care** a lot about their town. They
wanted to make something really **large** so everyone would
notice it.

The people had to **start** planning months **before** the
big day. First, they had to **order** all the things to go into
the salad. Then, for hours and hours, they chopped and
sliced everything. When they were finished, their salad
stretched out as long as a football field. It had one
thousand heads of lettuce and tons of tomatoes, olives,
cheese, peppers, and onions. There were gallons of dressing
to go with it, too.

On the day of the **party,** each guest lined up with a fork
and plate in hand. Then the mighty salad disappeared like
magic. No one in Milford is sure if it was really the world's
biggest salad, but for them, it was quite a mouthful!

 Look back at the words in dark print in the
selection. Say each word. What do you notice
about the way the vowels sound in each word?

On Your Mark
Take your Warm Up Test. Then check your spelling with
the List Words on the next page.

53

Pep Talk
When a vowel comes before the letter **r**
in a word, the sound of the vowel can
change. Each List Word contains one of
the vowel sounds represented by these
sound-symbols:
/är/ as in <u>start</u>   /ir/ as in <u>year</u>
/ôr/ as in <u>fork</u>   /er/ as in <u>chair</u>

LIST WORDS
1. year — *year*
2. care — *care*
3. large — *large*
4. start — *start*
5. before — *before*
6. order — *order*
7. party — *party*
8. fork — *fork*
9. cheer — *cheer*
10. chair — *chair*
11. garden — *garden*
12. morning — *morning*
13. compare — *compare*
14. clear — *clear*
15. appear — *appear*

Game Plan
Spelling Lineup
Write each List Word under the correct
heading.

/är/ as in <u>far</u>	/ir/ as in <u>ear</u>
1. large	9. year
2. start	10. cheer
3. party	11. clear
4. garden	12. appear

/ôr/ as in <u>for</u>	/er/ as in <u>air</u>
5. before	13. care
6. order	14. chair
7. fork	15. compare
8. morning	

54   Lesson 13 ▪ Vowels with r

Sound-Spellings

Write the List Word for each sound-spelling given. Use your dictionary if you need help.

> In a dictionary, a **sound-spelling** appears after each entry word. It tells how to pronounce the word. **start** (stärt)

1. (ôr´ dər) _order_
2. (bē fôr´) _before_
3. (ker) _care_
4. (yir) _year_
5. (lärj) _large_
6. (cher) _chair_
7. (klir) _clear_
8. (chir) _cheer_
9. (pär´ tē) _party_
10. (môrn´ iŋ) _morning_
11. (kəm per´) _compare_
12. (ə pir´) _appear_

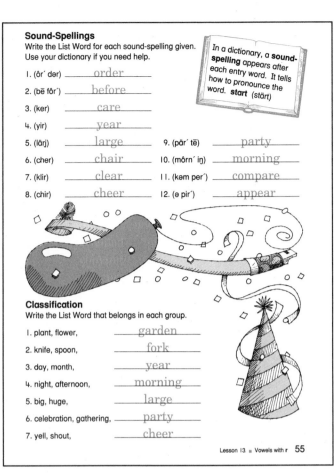

Classification

Write the List Word that belongs in each group.

1. plant, flower, _garden_
2. knife, spoon, _fork_
3. day, month, _year_
4. night, afternoon, _morning_
5. big, huge, _large_
6. celebration, gathering, _party_
7. yell, shout, _cheer_

Flex Your Spelling Muscles

Writing

Imagine that you have been chosen to make a salad for the 200th birthday of your own town. What are you going to put in it? Write a recipe telling how to make your salad. Use as many List Words as you can.

Proofreading

Each sentence below has two mistakes. Use the proofreading marks to fix each mistake. Write the misspelled List Words on the lines.

	Proofreading Marks
◯	spelling mistake
≡	capital letter

1. my mother planted a vegetable ⟨gardin⟩ last year.

2. she asked me to help take ⟨kare⟩ of it.

3. So I watered it ⟨befour⟩ school every ⟨mornin⟩.

4. i made sure to keep the weeds ⟨cler⟩.

5. The vegetables grew very ⟨larje⟩ that ⟨yer⟩.

1. _garden_
2. _care_
3. _before_
   morning
4. _clear_
5. _large_
   year

Now proofread your recipe. Fix any mistakes.

Go for the Goal

Take your Final Test. Then fill in your Scoreboard. Send your mistakes to the Word Locker.

SCOREBOARD

number correct	number wrong

★ ★ ★ ★ ★ ★ ★ All-Star Words ★ ★ ★ ★ ★ ★ ★

darkness   fear   airport   harm   forward

Write each All-Star Word and a clue to go with it. Then get together with a partner. Can you guess the All-Star Word that goes with each clue?

◉ **Spelling Strategy** Write each List Word on the board, leaving a blank for the letters that spell the /är/, /ir/, /ôr/, or /er/ sound. For each word, ask a volunteer to come to the board and
- fill in the missing letters
- write the symbol of the sound that the letters stand for beside the word.

You may need to help students identify and write the sound-symbols.

Flex Your Spelling Muscles   *Page 56*

As students complete the **Writing** activity, encourage them to brainstorm ideas, write a first draft, revise, and proofread their work. The **Proofreading** exercise will help them prepare to proofread their recipes. To publish their writing, students may want to make a class cookbook titled "Great Greens."

✍ Writer's Corner

> You may want to bring in recipes for various salads and share them with the class. Invite students to jot down their favorite recipe, take it home, and ask their parents or other family members to help them make the salad.

Go for the Goal/Final Test

1. Yesterday it rained, but today the sky is ***clear.***
2. Do you grow corn and beans in your ***garden?***
3. Uncle Kenji used a big ***fork*** to serve the fish.
4. Please put on your coat ***before*** you go outside.
5. The doctor will take ***care*** of your poison ivy.
6. Read the directions before you ***start*** the game.
7. What a great vacation we had last ***year!***
8. Please put your ***chair*** next to mine.
9. What games should we play at our class ***party?***
10. We ***compare*** things to tell how they are alike.
11. We hope to go fishing early tomorrow ***morning.***
12. Soon new leaves will ***appear*** on the trees.
13. Did Andrea put these pages in ***order?***
14. My father likes to ***cheer*** for his favorite team.
15. I'd like to drink a ***large*** glass of milk.

Remind students to complete the Scoreboard and write any misspelled words in their Word Locker.

★★ **All-Star Words** You may want to point out that the All-Star Words follow the spelling rule and model how to write a clue for a List Word.

Lesson 14

Objective
To spell words with /ʉr/

Correlated Phonics Lessons
MCP Phonics, Level C, Lessons 36–37
Silver Burdett Ginn *World of Reading,* 3/2, p. 310

Warm Up   **Page 57**
In "Give a Hoot," students read about a contest in
which people yell at the top of their lungs to honor the
past. After reading, invite students to suggest ideas
for contests that could be held in their city or town.

Encourage students to look back at the words in
dark print. Ask volunteers to say each word and
name the vowel sound with *r* that they hear.

On Your Mark/Warm Up Test
1. Steve was tired, so he went to bed *early.*
2. Cassandra sits in the *third* row.
3. Does each student have a *workbook?*
4. The runner slid into *first* base.
5. Don't *worry* about tomorrow's test.
6. Fernando *hurt* his leg when he fell on the ice.
7. We're going to a football game on *Saturday.*
8. "I have a *better* idea," said Fran.
9. I know the *farmer* who owns that cow.
10. Aretha had the *honor* of meeting Mayor Flynn.
11. Too much *sugar* may cause tooth decay.
12. My brother is a *nurse* at Emerson Hospital.
13. How far is it from the *earth* to the moon?
14. I took a stack of *paper* to the recycling center.
15. Our spelling words are fun to *learn!*

Pep Talk/Game Plan   **Pages 58–59**
Introduce the spelling rule and have students read
the List Words aloud. Encourage students to look
back at their Warm Up Tests and apply the spelling
rule to any misspelled words.

As students work through the **Spelling Lineup,**
Dictionary, and **Puzzle** exercises, remind them to
look back at their List Words or in their dictionaries if
they need help. For the **Spelling Lineup,** you may
want to complete the first item with students.

 See **Variant Spellings,** page 14

52

Vowels with r

Warm Up
Why do people come to the National Hollerin' Contest?

Give a Hoot
   Every year on the **third Saturday** in
June, folks gather to hoot and holler. The
place is Spivey's Corner, North Carolina. The
people come here to **honor** the past by yelling.
   Years ago around these parts, you could hear
hollering every day. **Early** in the morning on
their way to work, farmers would holler to
each other. **First,** one **farmer** would yell. Then
another would take a turn. Several more would
join in. Before long, people were hollerin' from miles
away. Each farmer tried to yell **better** and louder than
the last. Each one had a special style. Neighbors could
recognize one another's yells. It was a signal that the work
day was beginning, just like an early morning hello.
   Today, there's no need to yell in Spivey's Corner. Now
there are telephones! Once a year though, people still
holler. The best and the loudest yellers come from all
around. You could call Spivey's Corner the "hollerin'
capital of the world." But don't say it too loud, it might
hurt your ears.

 Say the words in dark print in the selection. What
vowel sound with **r** do you hear in each word?

On Your Mark

Take your Warm Up Test. Then check your spelling with
the List Words on the next page.

57

Pep Talk
Each List Word contains the /ʉr/ sound. It
can be spelled many ways. Look at each
List Word to see how the /ʉr/ sound is
spelled:
fi**r**st l**ea**rn w**o**rk sug**ar** p**a**per h**u**rt
When the /ʉr/ sound is found in a syllable
that is not accented, its sound-symbol is /ər/.

LIST WORDS

1. early	*early*
2. third	*third*
3. workbook	*workbook*
4. first	*first*
5. worry	*worry*
6. hurt	*hurt*
7. Saturday	*Saturday*
8. better	*better*
9. farmer	*farmer*
10. honor	*honor*
11. sugar	*sugar*
12. nurse	*nurse*
13. earth	*earth*
14. paper	*paper*
15. learn	*learn*

Game Plan
Spelling Lineup
Write each List Word under the correct
spelling of the /ʉr/ sound.

ir
1. third
2. first

ur
3. hurt
4. Saturday
5. nurse

ear
6. early
7. earth
8. learn

er
9. better
10. farmer
11. paper

or
12. workbook
13. worry
14. honor

ar
15. sugar

58   Lesson 14 ▪ Vowels with r

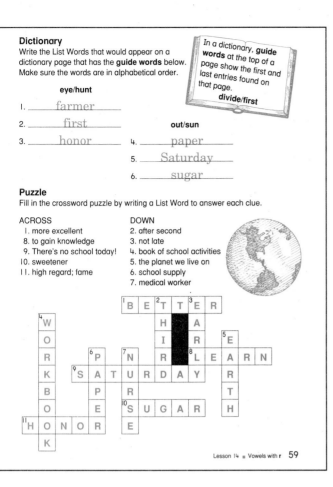

Dictionary

Write the List Words that would appear on a dictionary page that has the **guide words** below. Make sure the words are in alphabetical order.

In a dictionary, **guide words** at the top of a page show the first and last entries found on that page.
divide/first

eye/hunt

1. _farmer_
2. _first_
3. _honor_

out/sun

4. _paper_
5. _Saturday_
6. _sugar_

Puzzle

Fill in the crossword puzzle by writing a List Word to answer each clue.

ACROSS
1. more excellent
8. to gain knowledge
9. There's no school today!
10. sweetener
11. high regard; fame

DOWN
2. after second
3. not late
4. book of school activities
5. the planet we live on
6. school supply
7. medical worker

Crossword:
- 1 Across: BETTER
- 9 Across: SATURDAY
- 8 Across: LEARN
- 10 Across: SUGAR
- 11 Across: HONOR
- 4 Down: WORKBOOK
- 2 Down: THIRD
- 3 Down: EARLY
- 5 Down: EARTH
- 6 Down: PAPER
- 7 Down: NURSE

Lesson 14 ■ Vowels with r 59

Flex Your Spelling Muscles

Writing

Use the List Words to create a poster to advertise a contest you know about or would like to have. Remember to include important information such as what kind of contest it is, and when and where it will take place.

Proofreading

Each sentence below has two mistakes. Use the proofreading marks to fix each mistake. Write the misspelled List Words on the lines.

Proofreading Marks
⌒ spelling mistake
⊙ add period

1. Many years ago, people in Africa used drums instead of (papir) to communicate
2. They could (lurn) about other people (bettur) and faster with drums.
3. The drums could tell if someone was (hert) and if a doctor was needed
4. The drums held a special place of (honar) among the people

Now proofread your poster.
Fix any mistakes.

1. _paper_
2. _learn_
   better
3. _hurt_
4. _honor_

Go for the Goal

Take your Final Test. Then fill in your Scoreboard. Send your mistakes to the Word Locker.

SCOREBOARD
number correct	number wrong

★ ★ ★ ★ ★ ★ ★ ★ All-Star Words ★ ★ ★ ★ ★ ★ ★ ★

churn   earn   dessert   squirm   afford

Write a sentence for each word, then erase the All-Star Word. Trade papers with a partner. Write the word that belongs in each blank.

60 Lesson 14 ■ Vowels with r

⊙ **Spelling Strategy**   To help students recognize the different spellings of the /ur/ sound, invite them to get together with a partner and take turns pronouncing the List Words. As students say the words, they can point to the letters that stand for the /ur/ sound and stress them (l*ear*n, sug*ar*).

Flex Your Spelling Muscles   *Page 60*

As students complete the **Writing** activity, encourage them to brainstorm ideas, write a first draft, revise, and proofread their work. The **Proofreading** exercise will help them prepare to proofread their posters. To publish their writing, students may want to

• create a classroom display called "Contest Corner"
• hang their posters in local stores or businesses if they announce real contests.

✎ **Writer's Corner** _____

Students might enjoy entering local contests. Help them research contests for children in your area and fill out any entrance or application forms.

Go for the Goal/Final Test

1. The *farmer* milked the cows.
2. On *Saturday* we had a picnic.
3. Yesterday I was sick, but today I'm *better.*
4. The piñata is made of colorful *paper.*
5. Oceans cover much of the *earth.*
6. Which new words did you *learn* to spell?
7. I *hurt* my hand when I caught the ball.
8. This is the *first* time I have ridden in a plane.
9. Your parents will *worry* if you are late.
10. Please do the exercise in your *workbook.*
11. Thu arrived at school *early* this morning.
12. Are you in the *third* grade?
13. I like brown *sugar* on oatmeal.
14. The *nurse* put a fresh bandage on my cut.
15. What an *honor* it is to meet you!

Remind students to complete the Scoreboard and write any misspelled words in their Word Locker.

★ ★ **All-Star Words**   You may want to point out that the All-Star Words follow the spelling rule and model completing the activity with a List Word.

Lesson 15

Objective
To spell words in which the suffixes *ed* and *ing* have been added to root words

Correlated Phonics Lessons
MCP Phonics, Level C, Lesson 51
Silver Burdett Ginn *World of Reading*, 3/2, pp. 316–317

Warm Up   *Page 61*
Students learn how abandoned lookout towers have been converted into vacation houses in "Above the Crowds." Ask what they would and would not like about vacationing in one of these towers.

Call on volunteers to say the words in dark print and identify the root words that changed when a suffix was added.

On Your Mark/Warm Up Test
1. It *rained* hard all afternoon.
2. We *prayed* that the river would not overflow.
3. I *studied* all day Saturday for my math test.
4. The children are *cleaning* their bedroom.
5. She *thanked* everyone for the birthday presents.
6. Mitsu *acted* quickly during the emergency.
7. Julio *worried* about being late.
8. Everyone *helped* rake the leaves.
9. Are you *copying* the poem that you like?
10. That kite is *flying* right into a tree.
11. The twins *hurried* home after school.
12. The *married* couple cut the wedding cake.
13. The actors are *dressing* for the next scene.
14. Our *camping* trip was fantastic!
15. Have you *replied* to Marianne's invitation?

Pep Talk/Game Plan   *Pages 62–63*
Introduce the spelling rule and have students read the List Words aloud. Encourage students to look back at their Warm Up Tests and apply the spelling rule to any misspelled words.

As students work through the **Spelling Lineup**, **Classification,** and **Missing Words** exercises, remind them to look back at their List Words or in their dictionaries if they need help. Before students begin the **Spelling Lineup,** point out that each of the List Words is a verb. Explain that the verbs that end in *ing* tell about an action that is happening now, and that the verbs that end in *ed* tell about an action that happened in the past.

 See **Change or No Change,** page 15

Suffixes Added to Root Words   LESSON 15

Warm Up
What, other than fire detection, can a lookout tower be used for?

Above the Crowds
If you're in the mood for a mountain vacation, and you don't care to go **camping,** why not try a week in a lookout tower? In many national forests across the country people are doing just that—vacationing in old fire lookout towers.

At one time the Forest Service relied heavily on these towers. From them rangers **studied** the forest for signs of forest fire. Today, the Forest Service depends mostly on airplanes that are much more efficient and can pinpoint the exact locations of fires. As a result, many of the older lookout towers are no longer being used. However, volunteers have begun taking an interest in saving these buildings. They have started **cleaning** and repairing towers that need repairs.

If you like fancy hotels, you may not like a lookout tower. Many are five stories high, and the bathrooms are on the ground. There is no electricity and you have to haul up your own water. And if you are **worried** about lightning, stay home. Lightning strikes are a pretty common event. Although the towers are fairly safe, a lightning bolt can be shocking! As one visitor said, "It's like being on the inside of a light bulb when someone turns it on."

 Look back at the words in dark print. What do you notice about their spelling? Did the root words change when an ending, or suffix, was added?

On Your Mark
Take your Warm Up Test. Then check your spelling with the List Words on the next page.

Pep Talk
A **suffix** is added at the end of a **root word**. If a word ends in a vowel and **y**, add only the suffix—**stay + ed = stayed.** If a word ends in a consonant and **y**, change the **y** to **i** before adding the suffix unless the suffix begins with **i**.
worry + ed = worried
worry + ing = worrying

LIST WORDS

1. rained *rained*
2. prayed *prayed*
3. studied *studied*
4. cleaning *cleaning*
5. thanked *thanked*
6. acted *acted*
7. worried *worried*
8. helped *helped*
9. copying *copying*
10. flying *flying*
11. hurried *hurried*
12. married *married*
13. dressing *dressing*
14. camping *camping*
15. replied *replied*

Game Plan

Spelling Lineup
Write the List Words. In some List Words, you must change the **y** to **i.**

1. rain + ed = _____ rained
2. pray + ed = _____ prayed
3. study + ed = _____ studied
4. clean + ing = _____ cleaning
5. thank + ed = _____ thanked
6. act + ed = _____ acted
7. worry + ed = _____ worried
8. help + ed = _____ helped
9. copy + ing = _____ copying
10. fly + ing = _____ flying
11. hurry + ed = _____ hurried
12. marry + ed = _____ married
13. dress + ing = _____ dressing
14. camp + ing = _____ camping
15. reply + ed = _____ replied

62   Lesson 15 ■ Suffixes Added to Root Words

Classification

Write the List Word that belongs in each group.

1. school, tests, books, _____studied_____
2. tent, sleeping bag, backpack, _____camping_____
3. bride, groom, ring, _____married_____
4. stage, play, theater, _____acted_____
5. clouds, lightning, thunder, _____rained_____
6. said, answered, responded, _____replied_____
7. soap, water, dirt, _____cleaning_____
8. shirt, pants, jacket, _____dressing_____

Missing Words

Add **ing** or **ed** to a root word from the box to make List Words. Write a List Word to finish each sentence.

help	fly	copy	thank
study	hurry	worry	pray

1. I _____thanked_____ my grandparents for the gift.
2. David _____helped_____ his dad do the housework.
3. I am _____copying_____ the words onto my paper now.
4. The farmers _____prayed_____ for rain.
5. My parents were _____worried_____ when I came home late from school.
6. I _____hurried_____ to reach the store before it closed.
7. The pilot is _____flying_____ around the world.
8. Paul and I _____studied_____ together in the library.

Lesson 15 ▪ Suffixes Added to Root Words 63

Flex Your Spelling Muscles

Writing

Have you ever been on a camping trip, or wondered what it would be like? Write a story about a camping trip you've taken or would like to take. Use as many List Words as you can.

Proofreading

Each sentence below has two mistakes. Use the proofreading marks to fix each mistake. Write the misspelled List Words on the lines.

Proofreading Marks	
◯	spelling mistake
⊙	add period

1. Teddy Roosevelt was a president who (studyed) the environment⊙   1. _____studied_____
2. He (wooried) about what was happening to the wild lands in our country⊙   2. _____worried_____
3. He (helpet) save the forests and wildlife⊙   3. _____helped_____
4. Most people (tainked) him for what he did⊙   4. _____thanked_____

Now proofread your story. Fix any mistakes.

Go for the Goal

Take your Final Test. Then fill in your Scoreboard. Send your mistakes to the Word Locker.

SCOREBOARD

number correct	number wrong

★ ★ ★ ★ ★ ★ ★ All-Star Words ★ ★ ★ ★ ★ ★ ★

tossed   scolding   frying   satisfied   spied

Write a sentence using each All-Star Word, but erase the word's suffix. Trade papers with a partner. Finish each other's sentences.

64 Lesson 15 ▪ Suffixes Added to Root Words

◎ **Spelling Strategy**   Invite students to get together with a partner and take turns writing the List Words whose root words end with *y.* The partner who writes the word
- circles the suffix
- points to the *y* or *i*
- explains why the *y* was or was not changed to *i.*

Flex Your Spelling Muscles   *Page 64*

As students complete the **Writing** activity, encourage them to brainstorm ideas, write a first draft, revise, and proofread their work. The **Proofreading** exercise will help them prepare to proofread their stories. To publish their writing, encourage students to create a camping bulletin-board display, using their stories and original drawings or magazine art.

✍ **Writer's Corner**

Students might be interested in reading a book about forest rangers, such as *I Can Be a Forest Ranger* by Carol Greene. Encourage them to write a response to the book, telling why they would or wouldn't enjoy working as a ranger.

Go for the Goal/Final Test

1. Have they **replied** to your letter?
2. We finished **dressing** for the party.
3. Mom **hurried** to the airport to catch her plane.
4. Are you **copying** your homework neatly?
5. We were **worried** when you didn't call.
6. He **thanked** the man for returning his lost wallet.
7. I hope you **studied** enough for this test.
8. It **rained** all week, and the field was muddy.
9. I love to go **camping** in the mountains!
10. Dan and Susan have been **married** for a year.
11. The hawk was **flying** right over our heads.
12. The police officer **helped** the lost children.
13. Erica **acted** in a responsible way.
14. Will you start **cleaning** the garage tonight?
15. She **prayed** that her grandfather would get well.

Remind students to complete the Scoreboard and write any misspelled words in their Word Locker.

★★ **All-Star Words**   You may want to point out that the All-Star Words follow the spelling rule. Explain to students that the suffix in words that end in *ied* is *ed,* not *ied.*

55

Lesson 16

Objective
To spell words with the suffixes *ed, ing, er, est,* and *y*

Correlated Phonics Lessons
MCP Phonics, Level C, Lesson 48
Silver Burdett Ginn *World of Reading,* 3/2, pp. 316–317

Warm Up   **Page 65**
In this selection, students find out why Mark Spitz is considered the best swimmer in the world. Ask students what they think a swimmer has to do to become a world champion.

Encourage students to look back at the words in dark print. Ask volunteers to say each word and tell how the root word changed when the suffix was added.

On Your Mark/Warm Up Test
1. Mark Spitz was an Olympic *swimmer.*
2. That's the *biggest* horse I've ever seen!
3. Who is the *winner* of the spelling bee?
4. The barber is *cutting* Diego's hair.
5. The mountaintop is *foggy* this morning.
6. The sun is *setting* on the horizon.
7. The traffic *stopped* at the red light.
8. A rain forest is a *wetter* place than a desert.
9. The quarterback *slipped* on the muddy field.
10. The children are *stepping* in the puddles.
11. Mom was *beginning* to think you weren't coming.
12. He finally *admitted* that he ate the last piece.
13. The *jogger* ran around the track twenty times.
14. The athletes are *flexing* their muscles.
15. Was this floor just *waxed?*

Pep Talk/Game Plan   **Pages 66–67**
Introduce the spelling rule and have students read the List Words aloud. Encourage students to look back at their Warm Up Tests and apply the spelling rule to any misspelled words.

As students work through the **Spelling Lineup, Rhyming,** and **Definitions** exercises, remind them to look back at their List Words or in their dictionaries if they need help. For the **Spelling Lineup,** ask a volunteer to read both sets of directions aloud.

 See **Questions/Answers,** page 15

Suffixes Added to Root Words

Warm Up
Why would people call Mark Spitz the best swimmer in the world?

Golden Boy
Mark Spitz won nine Olympic gold medals in the 1968 and 1972 Olympic games. That means he came in first in nine races. He also won a silver medal for second place and a bronze medal for third place in two other races. With eleven Olympic medals, Mark Spitz became the most famous **swimmer** in the world and the **biggest** winner of Olympic medals.

At age six Mark was just **beginning** swimming lessons. By the time he was ten, he was known for **setting** a record. It was in the 50-yard race for nine- and ten-year-olds. He won that race in less time than anyone in that age group had ever done before.

To this day, no one has ever won as many Olympic medals as Mark Spitz. But when that day finally comes, it'll really be something to see!

Look back at the words in dark print. What do you notice about the spelling of the root words when the suffixes are added?

On Your Mark
Take your Warm Up Test. Then check your spelling with the List Words on the next page.

65

Pep Talk
When a short-vowel word ends with one consonant, double the consonant before adding a suffix that begins with a vowel.
swim + **er** = swimmer
cut + **ing** = cutting
Do not double final **x** in roots ending in **x**.
flex + **ing** = flexing

LIST WORDS

1. swimmer — *swimmer*
2. biggest — *biggest*
3. winner — *winner*
4. cutting — *cutting*
5. foggy — *foggy*
6. setting — *setting*
7. stopped — *stopped*
8. wetter — *wetter*
9. slipped — *slipped*
10. stepping — *stepping*
11. beginning — *beginning*
12. admitted — *admitted*
13. jogger — *jogger*
14. flexing — *flexing*
15. waxed — *waxed*

Game Plan
Spelling Lineup
Write each List Word whose final consonant was doubled before the suffix was added. Circle each suffix.

1. swimm(er)   8. wett(er)
2. bigg(est)   9. slipp(ed)
3. winn(er)   10. stepp(ing)
4. cutt(ing)   11. beginn(ing)
5. fogg(y)   12. admitt(ed)
6. sett(ing)   13. jogg(er)
7. stopp(ed)

Write each List Word that did not have the final consonant doubled before the suffix was added. Circle each suffix.

14. flex(ing)   15. wax(ed)

Rhyming

Write the List Word that rhymes with each word given.

1. netting _setting_   4. clipped _slipped_
2. taxed _waxed_   5. logger _jogger_
3. letter _wetter_   6. chopped _stopped_

Definitions

Write the List Word that matches the meaning given. Then read down the shaded boxes to answer the riddle.

1. largest			B	I	G	G	E	S	T
2. misty and cloudy		F	O	G	G	Y	
3. said to be true		A	D	M	I	T	T	E	D
4. dividing into parts	C	U	T	T	I	N	G	
5. one who moves in water	S	W	I	M	M	E	R	
6. walking		S	T	E	P	P	I	N	G
7. polished		W	A	X	E	D	
8. bending or tightening your muscles		F	L	E	X	I	N	G

Riddle: What does a boat eat for breakfast?

Answer: _BOATMEAL_

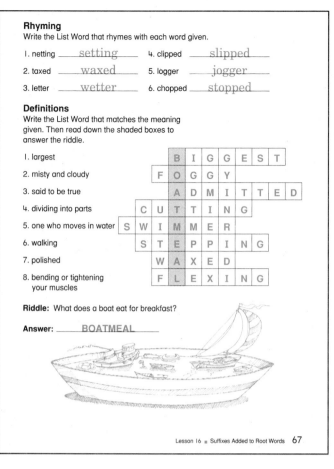

Flex Your Spelling Muscles

Writing

What is your favorite sport? Write a few sentences naming the sport you like best and why. Use as many List Words as you can.

Proofreading

Each sentence below has two mistakes. Use the proofreading marks to fix each mistake. Write the misspelled List Words on the lines.

Proofreading Marks	
◯	spelling mistake
≡	capital letter
⊙	add period

1. In the (beegining) the Olympic games were held in greece.

1. _beginning_

2. today, the (seting) of the Olympics changes each time they are held.

2. _setting_

3. Some cities have never (stopt) wanting to host the games

3. _stopped_

4. Maybe one day your town will have the top (swimar) in the Olympics

4. _swimmer_

Now proofread your sentences about sports. Fix any mistakes.

Goal for the Goal

Take your Final Test. Then fill in your Scoreboard. Send your mistakes to the Word Locker.

SCOREBOARD

number correct	number wrong

★ ★ ★ ★ ★ ★ ★ ★ **All-Star Words** ★ ★ ★ ★ ★ ★ ★ ★

stirred   dimmer   clapping   smoggy   maddest

Write a sentence for each All-Star Word. Trade papers with a partner. Circle the suffix in the All-Star Word in each sentence.

⊙ **Spelling Strategy** Write List Words on the board, one for each suffix presented in the lesson (*swimmer, cutting, biggest, admitted, foggy*). Then write short-vowel words that have two final consonants and a suffix (*helper, rushing, freshest, blinked, sandy*). Have students identify the root words in each list and compare their spellings when a suffix is added. Help students conclude that when a short-vowel word ends with one consonant, the consonant doubles when a suffix is added. Remind them that roots ending in *x* do not double the final *x*.

Flex Your Spelling Muscles   *Page 68*

As students complete the **Writing** activity, encourage them to brainstorm ideas, write a first draft, revise, and proofread their work. The **Proofreading** exercise will help them prepare to proofread their sentences. To publish their writing, students may want to
• read their sentences aloud to the class
• exchange their sentences with a partner.

✎ Writer's Corner

You may want to bring in the sports section of your local newspaper and read some of the articles. Afterward, invite students to make "sports" cards to share and trade with one another.

Go for the Goal/Final Test

1. The runner is *flexing* and stretching his muscles.
2. I never *admitted* how disappointed I was.
3. The small child is *stepping* in the flower bed.
4. The longer it rains, the *wetter* the soil gets.
5. The sun is *setting* on the horizon.
6. Why are you *cutting* out that news story?
7. That's the *biggest* pumpkin I've ever seen!
8. It takes practice to become a great *swimmer.*
9. The judge announced the *winner.*
10. Driving is difficult when it is *foggy.*
11. The music *stopped* when the curtain rose.
12. I *slipped* on the icy sidewalk.
13. How did you like the *beginning* of the movie?
14. The *jogger* looked tired as she passed by.
15. The car shone like new after it was *waxed.*

Remind students to complete the Scoreboard and write any misspelled words in their Word Locker.

★★ **All-Star Words** You may want to point out that the All-Star Words follow the spelling rule and model how to write a sentence using a List Word.

Lesson 17

Objective

To spell words with the suffixes *ed, ing, ly,* and *y*

Correlated Phonics Lessons

MCP Phonics, Level C, Lessons 49–50
Silver Burdett Ginn *World of Reading,* 3/2, pp. 316–317

Warm Up   **Page 69**

In this selection, students learn about an unusual car race in which the fuel is not gasoline—but sunshine. Afterward, ask students why they think it is important to develop solar-powered cars.

Encourage students to look back at the words in dark print. Ask volunteers to say each word and tell whether the root word changed when the suffix was added.

On Your Mark/Warm Up Test

1. He ***chased*** his wind-blown hat down the street.
2. My sister and I ***shared*** a room at camp.
3. Our neighbor is ***taking*** her pet for a walk.
4. Where is your uncle ***living*** now?
5. The class is ***making*** scenery for the play.
6. The bus station was crowded and ***noisy.***
7. The streets are ***icy***, so walk carefully.
8. The two horses are ***racing*** neck and neck.
9. My friends and I enjoy ***dancing.***
10. You wrapped that present so ***nicely.***
11. What a ***lovely*** spring day!
12. "Now watch me ***closely,***" said the magician.
13. We haven't been to the museum ***lately.***
14. Have you ***framed*** the sketches for the art show?
15. The stranded hikers ***hoped*** for a quick rescue.

Pep Talk/Game Plan   **Pages 70–71**

Introduce the spelling rule and have students read the List Words aloud. Point out to students that List Words with *ing* endings and *ed* endings are action words or verbs. Verbs that have *ing* added at the end tell about action that is going on now. Verbs that have *ed* added at the end tell about the past, or action that has already happened. Encourage students to look back at their Warm Up Tests and apply the spelling rule to any misspelled words.

As students work through the **Spelling Lineup, Suffixes,** and **Scrambled Letters** exercises, remind them to look back at their List Words or in their dictionaries if they need help.

 for ESL students See **Comparing/Contrasting,** page 15

58

Warm Up

Can cars really use sunlight as fuel?

Racing on Sunshine

In an unusual event called Sunrayce, a car that looked like a pizza box **chased** another car that looked like a torpedo on wheels. **Racing** up from behind was still another car that looked like a huge telephone handle. These cars had one thing in common—they were all solar-powered. Each car had dark, shiny photoelectric cells that sparkled in the sunlight—a **lovely** and energy-saving sight!

These cars were built by science and engineering students from thirty-two American and Canadian colleges. The idea of the race was for each team to turn sunlight into enough electrical power to drive a car about 1,600 miles. Because the motors were electric, the only thing **noisy** was the crowd of people watching!

Car manufacturers are **making** great progress with electric cars. However, it is unlikely that we will use solar-powered cars in our everyday lives. A solar car would have to carry enough battery power so that the car could run even when the sun isn't shining.

Events like Sunrayce give scientists a chance to study new ideas that could be put to use one day in the future.

 Look back at the boldfaced words in the selection. Name the root words. Which words changed their spelling when an **ed, ing, y,** or **ly** was added?

On Your Mark

Take your Warm Up Test. Then check your spelling with the List Words on the next page.

69

LIST WORDS

1. chased *chased*
2. shared *shared*
3. taking *taking*
4. living *living*
5. making *making*
6. noisy *noisy*
7. icy *icy*
8. racing *racing*
9. dancing *dancing*
10. nicely *nicely*
11. lovely *lovely*
12. closely *closely*
13. lately *lately*
14. framed *framed*
15. hoped *hoped*

Pep Talk

If a word ends in a silent e, drop the e before adding a suffix that begins with a vowel.

chase + **ed** = chased
make + **ing** = making

In some words ending with silent e, drop the e before adding y.

ice + **y** = icy

Keep the final **e** when adding the suffix **ly.**

nice + **ly** = nicely

Game Plan

Spelling Lineup

Write the List Words under the correct heading. Circle the suffixes.

words with **ing** that tell about present action

1. tak(ing)   4. rac(ing)
2. liv(ing)   5. danc(ing)
3. mak(ing)

words that tell about past action

6. chas(ed)   8. fram(ed)
7. shar(ed)   9. hop(ed)

words that end with the suffix **y**

10. nois(y)   11. ic(y)

words that end with the suffix **ly**

12. nice(ly)   14. close(ly)
13. love(ly)   15. late(ly)

70   Lesson 17 ■ Suffixes Added to Root Words

Suffixes

Make a List Word from the root in each sentence. Circle the root word and add a suffix from the box. Write the List Words.

ed	ing	ly	y

1. The road was (ice) .   _icy_
2. Maria has a (love) voice.   _lovely_
3. Mom and Dad watched the road (close) .   _closely_
4. Dan (nice) offered to set the table.   _nicely_
5. Tom (share) his piece of carrot cake with me.   _shared_
6. The loud music was (make) my head hurt.   _making_
7. Aunt Josie is (live) in a new city.   _living_
8. Kim and Jo are (race) to catch the school bus.   _racing_
9. We (hope) that Dad would win the contest, but he lost. _hoped_
10. Pat is (dance) in our school play.   _dancing_

Scrambled Letters

Unscramble the letters to spell List Words. Write the List Words.

1. mardef   _framed_
2. shcade   _chased_
3. gatkin   _taking_
4. teally   _lately_
5. inyso   _noisy_
6. cosylle   _closely_

Flex Your Spelling Muscles

Writing

Would you like to invent a new kind of transportation? Draw a picture of your invention. Write a brief description of it. Use as many List Words as you can.

Proofreading

This paragraph has nine mistakes. Use the proofreading marks to fix each mistake. Write the misspelled List Words on the lines.

Proofreading Marks	
◯	spelling mistake
∧	add something
≡	capital letter

   Do you like looking (clozely) at old cars? If you do, there is a (lovily) festival you can go to at the Henry Ford Museum in dearborn, Michigan. In august, you can see old (rasing) cars from the 1950s. Perhaps their owners will let you listen to the (noizy) engines! Will you be one of the visitors (takeng) lots of pictures?

1. _closely_   3. _racing_   5. _taking_
2. _lovely_   4. _noisy_

Now proofread your description. Fix any mistakes.

Goal for the Goal

Take your Final Test. Then fill in your Scoreboard. Send your mistakes to the Word Locker.

SCOREBOARD

number correct	number wrong

★ ★ ★ ★ ★ ★ ★ ★ All-Star Words ★ ★ ★ ★ ★ ★ ★ ★

losing   gazed   spicy   politely   serving

Write each All-Star Word. Then write a clue to go with it. Read each clue aloud to a partner. Ask your partner for the All-Star Word that goes with the clue.

◉ **Spelling Strategy**   Review the soft sound of *c* found in the List Words *icy, dancing,* and *nicely.* Point out that the *s* in *noisy* spells the sound for /z/ while the *s* in *closely* spells the sound for /s/. Then invite students to suggest other words in which *s* spells the sound for /s/.

Flex Your Spelling Muscles   *Page 72*

As students complete the **Writing** activity, encourage them to brainstorm ideas, write a first draft, revise, and proofread their work. The **Proofreading** exercise will help them prepare to proofread their descriptions. To publish their writing, students may want to read their descriptions and show their illustrations to the class, then role-play traveling in their vehicle.

✍ Writer's Corner

To find out more about solar power, students can request the fact sheet *Solar Energy and You—FS 118* from CAREIRS, P.O. Box 8900, Silver Spring, MD 20907. Have the class write its request on a postcard.

Go for the Goal/Final Test

1. Please don't be so **noisy!**
2. **Dancing** is good exercise.
3. Alex and I **shared** our lunches today.
4. That is a **lovely** picture of your mother.
5. I **hoped** you would come and visit me.
6. I haven't heard Dozer barking **lately.**
7. Our cat **chased** all the birds away.
8. The cars are **racing** around the track.
9. Dad is **making** homemade pizza for the party.
10. How **nicely** Justin read the poem!
11. The roads were **icy** after the freezing rain.
12. Antonia is **living** with relatives in Italy.
13. Follow the directions **closely.**
14. Have you **framed** the picture that you drew?
15. Chen is **taking** his baby sister for a walk.

Remind students to complete the Scoreboard and write any misspelled words in their Word Locker.

★★ **All-Star Words**   You may want to point out that the All-Star Words follow the spelling rule and model writing a clue for a List Word.

Lesson 18 • Instant Replay

Objective
To review spelling words with vowels with *r,* and suffixes added to root words

Time Out
Pages 73–76

Check Your Word Locker Based on your observations, note which words are giving students the most difficulty and offer assistance for spelling them correctly. Here are some frequently misspelled words to watch for: *before, sugar, early, replied, beginning,* and *making.*

To give students extra help and practice in taking standardized tests, you may want to have them take the Review Test for this lesson on pages 62–63. After scoring the tests, return them to students so that they can record their misspelled words in their Word Locker.

After practicing their troublesome words, students can work through the exercises for **Lessons 13–17.** Before they begin each exercise, you may want to go over the spelling rule.

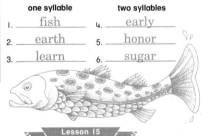 **Take It Home** Suggest that students and their family members write a story using List Words from **Lessons 13–17.** For a complete list of the words, encourage students to take their *Spelling Workout* books home. They can also use Take It Home Master 3 on pages 64–65 to help them do the activity. Invite students to read their story to the class.

Name _____

Instant Replay • Lessons 13–17

LESSON 18

Time Out
Take another look at vowels with **r** and suffixes added to root words.

Check Your Word Locker
Look at the words in your Word Locker. Which words for Lessons 13 through 17 did you have the most trouble with? Write them here.

_____

Practice writing your troublesome words with a partner. Take turns spelling the words aloud while your partner writes the words on the board.

Lesson 13
The letter **r** can change the sound of a vowel in a word. Listen for the vowel sounds in <u>party</u>, <u>fork</u>, <u>year</u>, and <u>care</u>.

List Words
large
start
before
morning
clear
appear

Write a List Word that means the opposite of each word given.

1. after ___before___
2. small ___large___
3. vanish ___appear___
4. finish ___start___
5. muddy ___clear___
6. evening ___morning___

73

Lesson 14
The /ʉr/ sound you hear in <u>hurt</u> can be spelled with **ir, or, er, ear, ar,** or **ur.** When the /ʉr/ sound is found in a syllable that is not accented, its sound-symbol is /ər/.

List Words
early
fish
honor
sugar
earth
learn

Write each List Word under the number of syllables it contains.

one syllable
1. ___fish___
2. ___earth___
3. ___learn___

two syllables
4. ___early___
5. ___honor___
6. ___sugar___

Lesson 15
Root words often change their spelling when a suffix is added. For a word ending with a vowel and **y,** add only the suffix, as in <u>prayed</u>. For a word ending with a consonant and **y,** change the **y** to **i** before adding the suffix unless the suffix begins with **i,** as in <u>married</u> and <u>marrying</u>.

List Words
rained
studied
worried
copying
hurried
replied

Write a List Word that matches each clue.

1. went faster ___hurried___
2. answered the question ___replied___
3. made the day wet ___rained___
4. did schoolwork ___studied___
5. doing the same thing again ___copying___
6. bothered ___worried___

74 Lesson 18 ■ Instant Replay

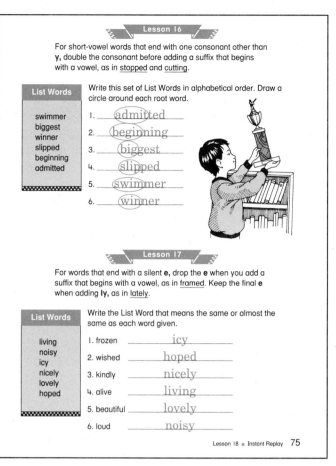

Lesson 16

For short-vowel words that end with one consonant other than **y**, double the consonant before adding a suffix that begins with a vowel, as in <u>stopped</u> and <u>cutting</u>.

List Words

swimmer
biggest
winner
slipped
beginning
admitted

Write this set of List Words in alphabetical order. Draw a circle around each root word.

1. admitted
2. beginning
3. biggest
4. slipped
5. swimmer
6. winner

Lesson 17

For words that end with a silent **e,** drop the **e** when you add a suffix that begins with a vowel, as in <u>framed</u>. Keep the final **e** when adding **ly,** as in <u>lately</u>.

List Words

living
noisy
icy
nicely
lovely
hoped

Write the List Word that means the same or almost the same as each word given.

1. frozen — icy
2. wished — hoped
3. kindly — nicely
4. alive — living
5. beautiful — lovely
6. loud — noisy

Lesson 18 ■ Instant Replay   75

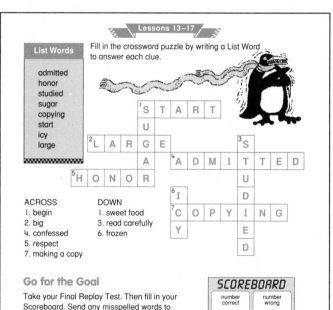

List Words

admitted
honor
studied
sugar
copying
start
icy
large

Fill in the crossword puzzle by writing a List Word to answer each clue.

ACROSS
1. begin
2. big
4. confessed
5. respect
7. making a copy

DOWN
1. sweet food
3. read carefully
6. frozen

Go for the Goal

Take your Final Replay Test. Then fill in your Scoreboard. Send any misspelled words to your Word Locker.

SCOREBOARD

number correct	number wrong

Clean Out Your Word Locker
Look in your Word Locker. Cross out each word you spelled correctly on your Final Replay Test. Circle the words you're still having trouble with. Add the words you circled to your Spelling Notebook. What do you notice about the words? Watch for those words as you write.

Go for the Goal/Final Replay Test   *Page 76*

1. My dog wakes me every ***morning.***
2. The water in the pond is so clean and ***clear.***
3. The whale will ***appear*** again when it needs air.
4. How much ***sugar*** does the recipe call for?
5. The farmer planted the seeds in the rich ***earth.***
6. Someday I want to ***learn*** a new language.
7. It has never ***rained*** on Jessica's birthday.
8. The test is on the words we ***studied*** last week.
9. My father ***worried*** about the approaching storm.
10. I almost ***slipped*** on the tile floor.
11. We missed the ***beginning*** of the play.
12. Finally, the driver ***admitted*** we were lost.
13. My cousin is now ***living*** near San Francisco.
14. The truck rumbling by made the room ***noisy.***
15. Throw some sand on those ***icy*** steps.
16. What a ***large*** school this is!
17. Our car is hard to ***start*** in cold weather.
18. May we have a snack ***before*** we leave?
19. The restaurant opens ***early*** in the morning.
20. You may have the ***first*** ride on the pony.
21. It is an ***honor*** to speak at graduation.
22. Make sure you are ***copying*** the notes correctly.
23. We ***hurried*** up the stairs and into the office.
24. Fred thought about the question and ***replied.***
25. That ***swimmer*** beat the world record!
26. Sometimes the ***biggest*** apples are not the best.
27. When will they name the ***winner*** of the contest?
28. Did you ask her ***nicely*** for the favor?
29. The dancers looked ***lovely*** in the soft light.
30. I ***hoped*** you would come and visit me.

Clean Out Your Word Locker   Before writing each word, students can say the word and pronounce the *r*-controlled vowel or identify the suffix.

Instant Replay Test

Side A

Read each sentence and set of words. Fill in the circle next to the word that is spelled correctly to complete the sentence.

1. Mark makes his bed every _____.
   - ⓐ morening
   - ⓒ mornning
   - ⓑ mornin
   - ⓓ morning

2. It is an _____ to receive this award.
   - ⓐ honor
   - ⓒ honer
   - ⓑ awner
   - ⓓ onar

3. The shy boy _____ quietly.
   - ⓐ replied
   - ⓒ repelied
   - ⓑ repliede
   - ⓓ replide

4. My bike _____ on the wet road.
   - ⓐ sliped
   - ⓒ slippt
   - ⓑ slipt
   - ⓓ slipped

5. The baby will _____ to walk soon.
   - ⓐ learn
   - ⓒ lern
   - ⓑ lernn
   - ⓓ lurn

6. Carmen planted a seed in the _____.
   - ⓐ erth
   - ⓒ urth
   - ⓑ erthe
   - ⓓ earth

7. An elephant is a _____ jungle animal.
   - ⓐ larej
   - ⓒ large
   - ⓑ larg
   - ⓓ larje

8. Tanya _____ for the spelling test.
   - ⓐ studyed
   - ⓒ studdied
   - ⓑ studied
   - ⓓ studeed

Name _____

Instant Replay Test

Side B

Read each sentence and set of words. Fill in the circle next to the word that is spelled correctly to complete the sentence.

9. Carla _____ about her lost dog.
   - ⓐ wurried
   - ⓒ worried
   - ⓑ wurryed
   - ⓓ worryed

10. That's the _____ building I've ever seen!
    - ⓐ bigist
    - ⓒ bigest
    - ⓑ biggest
    - ⓓ biggist

11. At dawn the sun will _____.
    - ⓐ appeer
    - ⓒ apeer
    - ⓑ appear
    - ⓓ apear

12. Tom _____ his mistake.
    - ⓐ admitted
    - ⓒ atmitted
    - ⓑ atmidded
    - ⓓ admited

13. The lunchroom was _____.
    - ⓐ noysy
    - ⓒ noizy
    - ⓑ nosie
    - ⓓ noisy

14. What a _____ day for a picnic!
    - ⓐ luvly
    - ⓒ lovely
    - ⓑ lovley
    - ⓓ luvely

15. John _____ he would win the prize.
    - ⓐ hopet
    - ⓒ hoped
    - ⓑ hoppd
    - ⓓ hoppt

TAKE IT HOME

3

Your child has learned to spell many new words and would like to share them with you and your family. Here are some great ways to turn your child's spelling review of Lessons 13–17 into family fun!

Happily Ever After!

With a little help from family members, your child can use the spelling words to write a story. You can make up a story of your own, or retell an old favorite. Your child will be spelling "happily ever after!"

large   morning   start
clear   before   appear   early
sugar   first   earth   honor
learn   rained   copying
studied   hurried   worried
replied   swimmer   slipped
biggest   beginning   winner
admitted   living   nicely
noisy   lovely   icy   hoped

One lovely morning before the sun was up, the first swimmer slipped into the icy water. A noisy ...

What's the Word?

Can you and your child solve "The Case of the Missing Letters"? Use the clues!

appear	hurried	soil	rained	start
said	until	large	wanted	honor

1. big! huge! humongous!

2. begin

3. When it _____, it poured!

4. wished

5. Don't open this present _____ your birthday!

6. At our family reunion, Great-Grandpa was the guest of _____ .

7. Plant the flower seeds in good, rich _____ .

8. The magician made a rabbit _____ , then disappear!

9. rushed

10. answered

1. __ a r __ __

2. __ __ a r __

3. __ __ __ __ e d

4. __ __ __ __ e d

5. __ __ __ i l

6. __ __ __ o r

7. s __ __ __

8. __ __ __ e a r

9. __ __ __ __ i e d

10. __ __ i d

Lesson 19

Objective
To spell regular plural nouns

Correlated Phonics Lessons
MCP Phonics, Level C, Lessons 42–43
Silver Burdett Ginn *World of Reading,* 3/2, p. 276

Warm up   ***Page 77***
In this selection, students discover how squirrels help hunters collect pine cones. After reading, invite students to read aloud the part of the selection they liked the best.

Encourage students to look back at the words in dark print. Ask volunteers to say each word and name the letter or letters that form the plural.

On Your Mark/Warm Up Test
1. *Cones* contain seeds of evergreen trees.
2. The *hunters* followed the tracks in the snow.
3. Please keep all your *desks* in neat rows.
4. Kangaroo *babies* stay in their mothers' pouches.
5. Adam likes *berries* on his cereal.
6. Will the *puppies* be big when they grow up?
7. What lovely rose *bushes* grow along that wall!
8. How many *bunches* of bananas should we buy?
9. The students in art class cleaned their *brushes.*
10. The tree *branches* were bare all winter long.
11. Twelve *inches* equals one foot.
12. We pay *taxes* to get government services.
13. My sister is taking three *classes* in college.
14. Thanks for helping me wash the *dishes.*
15. All three of these *watches* tell different times!

Pep Talk/Game Plan   ***Pages 78–79***
Introduce the spelling rule and have students read the List Words aloud. Encourage students to look back at their Warm Up Tests and apply the spelling rule to any misspelled words.

As students work through the **Spelling Lineup, Rhyming,** and **Scrambled Letters Puzzle** exercises, remind them to look back at their List Words or in their dictionaries if they need help. For the **Rhyming** exercise, remind students to pay more attention to the sounds of the List Words than to their spellings.

 for ESL students See **Picture Clues,** page 15

Name _____

Regular Plurals: Adding s or es

LESSON 19

Warm Up
What are these hunters gathering?

Hide and Seek

It is early fall in the forests of Oregon and Washington. For six weeks every year, armies of cone **hunters** search the woods here. They look for **cones** with plenty of seeds. Lumber and seed companies pay them for the best cones. The seeds are then used to plant new forests around the world.

The best cones are hard to find. They grow on **branches** high in the trees. The hunters don't need to climb the trees to get the cones. They just let the squirrels do the job. Then they find the places where the squirrels hide them. To do this, a good hunter must think like a squirrel.

Are the hunters stealing food from squirrels? "The squirrels will never go hungry," says one cone hunter. "They are too clever. We never find all their hiding places. We might be just a few **inches** away from one place and not find it. If I thought I was starving a squirrel, I'd bring the squirrel some nuts and trade them for the cones. Squirrels also eat **berries** and nuts. We may be taking some pine cones, but we're giving the squirrels more trees in the years to come."

 Look back at the words in dark print. They are all nouns that name more than one. What do you notice about their spelling?

On Your Mark
Take your Warm Up Test. Then check your spelling with the List Words on the next page.

77

Pep Talk
Singular nouns name one person, place, or thing. Plural nouns name more than one. Add **s** to most singular nouns to make them plural.
If a noun ends in **x, s, sh,** or **ch,** add **es** to make it plural. If a noun ends with a consonant and **y,** change the **y** to **i** and add **es.**

LIST WORDS
1. cones
2. hunters
3. desks
4. babies
5. berries
6. puppies
7. bushes
8. bunches
9. brushes
10. branches
11. inches
12. taxes
13. classes
14. dishes
15. watches

Game Plan
Spelling Lineup
Write each List Word under the correct heading. The heading tells what to do to a singular word to form the plural List Word.

add **s**	add **es**
1. cones	7. bushes
2. hunters	8. bunches
3. desks	9. brushes
	10. branches
change y to i, and add es	11. inches
4. babies	12. taxes
5. berries	13. classes
6. puppies	14. dishes
	15. watches

78   Lesson 19 ▪ Regular Plurals: Adding **s** or **es**

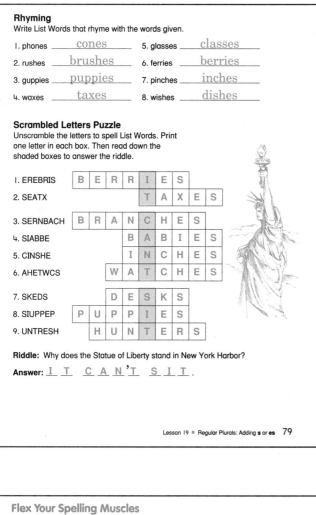

Rhyming
Write List Words that rhyme with the words given.

1. phones ___cones___   5. glasses ___classes___
2. rushes ___brushes___   6. ferries ___berries___
3. guppies ___puppies___   7. pinches ___inches___
4. waxes ___taxes___   8. wishes ___dishes___

Scrambled Letters Puzzle
Unscramble the letters to spell List Words. Print one letter in each box. Then read down the shaded boxes to answer the riddle.

1. EREBRIS   B E R R I E S
2. SEATX   T A X E S
3. SERNBACH B R A N C H E S
4. SIABBE   B A B I E S
5. CINSHE   I N C H E S
6. AHETWCS   W A T C H E S
7. SKEDS   D E S K S
8. SIUPPEP   P U P P I E S
9. UNTRESH   H U N T E R S

Riddle: Why does the Statue of Liberty stand in New York Harbor?

Answer: I T   C A N ' T   S I T .

Flex Your Spelling Muscles

Writing
Have you ever watched a squirrel or other wild animal? Write a description about what you saw. Use as many List Words as you can.

Proofreading
This article about squirrels has eight mistakes. Use the proofreading marks to fix the mistakes. Then write the misspelled List Words on the lines.

Proofreading Marks
◯ spelling mistake
⌄ take out something

Baby squirrels hide in tree (branchs) until they feel brave enough to ⅛ climb down. The mother (wachis) over them as they explore. She shows them in which (bushs) tasty (buntchas) of (beries) can be found and how to gather (coans) for the winter. If danger is is near, the mother squirrel bravely drives off the enemy to protect her young.

1. ___branches___
2. ___watches___
3. ___bushes___
4. ___bunches___
5. ___berries___
6. ___cones___

Now proofread your description. Fix any mistakes.

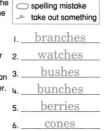

Go for the Goal
Take your Final Test. Then fill in your Scoreboard. Send your mistakes to the Word Locker.

SCOREBOARD	
number correct	number wrong

★ ★ ★ ★ ★ ★ **All-Star Words** ★ ★ ★ ★ ★ ★

sweaters   butterflies   polishes   businesses   mixes

Write a sentence for each word. Swap papers with your partner. Circle the plural endings of the All-Star Words.

◉ **Spelling Strategy**   To help students understand how *es* facilitates pronunciation of some words, ask them to try to pronounce the plural of *bunch, dish, inch,* and *class* by adding only the *s* ending, rather than *es.* Then review the rule about changing a final *y* to *i* if it is preceded by a consonant. Write *berries* and *babies* on the board and explain how they follow the rule.

Flex Your Spelling Muscles   *Page 80*
As students complete the **Writing** activity, encourage them to brainstorm ideas, write a first draft, revise, and proofread their work. The **Proofreading** exercise will help them prepare to proofread their descriptions. To publish their writing, students may want to illustrate their work and compile a collection called "Wildlife Wonders."

✍ Writer's Corner

> To learn more about forest animals, students can read books such as *The Hidden Life of the Forest* by Dwight Kuhn and David M. Schwartz. Encourage them to make animal posters based on what they learn from their reading.

Go for the Goal/Final Test
1. Don't scratch yourself on those low **branches!**
2. Are **hunters** allowed in this game preserve?
3. We planted some **bushes** in the yard.
4. Some **watches** can be read in the dark.
5. People pay **taxes** on the money they earn.
6. After the fire drill, **classes** continued.
7. The florist selected two **bunches** of daisies.
8. After I painted the room, I cleaned the **brushes.**
9. Let's use the blue **dishes** for a change.
10. We like having **berries** and cream for dessert.
11. Help me move the **desks** out of the front row.
12. Let's stop and buy ice cream **cones!**
13. Please cut a piece of paper eight **inches** wide.
14. Does your dog mind if you pick up her **puppies?**
15. Some animals get mad if you touch their **babies.**

Remind students to complete the Scoreboard and write any misspelled words in their Word Locker.

★★ **All-Star Words**   You may want to point out that the All-Star Words follow the spelling rule. Remind students that when a *y* has been changed to *i* to help form the plural, the *i* is not part of the plural ending.

Lesson 20

Objective
To spell irregular plural nouns

Correlated Phonics Lesson
MCP Phonics, Level C, Lesson 44

Warm Up   **Page 81**
In "Trick Feet," students find out how a man named Rant Mullens created Bigfoot tracks using huge wooden feet. After reading, invite students to describe other monsters they may be familiar with.

Encourage students to look back at the words in dark print. Ask volunteers to say each word and identify its singular form.

On Your Mark/Warm Up Test
1. All the *men* looked forward to their rugby game.
2. Six *women* waited for the elevator.
3. Does the jump rope belong to those *children?*
4. We have two *loaves* of rye bread.
5. For healthy *teeth,* brush after meals.
6. Two field *mice* ran into the barn.
7. Male *deer* have horns called *antlers.*
8. We get wool from *sheep.*
9. Astronauts' *lives* must be so exciting!
10. Chris has a tank full of tropical *fish.*
11. Many trees lose their *leaves* in the fall.
12. Did you put *knives* and forks on the table?
13. Pet dogs are related to wild *wolves.*
14. Those big animals are *oxen,* not cows.
15. How many presidents' *wives* can you name?
16. The *heroes* were honored with a parade.
17. I'd like some more mashed *potatoes,* please.
18. They look like ducks, but they are *geese.*
19. Viona built two extra *shelves* in the closet.
20. The Davidsons raise *cattle* on their ranch.

Pep Talk/Game Plan   **Pages 82–83**
Introduce the spelling rule and have students read the List Words aloud, helping them identify the singular form of each word. Then encourage students to look back at their Warm Up Tests and apply the spelling rule to any misspelled words.

As students work through the **Spelling Lineup, Word Building,** and **Word Puzzle** exercises, remind them to look back at their List Words or in their dictionaries if they need help.

 See **Words in Context,** page 14

Name _____

Warm Up
What did Rant Mullens use to make Bigfoot's "footprints"?

Trick Feet
In the state of Washington, folks tell about a giant monster. It's called Bigfoot of Mount Saint Helens. Over the years, its giant footprints have been seen by **men, women,** and **children.** Stories about the scary monster are still told everywhere.

A few years ago, Rant Mullens claimed to know the truth about Bigfoot. He said he started it himself as a joke in 1928. Using some **knives** and other tools, he cut two huge feet out of wood. Then he used the wooden feet to make the big footprints. Mr. Mullens explained that there is no real Bigfoot. It seems his joke may have fooled a lot of people for almost sixty years!

The joke may be on Mr. Mullens himself. By creating fake tracks, Mr. Mullens encouraged research into the possibility of a real Bigfoot. A scientist named Dr. Krantz studied many Bigfoot stories and tracks. He said the footprints made by Rant Mullens didn't match other Bigfoot tracks. Before Mr. Mullens told his story, scientists couldn't figure that out. In fact, Mr. Mullens' story may help to prove that perhaps a Bigfoot really does exist.

 Look back at the words in dark print. All the words are plural nouns. What is the singular form of each word?

On Your Mark
Take your Warm Up Test. Then check your spelling with the List Words on the next page.

Pep Talk
Singular nouns ending with **f** or **fe** often form plurals by changing the **f** or **fe** to **v** and adding **es.**
Some nouns have irregular plurals that do not end with **s.** Irregular plurals change their spelling or stay the same.

LIST WORDS

1. men
2. women
3. children
4. loaves
5. teeth
6. mice
7. deer
8. sheep
9. lives
10. fish
11. leaves
12. knives
13. wolves
14. oxen
15. wives
16. heroes
17. potatoes
18. geese
19. shelves
20. cattle

Game Plan
Spelling Lineup
Write the List Words that do not end with **s.**

1. men   7. sheep
2. women   8. fish
3. children   9. oxen
4. teeth   10. geese
5. mice   11. cattle
6. deer

Write the List Words that have singular forms that end with **f** or **fe.**

12. loaves   16. wolves
13. lives   17. wives
14. leaves   18. shelves
15. knives

Write the List Words that have singular forms that end with the letter **o.**

19. heroes   20. potatoes

Word Building

Build List Words by adding and subtracting letters. Write the List Words.

1. deal – al + er ___deer___
2. worn – rn + men ___women___
3. shell – l + ves ___shelves___
4. tomatoes – tom + pot ___potatoes___
5. loan – n + ves ___loaves___
6. twice – tw + m ___mice___
7. with – wi + tee ___teeth___
8. lives – l + w ___wives___
9. little – li + ca ___cattle___
10. lift – ft + ves ___lives___

Word Puzzle

Write the List Word that matches each clue given.
Then read down the shaded boxes to answer the riddle.
Here's what they can do . . .

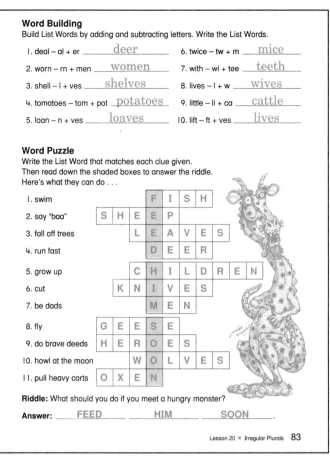

1. swim — F I S H
2. say "baa" — S H E E P
3. fall off trees — L E A V E S
4. run fast — D E E R
5. grow up — C H I L D R E N
6. cut — K N I V E S
7. be dads — M E N
8. fly — G E E S E
9. do brave deeds — H E R O E S
10. howl at the moon — W O L V E S
11. pull heavy carts — O X E N

Riddle: What should you do if you meet a hungry monster?

Answer: ___FEED___ ___HIM___ ___SOON___ .

Lesson 20 ■ Irregular Plurals 83

Flex Your Spelling Muscles

Writing

Finding a real Bigfoot would be an amazing story. Use the List Words to write a make-believe newspaper story telling about your discovery of Bigfoot.

Proofreading

This informational story has nine mistakes. Use the proofreading marks to fix the mistakes. Then write the misspelled List Words on the lines.

Proofreading Marks
◯ spelling mistake
^ add something
/ make small letter

In some parts of Asia, (man) women, and (childrun) talk about the yeti, or the abominable snowman. The yeti supposedly (livz) in the high mountains. Those who claim to have seen it say that it is big and covered with hair like an Ape. What a sight /It would be to see one! Some people think The yeti may just be large (woolvs) or some other animals that eat (catel). What do you think

1. ___men___
2. ___children___
3. ___lives___
4. ___wolves___
5. ___cattle___

Now proofread your newspaper story. Fix any mistakes.

Go for the Goal

Take your Final Test. Then fill in your Scoreboard.
Send your mistakes to the Word Locker.

SCOREBOARD
number correct | number wrong

★ ★ ★ ★ ★ ★ ★ All-Star Words ★ ★ ★ ★ ★ ★ ★

bison   halves   scarves   buffaloes   thieves

Work with a partner to write a story, using each word. Then erase the All-Star Words. Trade stories with other students. Write the All-Star Words in the story.

84 Lesson 20 ■ Irregular Plurals

Page 84

◎ **Spelling Strategy** Explain to students that words ending with the letter *o* usually add *es* to form the plural if the final *o* follows a consonant. Then write *potato, mosquito, patio, tomato, igloo,* and *hero* on the board. Call on volunteers to write the plural form of each word and to explain the rule that applies to the pluralization process.

Flex Your Spelling Muscles

As students complete the **Writing** activity, encourage them to brainstorm ideas, write a first draft, revise, and proofread their work. The **Proofreading** exercise will help them prepare to proofread their newspaper stories. To publish their writing, students may want to
• create a class newspaper
• read their stories aloud as news broadcasts.

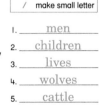

Writer's Corner

To learn more about monster myths, students can read a book such as *America's Very Own Monsters* by Daniel Cohen. Encourage students to write a poem about their favorite monster and to read it to the class.

Go for the Goal/Final Test

1. There are many **fish** in that river.
2. Do you know the **children** who live next door?
3. I straightened the books on those **shelves.**
4. The **men** on the porch are my uncles.
5. **Cattle** need lots of water and lots of hay.
6. We took many pictures of the beautiful **deer.**
7. My baby sister just got her first two **teeth!**
8. Several of the **sheep** have new lambs.
9. What a racket the honking of the **geese** makes!
10. Those **oxen** are much bigger than our cows.
11. **Wolves** are smart, social animals.
12. Don't cut yourself on those sharp **knives.**
13. The **wives** of the lost men waited for news.
14. How many baked **potatoes** did you eat?
15. We have four white **mice** as classroom pets.
16. I love hearing about my grandparents' **lives.**
17. The **women** use this gym for aerobics class.
18. The astronauts are true modern **heroes.**
19. Would you like two **loaves** of homemade bread?
20. Working together, we can rake up those **leaves.**

Remind students to complete the Scoreboard and write any misspelled words in their Word Locker.

★★ **All-Star Words** You may want to point out that the All-Star Words follow the spelling rule and help students brainstorm ideas for their stories.

Lesson 21

Objective
To spell words with vowel pairs

Correlated Phonics Lessons
MCP Phonics, Level C, Lessons 56–57
Silver Burdett Ginn *World of Reading,* 3/2, p. 403

Warm Up   *Page 85*
In this selection, students discover that many people are afraid of speaking in public. Ask students to share their own experiences with public speaking and to provide tips on how to deal with being nervous.

Call on volunteers to say each word in dark print, name the vowel pair in it, and identify the sound the vowels make.

On Your Mark/Warm Up Test
1. We have the nicest *teacher* in the world!
2. I *feel* proud when I run my fastest.
3. S*peak* slowly when you give a speech.
4. The detective found a *clue* in the old trunk.
5. Students who work hard will not *fail.*
6. *Soak* the dirty rug in a tub of cold water.
7. Whales live *below* the surface of the sea.
8. I will *lie* down and take a rest.
9. Grandmother took out her *needle* and thread.
10. Did you hear what I just *said?*
11. Everyone in the *group* knows the answer.
12. We sat down to a *feast* of roast turkey.
13. Get *ready* to spell the next word.
14. A *cheap* pair of shoes may not last very long.
15. I would like to see that movie *again.*
16. Connie has a sore *throat* today.
17. I'm *eager* to find out who made the team.
18. *Sooner* or later, Naomi will learn the truth.
19. Tom has at *least* twenty newspaper customers.
20. Does the letter *contain* good news?

Pep Talk/Game Plan   *Pages 86–87*
Introduce the spelling rule and have students read the List Words aloud. Point out that in the word *below,* the letter *w* acts as a vowel in the vowel pair *ow.* Then encourage students to look back at their Warm Up Tests and apply the spelling rule to any misspelled words.

As students work through the **Spelling Lineup, Classification, Syllables,** and **Definitions** exercises, remind them to look back at their List Words or in their dictionaries if they need help.

 See **Student Dictation,** page 14

70

Vowel Digraphs   LESSON 21

Warm Up
What are many people afraid of?

Speak Up!
What happens when the **teacher** calls on you? Do your mouth and throat get dry? Do you start to shake and forget everything you know? If so, you are not alone. Many people feel the same way.

Some scientists asked people what things made them afraid. Some people **said** they were afraid of bugs. Others said they were afraid of being in high places. Many people said they were afraid to **speak** in front of a **group** of people.

Is this true for you? Is speaking in front of your class one of your great fears? You don't have to be afraid. Here are some tips that will help you:
1. Be prepared. If you are **ready,** you will know what to say or have a good answer.
2. Be proud. You have something important to say.
3. Remember that you are not alone. Sooner or later, everyone gets called on. Your classmates don't want you to **fail,** because they don't want to fail either.
4. Last, but not least, speak up. Talk in a loud and clear voice.

> Say each word in dark print in the selection. Each word has two vowels that come together. What sounds do the vowel pairs make in the words?

On Your Mark
Take your Warm Up Test. Then check your spelling with the List Words on the next page.

85

Pep Talk
In a vowel digraph, the first vowel usually stands for a long sound and the second vowel is silent. teacher = /ē/ fail = /ā/
Some words do not follow this rule.
group = /o͞o/
Vowel pairs may also have a short sound.
said = /e/   ready = /e/

LIST WORDS
1. teacher
2. feel
3. speak
4. clue
5. fail
6. soak
7. below
8. lie
9. needle
10. said
11. group
12. feast
13. ready
14. cheap
15. again
16. throat
17. eager
18. sooner
19. least
20. contain

Spelling Lineup
Write each List Word under the correct heading.
One word is used twice.

/ā/ as in <u>day</u>	/o/ as in <u>home</u>
1. ___fail___	13. ___soak___
2. ___contain___	14. ___throat___
/ē/ as in <u>meet</u>	15. ___below___
3. ___teacher___	**/e/ as in <u>red</u>**
4. ___feel___	16. ___said___
5. ___speak___	17. ___ready___
6. ___below___	18. ___again___
7. ___needle___	**/o͞o/ as in <u>tool</u>**
8. ___least___	19. ___group___
9. ___cheap___	20. ___sooner___
10. ___eager___	21. ___clue___
11. ___feast___	
/ī/ as in <u>mile</u>	
12. ___lie___	

86   Lesson 21 ■ Vowel Digraphs

Classification

Write the List Word that belongs in each group.

1. touch, taste, **feel**   5. hint, suggestion, **clue**
2. anxious, willing, **eager**   6. sit, stand, **lie**
3. spoke, talked, **said**   7. neck, mouth, **throat**
4. wash, scrub, **soak**   8. crowd, gang, **group**

Syllables

Write each two-syllable List Word.

1. **teacher**   5. **again**
2. **below**   6. **eager**
3. **needle**   7. **sooner**
4. **ready**   8. **contain**

Definitions

Write the List Word that matches the meaning given. Use the number code to answer the riddle. Find the letter with the number 1 under it. Put that letter on each line below with the number 1 under it. Do the same for numbers 2 through 8.

1. a person who works at a school t e a c h e r
                             8   1 2

2. not to win or succeed f a i l
                      6

3. smallest in size or amount l e a s t
                          3 4

4. to say, tell, whisper, or shout s p e a k
                              7 5

Riddle: What did the goat have when it ate the dollar bill?

Answer: It had a c h e a p   f e a s t !
                   1 2 3 4 5   6 3 4 7 8

Lesson 21 ▪ Vowel Digraphs   87

Flex Your Spelling Muscles

Writing

Have you ever had to give a book report, read, or speak in front of a group of people? How did it make you feel? Use the List Words to write a paragraph sharing your feelings.

Proofreading

The diary entry below has ten mistakes. Use the proofreading marks to fix the mistakes. Write the misspelled List Words on the lines.

> **Proofreading Marks**
> ◯ spelling mistake
> ≡ capital letter
> � take out something

september 12, 1993

  Am I glad this day is over! today my ⟨teecher⟩ asked me to ⟨speke⟩ in front of the class. When she called my name, I started to ⟨fele⟩ nervous. Then my my ⟨throet⟩ felt like it was closing up and my legs started to shake. Finally, I ⟨sed⟩ to myself, "The ⟨souner⟩ I get started, the sooner I'll be done." Now that it's all over, I'm not not quite sure why I was so nervous—it really wasn't too bad.

1. **teacher**
2. **speak**
3. **feel**
4. **throat**
5. **said**
6. **sooner**

Now proofread your paragraph. Fix any mistakes.

Go for the Goal

Take your Final Test. Then fill in your Scoreboard. Send your mistakes to the Word Locker.

> **SCOREBOARD**
> | number correct | number wrong |
> | --- | --- |

★ ★ ★ ★ ★ ★ ★ **All-Star Words** ★ ★ ★ ★ ★ ★ ★

bouquet   beneath   steady   stain   mood

Try to use all five All-Star Words in a single sentence. Then get together with a partner and compare sentences.

88   Lesson 21 ▪ Vowel Digraphs

◉ **Spelling Strategy**   Write these words on the board to exemplify the rule in the Pep Talk box: *rain, seat, tie, coat,* and *clue.* Then write each List Word and ask a volunteer to identify the vowel pair and the sound it stands for. Point out words that do not follow the rule (*said, ready, again, group, sooner*) and emphasize that certain vowel pairs (*ea, ai*) stand for both the long- and the short-vowel sound.

Flex Your Spelling Muscles   *Page 88*

As students complete the **Writing** activity, encourage them to brainstorm ideas, write a first draft, revise, and proofread their work. The **Proofreading** exercise will help them prepare to proofread their paragraphs. To publish their writing, students may want to
• get together with a group and share their ideas
• read their paragraphs to the class.

✍ Writer's Corner

You may want to invite a drama coach or a speech teacher to come to your class and offer advice on speaking in front of a group. Encourage students to take notes; also provide time in which they can practice public speaking, applying what they learned.

Go for the Goal/Final Test

1. Food travels down your **throat** to your stomach.
2. I am **ready** for a vacation.
3. Where can I buy a **cheap** pair of sunglasses?
4. Please say that **again** because I didn't hear you.
5. Do these jars **contain** applesauce?
6. We are **eager** to meet your new music teacher.
7. We arrived **sooner** than we had planned.
8. I thought I had at **least** four dollars.
9. My dog likes to **lie** at my feet while I read.
10. **Soak** the vegetables in fresh water.
11. Mrs. Franklin lives in the apartment **below** us.
12. I **fail** to see the point of doing that.
13. Who will **speak** for us at the meeting?
14. Mr. Gleason is the best **teacher** I've ever had!
15. I don't have a **clue** where I left my keys.
16. I was ill, but I **feel** better now.
17. At Thanksgiving, we have a great **feast.**
18. Please help me thread my **needle.**
19. A **group** of children came to visit me today.
20. You haven't heard a word I've **said**!

Remind students to complete the Scoreboard and write any misspelled words in their Word Locker.

★★ **All-Star Words**   You may want to point out that the All-Star Words follow the spelling rule. Tell students that there are two pronunciations for the word *bouquet* (bo͞o kā′/bō kā′).

Lesson 22

Objective
To spell words with double *o*

Correlated Phonics Lesson
MCP Phonics, Level C, Lesson 58

Warm Up   **Page 89**
In this selection, students discover what it means to Slip! Slop! Slap! Before reading, be sure they understand the meaning of the phrase *Down Under.* Ask students which information they found useful and what else they know about protecting the skin.

Call on volunteers to say the words in dark print and identify the different vowel sounds they hear.

On Your Mark/Warm Up Test
1. Add a *scoop* of flour to the muffin batter.
2. Take aim before you *shoot* the basketball.
3. This *afternoon* we will ride our bikes.
4. Does today seem *cooler* than yesterday?
5. The storm was so strong it blew off the *roof!*
6. Use a *broom* to sweep the kitchen floor.
7. Ahmed held his nose and jumped into the *pool.*
8. I hope that I'll *choose* the right answers.
9. A *goose* is usually bigger than a duck.
10. A glass of warm milk may *soothe* you.
11. My tooth is *loose* and will come out soon.
12. We *stood* on the corner and waited for Paco.
13. She spoke of the *goodness* of her Aunt Sarah.
14. We get *wool* from sheep.
15. Can we catch fish in the *brook?*
16. Ebony ate a *cookie* with her applesauce.
17. Did you say *goodbye* to your uncle?
18. My grandfather has an old *wooden* boat.
19. The *soot* from the chimney made the rug dirty.
20. *Blood* carries nourishment throughout your body.

Pep Talk/Game Plan   **Pages 90–91**
Introduce the spelling rule and have students read the List Words aloud. Point out that the pronunciation of *roof* may vary with geographical area, with *oo* as in *cool* or as in *book.* Then encourage students to look back at their Warm Up Tests and apply the spelling rule to any misspelled words.

As students work through the **Spelling Lineup, Alphabetical Order,** and **Comparing Words** exercises, remind them to look back at their List Words or in their dictionaries if they need help.

 See **Charades/Pantomime,** page 15

72

Name _____

 LESSON **22**

Double o

Warm Up
What does Slip! Slop! Slap! mean?

Save Your Skin!
Did you know that the sun can damage your skin? The sun's ultraviolet rays cause sunburn, which can harm, dry, and age your skin. But, if you follow these safety tips, you won't have to say **goodbye** to the sun.
• Avoid direct sunlight, especially at midday. The sun is the hottest in the late morning or early **afternoon.** It doesn't mean that you have to stay away from the beach or **pool.** Just stay in a shady spot. It's **cooler** in the shade!
• Bring an umbrella, or wear a big hat.
• Use sunscreen. **Choose** one that has a high SPF. *SPF* means sunburn protection factor. A SPF of 30 protects the skin 30 times longer than with no protection at all.
• If you do get burned, **soothe** the ache with aloe cream.
Even in Australia, where there is so much sunny weather, people are beginning to pay attention to the warnings, especially lifeguards. At the beach, they always try to sit in shaded areas and wear t-shirts that read Slip! Slop! Slap! Almost everybody "Down Under" understands that to mean, "Slip on a shirt. Slop on some sunscreen. Slap on a hat!"

 Look back at the words in dark print. Notice that each word has the vowel pair **oo.** Say each word. How many different vowel sounds do you hear?

On Your Mark
Take your Warm Up Test. Then check your spelling with the List Words on the next page.

89

Pep Talk
The vowel pair **oo** stands for three sounds.
/o͞o/ as in <u>cooler</u>   /o͝o/ as in <u>brook</u>
/u/ as in <u>blood</u>
Listen for the sound the vowel pair **oo** stands for in each List Word.

LIST WORDS
1. scoop
2. shoot
3. afternoon
4. cooler
5. roof
6. broom
7. pool
8. choose
9. goose
10. soothe
11. loose
12. stood
13. goodness
14. wool
15. brook
16. cookie
17. goodbye
18. wooden
19. soot
20. blood

Game Plan
Spelling Lineup
Write each List Word under the correct heading.

/o͞o/ as in <u>cool</u>   /o͝o/ as in <u>book</u>
1. scoop   12. stood
2. shoot   13. goodness
3. afternoon   14. wool
4. cooler   15. brook
5. roof   16. cookie
6. broom   17. goodbye
7. pool   18. wooden
8. choose   19. soot
9. goose
10. soothe   /u/ as in <u>flood</u>
11. loose   20. blood

90   Lesson 22 ▪ Double o

Alphabetical Order

Write each group of List Words in alphabetical order.

pool	soothe	wooden
shoot	stood	wool

1. pool
2. shoot
3. soothe
4. stood
5. wooden
6. wool

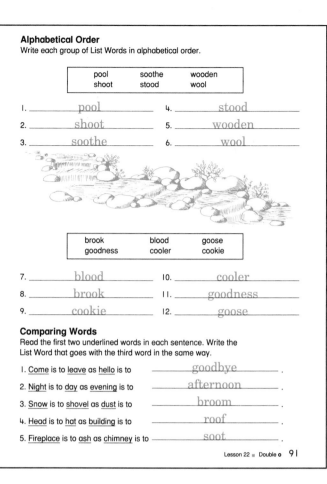

brook	blood	goose
goodness	cooler	cookie

7. blood
8. brook
9. cookie
10. cooler
11. goodness
12. goose

Comparing Words

Read the first two underlined words in each sentence. Write the List Word that goes with the third word in the same way.

1. Come is to leave as hello is to _goodbye_ .
2. Night is to day as evening is to _afternoon_ .
3. Snow is to shovel as dust is to _broom_ .
4. Head is to hat as building is to _roof_ .
5. Fireplace is to ash as chimney is to _soot_ .

Lesson 22 ■ Double o 91

Flex Your Spelling Muscles

Writing

The danger of ultraviolet rays makes sunscreen important for everyone. Use the List Words to write a persuasive ad that will convince people to use sunscreen.

Proofreading

The recipe below has nine mistakes. Use the proofreading marks to fix the mistakes. Then write the misspelled List Words on the lines.

Proofreading Marks	
◯	spelling mistake
☰	capital letter
/	make small letter

Summer Salad
Here's a recipe that will make a warm summer (afternun) just a little bit (cooler.)
• First, (chooz) your favorite kinds of melons. watermelon, Honeydew, and cantaloupe are the best.
• next, cut them in half and (scoope) out the insides using a melon baller.
• Then, use the Hollowed out skin of one of the melons as a bowl for the melon balls.
• finally, enjoy!

1. afternoon
2. cooler
3. choose
4. scoop

Now proofread your sunscreen ad. Fix any mistakes.

Go for the Goal

Take your Final Test. Then fill in your Scoreboard. Send your mistakes to the Word Locker.

SCOREBOARD

number correct	number wrong

★ ★ ★ ★ ★ ★ ★ ★ **All-Star Words** ★ ★ ★ ★ ★ ★ ★ ★

bamboo flood raccoon crooked gloomy

Draw a picture to give a clue for each All-Star Word. Trade drawings with a partner. Can you write a caption for each picture using the correct All-Star Word?

92 Lesson 22 ■ Double o

⊚ **Spelling Strategy** Invite students to get together with a partner and to take turns
• writing the List Words
• pointing to the vowel pair *oo* in each word
• pronouncing the word, emphasizing the sound that *oo* stands for
• suggesting another word in which *oo* makes the same sound.

Remind students that *roof* can be pronounced /o͞o/ or /o͝o/.

Flex Your Spelling Muscles *Page 92*

As students complete the **Writing** activity, encourage them to brainstorm ideas, write a first draft, revise, and proofread their work. The **Proofreading** exercise will help them prepare to proofread their persuasive ads. To publish their writing, students may want to
• illustrate their ads
• read their ads aloud as a radio advertisements.

✎ Writer's Corner

You may want to bring in a few containers of sunscreen and read some of the information on the containers to students. Then invite them to create their own sunscreen product. Students can write a description of their product and draw a picture of it.

Go for the Goal/Final Test

1. Kathy dove into the swimming **pool.**
2. My favorite kind of **cookie** has nuts and raisins.
3. Please sweep the floor with the new **broom.**
4. A small **brook** runs behind my house.
5. This chimney is full of **soot!**
6. Is your new belt too **loose?**
7. A gentle hug may **soothe** a frightened child.
8. **Blood** is red.
9. My mittens are made of **wool.**
10. They put new shingles on the **roof.**
11. I admire the hard work and **goodness** of doctors.
12. Marisol **stood** in the rain, waiting for the bus.
13. Tomorrow **afternoon** I will paint the fence.
14. He will **shoot** the arrow at the target.
15. Ice cubes will make your juice **cooler.**
16. Do you want a **scoop** of ice cream?
17. In this famous tale, a **goose** lays a golden egg.
18. We will **choose** partners and share our stories.
19. Jeff forgot to say **goodbye** before he left home.
20. They made a **wooden** gate for the new pig pen.

Remind students to complete the Scoreboard and write any misspelled words in their Word Locker.

★★ **All-Star Words** You may want to point out that the All-Star Words follow the spelling rule and model completing the activity with a List Word.

Lesson 23

Objective
To spell words with silent consonants *l* and *gh*

Correlated Phonics Lesson
Silver Burdett Ginn *World of Reading,* 3/2, p. 424

Warm Up   *Page 93*
In "Sign of the Times," students discover the connection between the dollar sign and two high rocks called the Pillars of Hercules. After reading, ask students which part of the selection they liked the best, and why.

Encourage students to look back at the words in dark print. Ask volunteers to say each word and name the silent letter or letters.

On Your Mark/Warm Up Test
1. "Do not **fight** over the front seat," Mom said.
2. Nathan drank **half** a glass of juice.
3. The detective never let the suspect out of **sight**.
4. I **would** like to introduce you to my parents.
5. What a cold **night** this is!
6. Please turn off the **light** to save electricity.
7. A **calf** is a young cow or ox.
8. I **might** not be able to come to your party.
9. A **highway** is a main road.
10. **Moonlight** shone through the window.
11. Candlelight is not very **bright**.
12. **Eight** is the number that comes before nine.
13. Have you given any **thought** to the project yet?
14. We drove **through** the tunnel without stopping.
15. You need a big truck to haul a heavy **weight**.
16. The loud clap of thunder gave me such a **fright!**
17. Judy frowned and gave a loud **sigh**.
18. There is a **slight** chance it will rain tomorrow.
19. Paul **fought** to build a new park for the city.
20. The **knight** put on a suit of armor.

Pep Talk/Game Plan   *Pages 94–95*
Introduce the spelling rule and have students read the List Words aloud, calling their attention to the different vowel sounds in *thought* and *through*. Then encourage them to look back at their Warm Up Tests and apply the spelling rule to any misspelled words.

As students work through the **Spelling Lineup, Dictionary, Homonyms,** and **Puzzle** exercises, remind them to look back at their List Words or in their dictionaries if they need help.

 See **Spelling Aloud,** page 14

Silent Consonants

Warm Up
What were the Pillars of Hercules?

Sign of the Times
What does this dollar sign look like? It looks something like a figure **eight**. That's because long ago, in the days of pirates, an eight was printed on Spanish coins called "pieces of eight." Each of these coins could be cut into eight pieces. One or more pieces could be used when something cost less money.

Why do two lines cut the eight in **half?** These lines stand for two high rocks at the southern tip of Spain. A long, long time ago, people told a story about a strong man named Hercules. They **thought** he might have split a big mountain in two with his bare hands. They claimed this opened a doorway to the Mediterranean Sea from the Atlantic Ocean. The two high rocks on either side of the doorway came to be called the Pillars of Hercules. Spanish sailors **would** often pass **through** the Pillars of Hercules. Therefore, the two lines were added to the sign to mark the coins as Spanish money.

Soon the $ came to mean dollar. And, of course, that's what it still means today.

 Say each word in dark print in the selection. Which letters do not make a sound?

On Your Mark
Take your Warm Up Test. Then check your spelling with the List Words on the next page.

93

Pep Talk
In each List Word you will find that **gh** or **l** is not heard. Look for these spelling patterns in your List Words:

al is /a/ as in <u>calf</u>
igh is /ī/ as in <u>light</u>
oul is /oo/ as in <u>would</u>
eigh is /ā/ as in <u>eight</u>
ough is /oo/ as in <u>through</u>
ough is /ô/ as in <u>fought</u>

LIST WORDS
1. fight
2. half
3. sight
4. would
5. night
6. light
7. calf
8. might
9. highway
10. moonlight
11. bright
12. eight
13. thought
14. through
15. weight
16. fright
17. sigh
18. slight
19. fought
20. knight

Game Plan
Spelling Lineup
Write each List Word under the correct heading. Circle the silent consonant or consonants in each word.

igh spells /ī/
1. fight
2. sight
3. night
4. light
5. might
6. highway
7. moonlight
8. bright
9. fright
10. sigh
11. slight
12. knight

al spells /a/
13. half
14. calf

oul spells /oo/
15. would

eigh spells /ā/
16. eight
17. weight

ough spells /oo/
18. through

ough spells /ô/
19. thought
20. fought

94 Lesson 23 ▪ Silent Consonants

Dictionary

Write the List Word for each sound-spelling given.

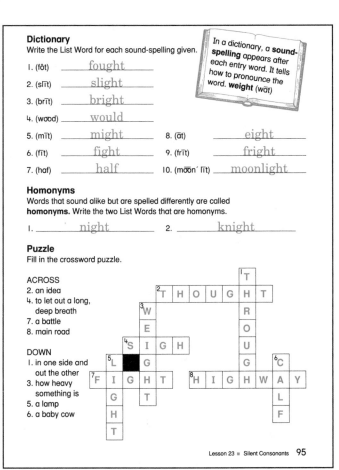

In a dictionary, a **sound-spelling** appears after each entry word. It tells how to pronounce the word. **weight** (wāt)

1. (fôt) _fought_
2. (slīt) _slight_
3. (brīt) _bright_
4. (wood) _would_
5. (mīt) _might_
6. (fīt) _fight_
7. (haf) _half_
8. (āt) _eight_
9. (frīt) _fright_
10. (moon' līt) _moonlight_

Homonyms

Words that sound alike but are spelled differently are called **homonyms.** Write the two List Words that are homonyms.

1. _night_
2. _knight_

Puzzle

Fill in the crossword puzzle.

ACROSS
2. an idea
4. to let out a long, deep breath
7. a battle
8. main road

DOWN
1. in one side and out the other
3. how heavy something is
5. a lamp
6. a baby cow

					T	
	T	H	O	U	G	H	T
		W			R	
		E			O	
	S	I	G	H		U	
	L		G			G	C
F	I	G	H	T		H	I	G	H	W	A	Y
	G		T				L
	H						F
	T						

Flex Your Spelling Muscles

Writing

Can you think of a different symbol that might be used to represent the dollar? Draw your idea. Then use the List Words to write a paragraph explaining why you chose your symbol.

Proofreading

This article has ten mistakes. Use the proofreading marks to fix each mistake. Write the misspelled List Words on the lines.

Proofreading Marks
◯ spelling mistake
≡ capital letter
⊙ add period

The United states (haff) dollar is worth 50 cents. This (brite) silver-and-copper coin was first made in February of 1964 In 1975, the government (thaut) it (woode) be a good idea to issue a special half dollar for our country's 200th birthday This special coin, which showed independence Hall on one side, was made from 1975 (thruw) 1976. Although hard to find, half dollars are still being used today

1. _half_
2. _bright_
3. _thought_
4. _would_
5. _through_

Now proofread your paragraph. Fix any mistakes.

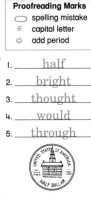

Go for the Goal

Take your Final Test. Then fill in your Scoreboard. Send your mistakes to the Word Locker.

SCOREBOARD
number correct | number wrong

★ ★ ★ ★ ★ ★ ★ ★ **All-Star Words** ★ ★ ★ ★ ★ ★ ★ ★

flight   behalf   freight   although   sought

Write a sentence for each word, but leave a blank where the All-Star Word should be. Trade sentences with your partner. Write the correct words in the blanks.

◉ **Spelling Strategy**   Write the spelling patterns *al, igh, oul, eigh,* and *ough* on the board as separate column headings. Then have students examine each List Word and tell you which pattern the word contains. Write the word in the correct column and ask a volunteer to circle its silent consonant or consonants. Help students notice that *knight* contains not only silent *gh,* but also silent *k.*

Flex Your Spelling Muscles   *Page 96*

As students complete the **Writing** activity, encourage them to brainstorm ideas, write a first draft, revise, and proofread their work. The **Proofreading** exercise will help them prepare to proofread their paragraphs. To publish their writing, students may want to create a collage incorporating their paragraphs and their different symbols for the dollar.

✍ **Writer's Corner** _____

Students might enjoy reading *Money* by Benjamin Elkin, or a similar book. Encourage them to create text for a bulletin-board display depicting the history of money.

Go for the Goal/Final Test

1. Joe ate **half** a pizza all by himself!
2. Kim **would** like to go to the movies tonight.
3. Please turn out the **light** and go to sleep.
4. The **calf** stayed close to its mother.
5. There was a huge traffic jam on the **highway.**
6. Jon wore a **bright** yellow shirt to the dance.
7. Have you **thought** about becoming a scientist?
8. Some people can lift their own **weight.**
9. I heard her loud **sigh** from across the room.
10. My little brothers **fought** over the last apple.
11. I always feel bad after we **fight.**
12. The **sight** of blood makes me weak.
13. The dog's barking kept me up all **night.**
14. We **might** perform the play on stage.
15. The **moonlight** cast shadows on the sidewalk.
16. I have saved **eight** dollars.
17. Are you **through** with that book yet?
18. Your costume gave me quite a **fright.**
19. Danielle has a **slight** cold, so she can't go.
20. We read a story about a very brave **knight.**

Remind students to complete the Scoreboard and write any misspelled words in their Word Locker.

★ ★ **All-Star Words**   You may want to point out that the All-Star Words follow the spelling rule and review how to write a cloze sentence.

Lesson 24 • Instant Replay

Objective

To review spelling words with regular plurals: adding *s* or *es;* irregular plurals; vowel digraphs; double *o;* and silent consonants

Time Out   *Pages 97–100*

Check Your Word Locker Based on your observations, note which words are giving students the most difficulty and offer assistance for spelling them correctly. Here are some frequently misspelled words to watch for: *teacher, loose, thought, through,* and *weight.*

To give students extra help and practice in taking standardized tests, you may want to have them take the Review Test for this lesson on pages 78–79. After scoring the tests, return them to students so that they can record their misspelled words in their Word Locker.

After practicing their troublesome words, students can work through the exercises for **Lessons 19–23.** Before they begin each exercise, you may want to go over the spelling rule.

🏠 Take It Home Invite students to locate List Words from **Lessons 19–23** in newsapers, books, magazines, and games. For a complete list of the words, encourage them to take their *Spelling Workout* books home. Students can also use Take It Home Master 4 on pages 80–81 to help them do the activity. Invite students to bring their lists to school and compare them with their classmates' lists.

Name _____

Time Out
Take another look at plurals, vowel pairs, and words with silent letters.

Check Your Word Locker
Look back at the words in your Word Locker. Write your troublesome words for Lessons 19–23.

_____

Practice writing your troublesome words with a partner. Form the letters of each word using clay. Your partner can spell the words aloud as you form the letters.

Lesson 19

Add **s** to most nouns to make them plural, as in <u>hunters</u>. If a noun ends in **x, s, sh,** or **ch,** add **es** to make it plural, as in <u>bunches</u>. If a noun ends in a consonant and **y,** change the **y** to **i** and add **es,** as in <u>berries</u>.

List Words	Write the List Words in alphabetical order.

inches
desks
watches
bushes
puppies
babies

1. babies   4. inches
2. bushes   5. puppies
3. desks   6. watches

97

Lesson 20

If a word ends in **f** or **fe,** usually change the **f** or **fe** to **v** and add **es,** as in <u>leaves</u>. Some words change their vowel sound or spelling to make the plural form, as in <u>men</u>. Others have the same form for singular and plural, as in <u>deer</u>.

List Words	Write each List Word under the correct heading.

children
geese
sheep
wolves
heroes
women

animals
1. geese
2. sheep
3. wolves

people
4. children
5. heroes
6. women

Lesson 21

Most vowel digraphs spell long-vowel sounds, as in <u>least</u>. A few words, such as <u>said</u>, do not follow this rule. Some vowel digraphs spell short-vowel sounds, as in <u>again</u>.

List Words

group
soak
clue
speak
said
least

Write a List Word that rhymes with each word given.

1. fed _____ said
2. peek _____ speak
3. feast _____ least
4. poke _____ soak
5. loop _____ group
6. flew _____ clue

98 Lesson 24 ■ Instant Replay

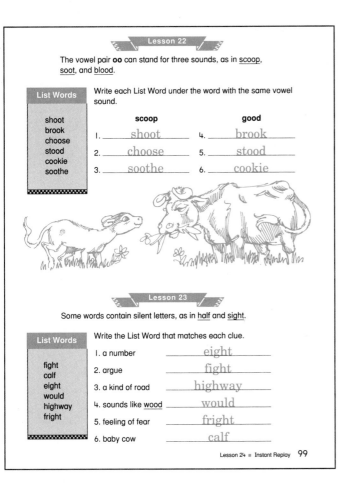

Lesson 22

The vowel pair **oo** can stand for three sounds, as in <u>scoop</u>, <u>soot</u>, and <u>blood</u>.

List Words

shoot
brook
choose
stood
cookie
soothe

Write each List Word under the word with the same vowel sound.

scoop
1. shoot
2. choose
3. soothe

good
4. brook
5. stood
6. cookie

Lesson 23

Some words contain silent letters, as in <u>half</u> and <u>sight</u>.

List Words

fight
calf
eight
would
highway
fright

Write the List Word that matches each clue.

1. a number — eight
2. argue — fight
3. a kind of road — highway
4. sounds like <u>wood</u> — would
5. feeling of fear — fright
6. baby cow — calf

Lesson 24 ■ Instant Replay 99

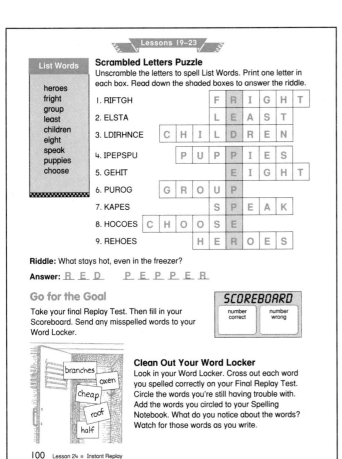

Lessons 19–23

List Words

heroes
fright
group
least
children
eight
speak
puppies
choose

Scrambled Letters Puzzle

Unscramble the letters to spell List Words. Print one letter in each box. Read down the shaded boxes to answer the riddle.

1. RIFTGH — F R I G H T
2. ELSTA — L E A S T
3. LDIRHNCE — C H I L D R E N
4. IPEPSPU — P U P P I E S
5. GEHIT — E I G H T
6. PUROG — G R O U P
7. KAPES — S P E A K
8. HOCOES — C H O O S E
9. REHOES — H E R O E S

Riddle: What stays hot, even in the freezer?

Answer: R E D P E P P E R

Go for the Goal

Take your final Replay Test. Then fill in your Scoreboard. Send any misspelled words to your Word Locker.

SCOREBOARD
number correct
number wrong

Clean Out Your Word Locker

Look in your Word Locker. Cross out each word you spelled correctly on your Final Replay Test. Circle the words you're still having trouble with. Add the words you circled to your Spelling Notebook. What do you notice about the words? Watch for those words as you write.

branches
oxen
cheap
roof
half

100 Lesson 24 ■ Instant Replay

Go for the Goal/Final Replay Test   *Page 100*

1. Both the ***children*** are in third grade.
2. In gym class, I learned to ***shoot*** an arrow.
3. The two birds began to ***fight*** over the corn.
4. One ***group*** walked and the other took the bus.
5. Cut the paper so that it is six ***inches*** long.
6. Are those two ***women*** your aunts?
7. Jose can ***speak*** four languages.
8. What cute ***puppies*** those are!
9. This recipe tells how to make one large ***cookie.***
10. The ***calf*** has soft brown eyes.
11. The ***geese*** chased people away from their nest.
12. Did you put the dirty clothes in to ***soak?***
13. I looked at dozens of ***watches*** before buying one.
14. Each of you may ***choose*** one book to buy.
15. My brother ***would*** like to come with us.
16. All the firefighters were treated like ***heroes.***
17. We need at ***least*** two cups of flour.
18. Mr. Matsudo planted two ***bushes*** near his door.
19. The bus seats were full, so we ***stood*** all the way.
20. An octopus has ***eight*** arms.
21. Is there a bridge across the ***brook?***
22. Our house is not on a busy ***highway.***
23. The ***desks*** in the front row are all taken.
24. The ***wolves*** at the zoo look like big dogs.
25. Would you like a ***clue*** to the riddle's answer?
26. This soup will ***soothe*** your upset stomach.
27. What a ***fright*** that loud noise gave me!
28. Those ***babies*** have not yet learned to walk.
29. In Australia, many people raise ***sheep.***
30. My parents ***said*** I could have dinner with you.

Clean Out Your Word Locker For each word, students can tell how the plural is formed, name the vowel digraph or the vowel pair, or identify the silent consonant or consonants.

77

Instant Replay Test

Side A

Read each set of words. Fill in the circle next to the word that is spelled wrong.

1. (a) said   (c) sheap
   (b) stood   (d) desks

2. (a) pupies   (c) eight
   (b) cookie   (d) geese

3. (a) highway   (c) brook
   (b) shute   (d) children

4. (a) deer   (c) heroas
   (b) bushes   (d) wool

5. (a) goose   (c) knight
   (b) leist   (d) would

6. (a) desks   (c) bright
   (b) again   (d) clew

7. (a) sooh   (c) moonlight
   (b) watches   (d) roof

8. (a) knives   (c) fish
   (b) choose   (d) frigt

9. (a) soak   (c) intches
   (b) wolves   (d) group

10. (a) weight   (c) fite
    (b) soot   (d) speak

Name _____

Instant Replay Test

Side B

Read each set of words. Fill in the circle next to the word that is spelled wrong.

11. (a) teeth   (c) cones
     (b) caff   (d) fought

12. (a) highway   (c) speek
     (b) deer   (d) children

13. (a) shoot   (c) bunches
     (b) waches   (d) soak

14. (a) said   (c) brook
     (b) soothe   (d) woold

15. (a) inches   (c) puppies
     (b) calf   (d) cookiy

16. (a) choos   (c) desks
     (b) heroes   (d) sheep

17. (a) stood   (c) babys
     (b) broom   (d) geese

18. (a) wolfes   (c) bright
     (b) brushes   (d) half

19. (a) eight   (c) least
     (b) groop   (d) again

20. (a) wimen   (c) bushes
     (b) ready   (d) branches

4 TAKE IT HOME

Your child will enjoy trying out new spelling words with you and your family. Here are some ways to help your child review the spelling words from Lessons 19–23 and have fun, too!

Read All About It!

Extra! Extra! Encourage your child to find some of his or her spelling words in newspapers, magazines, and even in books, magazines, and even in some computer games. Kids' encyclopedias are another great source! See how long a list your child can make.

Picture This!

With your child, use the clues to help you label the pictures in the art that represent spelling words.

- animals that honk and fly
- wool comes from these animals
- baby dogs
- animals that live in the forest
- used to sweep the floor
- cowhands herd these

- a baby cow
- you need this when it's dark
- plants, trees, _____
- something you can eat
- these animals are very strong
- water that babbles

Lesson 25

Objective
To spell words with the vowel sound /ô/

Correlated Phonics Lesson
MCP Phonics, Level C, Lesson 59

Warm Up   **Page 101**
In this selection, students discover why the hobby of coin collecting started with kings. Afterward, ask whether anyone has a collection and invite students to discuss other hobbies they enjoy.

Ask volunteers to say each word in dark print and name the letter or letters that stand for /ô/.

On Your Mark/ Warm Up Test
1. We *already* have a kitten, but thanks anyway.
2. Everyone is quiet *because* Dad is sleeping.
3. Whoops! You *almost* fell down!
4. The old vase has a small dent, or *flaw.*
5. How much does that ten-speed bike *cost?*
6. You dropped your *wallet* when you leaned over.
7. *Laws* are rules that nations follow.
8. Where were you when you *lost* your pen?
9. We had a *long* wait for the bus.
10. This book doesn't *belong* on the science shelf.
11. Look both ways before going *across* the street.
12. The doctor said Tom's leg was *all right.*
13. Dad *bought* milk, fruit, and vegetables.
14. September comes after *August.*
15. The teacher put some new *chalk* on the ledge.
16. The tugboats *haul* the barges across the river.
17. What an *awful* movie that was!
18. I'm watching this spider *crawl* up its web.
19. Mom mows the *lawn,* and I rake it.
20. Who *caught* the fly ball?

Pep Talk/Game Plan   **Pages 102–103**
Introduce the spelling rule and have students read the List Words aloud. Discuss the meanings of words that may be unfamiliar to students, such as *flaw, haul,* and the different meanings of *all right.* Then encourage students to look back at their Warm Up Tests and apply the spelling rule to any misspelled words.

As students work through the **Spelling Lineup, Word Shape Puzzle,** and **Definitions** exercises, remind them to look back at their List Words or in their dictionaries if they need help.

 See **Variant Spellings,** page 14

82

Name _____

/ô/

Warm Up
What hobby was known as "the hobby of kings"?

Royal Hobby
Many people like to save coins. Some people call coin collecting "the hobby of kings," **because**, at one time, only a king could afford to keep money. Most people had to spend all their money to live. Today, many people find coin collecting an easy and interesting hobby. Over five million North Americans collect coins.

To begin, all you need are a few coins and a folder in which to keep them. **Almost** any hobby shop can sell you this special kind of folder. You can keep each coin in its own special place. You might start by saving pennies. Try to get one for each year of your life.

As you learn more about coins, you will know which ones are the best to save. Look for a coin without a scratch, or **flaw.** A coin without flaws is worth more than others. However, it is not **all right** to clean a dirty coin. Rubbing wears down its face and makes it less valuable. Of course, everyone wants to find very old coins. These are hard to find and could **cost** a lot of money if you **bought** one. You could get lucky, though. You could find a valuable coin right in your own pocket.

 Say each word in dark print in the selection. Can you hear the /ô/ sound in each word?

On Your Mark
Take your Warm Up Test. Then check your spelling with the List Words on the next page.

Pep Talk
The /ô/ sound can be spelled many ways:
au as in <u>because</u>   **aw** as in <u>flaw</u>
o as in <u>cost</u>   **ou** as in <u>bought</u>
a followed by **l** as in <u>already</u>

Look at the spelling of /ô/ in each List Word.

LIST WORDS
1. already
2. because
3. almost
4. flaw
5. cost
6. wallet
7. laws
8. lost
9. long
10. belong
11. across
12. all right
13. bought
14. August
15. chalk
16. haul
17. awful
18. crawl
19. lawn
20. caught

Game Plan
Spelling Lineup
Write each List Word under the correct spelling of its /ô/ sound.

au
1. because   3. haul
2. August   4. caught

aw
5. flaw   8. crawl
6. laws   9. lawn
7. awful

a followed by l
10. already   13. all right
11. almost   14. chalk
12. wallet

o or ou
15. cost   18. belong
16. lost   19. across
17. long   20. bought

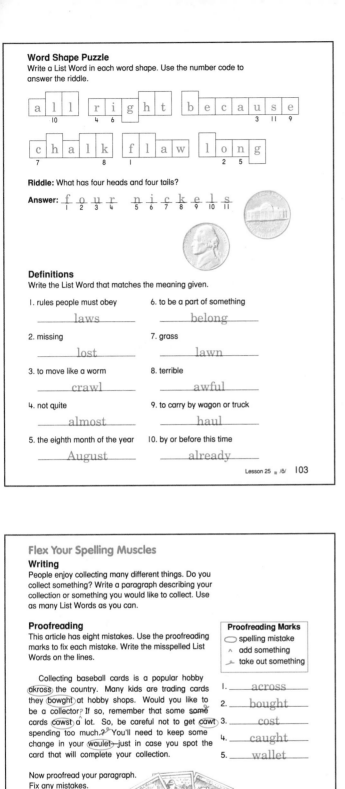

Word Shape Puzzle
Write a List Word in each word shape. Use the number code to answer the riddle.

a	l	l		r	i	g	h	t		b	e	c	a	u	s	e
		10		4		6							3	11		9

c	h	a	l	k		f	l	a	w		l	o	n	g
7			8				1					2		5

Riddle: What has four heads and four tails?

Answer: f o u r   n i c k e l s
1 2 3 4   5 6 7 8 9 10 11

Definitions
Write the List Word that matches the meaning given.

1. rules people must obey
   laws
2. missing
   lost
3. to move like a worm
   crawl
4. not quite
   almost
5. the eighth month of the year
   August
6. to be a part of something
   belong
7. grass
   lawn
8. terrible
   awful
9. to carry by wagon or truck
   haul
10. by or before this time
    already

Lesson 25 ■ /ô/ 103

Flex Your Spelling Muscles
Writing
People enjoy collecting many different things. Do you collect something? Write a paragraph describing your collection or something you would like to collect. Use as many List Words as you can.

Proofreading
This article has eight mistakes. Use the proofreading marks to fix each mistake. Write the misspelled List Words on the lines.

Proofreading Marks
◯ spelling mistake
∧ add something
⌐ take out something

Collecting baseball cards is a popular hobby akross the country. Many kids are trading cards they bowght at hobby shops. Would you like to be a collector? If so, remember that some some cards cawst a lot. So, be careful not to get cawt spending too much.? You'll need to keep some change in your wallet—just in case you spot the card that will complete your collection.

1. across
2. bought
3. cost
4. caught
5. wallet

Now proofread your paragraph. Fix any mistakes.

Go for the Goal
Take your Final Test. Then fill in your Scoreboard. Send your mistakes to the Word Locker.

SCOREBOARD	
number correct	number wrong

★ ★ ★ ★ ★ ★ *All-Star Words* ★ ★ ★ ★ ★ ★

moth   sausage   awkward   altogether   brought

Write a song title for each All-Star Word. Then get together with a partner and compare titles.

◎ **Spelling Strategy**   Write the different ways to spell /ô/ on the board: *au, o, aw, ou,* and *a* followed by *l.* Then say each List Word and have a volunteer write the word on the board under the correct heading. After each word has been written, repeat the word aloud and point to the letter or letters that spell /ô/.

Flex Your Spelling Muscles   *Page 104*
As students complete the **Writing** activity, encourage them to brainstorm ideas, write a first draft, revise, and proofread their work. The **Proofreading** exercise will help them prepare to proofread their paragraphs. To publish their writing, students may want to use their paragraphs as well as items from their collections to create a display.

✍ **Writer's Corner**

> The class can receive information about starting a coin collection by sending a letter and a long, self-addressed stamped envelope (with two first-class stamps) to the American Numismatic Association, Membership Department—KS, 818 North Cascade Avenue, Colorado Springs, CO 80903. Explain that *numismatic* means "of coins or medals."

Go for the Goal/Final Test
1. If you follow my directions, you'll be *all right.*
2. It's *almost* dark now, so let's go inside.
3. Sharelle has *already* finished her work.
4. It was a *long* book, but I enjoyed it.
5. Do you *belong* to any clubs?
6. What a lot of fish she *caught!*
7. The teacher looked for a new piece of *chalk.*
8. After so much rain, the *lawn* needed mowing.
9. Let's *haul* these leaves away.
10. My baby brother has just learned to *crawl.*
11. *Because* of the heat, we decided to swim.
12. The sweater had a tiny *flaw,* so it was on sale.
13. How much does each ticket *cost?*
14. My birthday is *August* 17.
15. Eric *bought* a new bulletin board for his wall.
16. Do you have any coins in your *wallet?*
17. Our country's *laws* were written to protect us.
18. Let's bring the map so that we don't get *lost.*
19. The guard helped us get safely *across* the road.
20. When the shelf fell, it made an *awful* noise.

Remind students to complete the Scoreboard and write any misspelled words in their Word Locker.

★★ **All-Star Words**   You may want to point out that the All-Star Words follow the spelling rule and model writing a song title for a List Word.

Lesson 26

Objective
To spell words with vowel digraphs *oi* or *oy* and *ou* or *ow*

Correlated Phonics Lesson
MCP Phonics, Level C, Lesson 61

Warm Up   **Page 105**
In this selection, students read about a special school in Florida called Clown College. Ask students whether they would like to be clowns and invite them to discuss clowns they have seen.

Encourage students to look back at the words in dark print. Ask volunteers to say each word and identify the spelling of the /oi/ or /ou/ sound.

On Your Mark/ Warm Up Test
1. The **clown** made a funny face.
2. Will you **join** my soccer team?
3. Do you live in a city or a **town?**
4. The **crowd** cheered when we scored a goal.
5. I **enjoy** hiking in the mountains.
6. A circle is a **round** shape.
7. The lion's **loud** roar startled me!
8. This pencil has a sharp **point.**
9. A dime is a small **coin.**
10. Did your brother get many **toys** for his birthday?
11. Tell me the story **about** Cinderella.
12. Jim was **proud** when he won the race.
13. Uncle Roland will **allow** us to help him paint.
14. Cover the bowl of applesauce with **foil.**
15. The engine has a lot of **power.**
16. Carlos gained one **pound** over the holidays.
17. Dolores wore a red **blouse** to the picnic.
18. The queen wears a **crown.**
19. Make a **choice** about which program to watch.
20. The **loyal** dog followed its master home.

Pep Talk/Game Plan   **Pages 106–107**
Introduce the spelling rule and have students read the List Words aloud. Encourage students to look back at their Warm Up Tests and apply the spelling rule to any misspelled words.

As students work through the **Spelling Lineup, Word Building,** and **Rhyming** exercises, remind them to look back at their List Words or in their dictionaries if they need help.

 See **Letter Cards,** page 15

Warm Up
Where is Clown College?

Clowning Around
Have you ever wanted to be a **clown?** Before you **join** the circus, you have to go to a very special school for clowns in Venice, Florida. Clown College takes only sixty students each year. They learn to juggle and to walk on tall poles called stilts. They also learn how to tumble head over heels and to ride a unicycle. That's a bike with only one wheel. Of course, they learn to fall down and make the **crowd** laugh.

The special students who go to Clown College really **enjoy** it. Learning to be a clown is hard work. For ten weeks, each student must prepare a special clown character. One clown may be fat with a big **round** face. Another may be tall with a head that comes to a **point.** The students must plan and make their own clothes and tricks. Most important is their makeup. Each clown has to have a different face. One will have a big, fat nose. Another will make a giant mouth or big ears. The students wear their "faces" all day at school to get used to being a clown.

Clown college is part of the Ringling Brothers and Barnum and Bailey Circus. They call it "The Greatest Show on Earth." They're not just clowning around!

 Say each word in dark print in the selection. How are the words with the /oi/ sound spelled? How are the words with the /ou/ sound spelled?

On Your Mark
Take your Warm Up Test. Then check your spelling with the List Words on the next page.

Pep Talk
The /oi/ sound may be spelled **oy** as in <u>toys</u> or oi as in <u>coin</u>. The /ou/ sound may be spelled **ow** as in <u>town</u> or ou as in <u>proud</u>. Each List Word has the /oi/ or /ou/ sound. Look at how the sound is spelled in each List Word.

LIST WORDS
1. clown
2. join
3. town
4. crowd
5. enjoy
6. round
7. loud
8. point
9. coin
10. toys
11. about
12. proud
13. allow
14. foil
15. power
16. pound
17. blouse
18. crown
19. choice
20. loyal

Game Plan
Spelling Lineup
Write each List Word under the correct heading.

oi as in <u>oil</u>
1. join
2. point
3. coin
4. foil
5. choice

ow as in <u>how</u>
6. clown
7. town
8. crowd
9. allow
10. power
11. crown

oy as in <u>boy</u>
12. enjoy
13. toys
14. loyal

ou as in <u>sound</u>
15. round
16. loud
17. about
18. proud
19. pound
20. blouse

84

Word Building

Build List Words by adding or subtracting letters. Write
the List Words.

1. enter – ter + joy = _enjoy_
2. alone – one + low = _allow_
3. black – ack + ouse = _blouse_
4. crown – n + d = _crowd_
5. pouch – ch + nd = _pound_
6. above – ve + ut = _about_
7. boys – b + t = _toys_
8. voice – v + ch = _choice_
9. sound – s + r = _round_
10. joint – j + p = _point_
11. royal – r + l = _loyal_
12. brown – br + cl = _clown_
13. coil – l + n = _coin_
14. jolly – lly + in = _join_

Rhyming

Write a List Word that rhymes with the underlined
clue word to complete each silly definition.

1. A place where funny people live is a <u>clown</u> _town_ .
2. A group of noisy people is a _loud_ <u>crowd</u>.
3. A monster who cooks and eats metal things might <u>boil</u> _foil_ .
4. A cloud that is pleased with itself is a _proud_ <u>cloud</u>.
5. A sad or angry king might wear a <u>frown</u> _crown_ .
6. A king who is true to his country is a _loyal_ <u>royal</u>.
7. A king who rules from the top of a castle has <u>tower</u> _power_ .

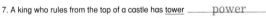

Flex Your Spelling Muscles

Writing

If you could be a clown, what kind of clown would
you be? How would you look? What would you
do to make people laugh? Draw a picture of you
as a clown. Then use the List Words to write a
few sentences describing your act.

Proofreading

This poem has eleven mistakes. Use the proofreading
marks to fix each mistake. Write the misspelled List
Words on the lines.

the circus is coming to (toun)
I can't wait to to see a (clooun)
i've heard there will be lots of (toiys)
For all of the happy girls and boys.
I can't wait to (joyn) the the (croud)
And laugh and cheer and clap out (lowd)

Now proofread your sentences. Fix any mistakes.

Proofreading Marks
◯ spelling mistake
≡ capital letter
⌐ take out something

1. _town_
2. _clown_
3. _toys_
4. _join_
5. _crowd_
6. _loud_

Go for the Goal

Take your Final Test. Then fill in your Scoreboard.
Send your mistakes to the Word Locker.

SCOREBOARD

number correct	number wrong

★ ★ ★ ★ ★ ★ ★ **All-Star Words** ★ ★ ★ ★ ★ ★ ★

avoid   doubt   destroy   spoil   drown

Work with a partner to write a story using the All-Star Words.
Swap stories with other students. How did they use the
All-Star Words?

◎ **Spelling Strategy**   Invite students to get
together with a partner and take turns pronouncing
the List Words. As students say the words, they can
stress the vowel digraph (c*oi*n, t*oy*s, p*ow*er, ab*ou*t)
and name the letters that stand for the /oi/ and /ou/
sounds they hear.

Flex Your Spelling Muscles   *Page 108*

As students complete the **Writing** activity, encourage
them to brainstorm ideas, write a first draft, revise,
and proofread their work. The **Proofreading** exercise
will help them prepare to proofread their sentences.
To publish their writing, students may want to post
their pictures and sentences in a "Just Clowning
Around" bulletin-board display.

✍ **Writer's Corner**

Students might enjoy watching a videotape, such as
Clowns: The Laugh Makers, which can be rented
from Britannica Films (312-347-7958). Encourage
them to make posters or flyers to advertise a
second showing of the film, which can be arranged
for another class.

Go for the Goal/Final Test

1. Which of your talents are you most ***proud*** of?
2. What a lot of ***toys*** the baby has!
3. Put this ***coin*** in your piggy bank.
4. Tell me all ***about*** your vacation.
5. Her new ***blouse*** has a lace collar.
6. The king's ***crown*** was made of gold.
7. The ***loyal*** soldier marched on.
8. Do I have a ***choice*** of soup or salad?
9. We wrapped the leftovers in ***foil.***
10. I ordered a ***pound*** of cheese for the party.
11. We use electric ***power*** to run our appliances.
12. Please ***allow*** me to help you.
13. The ***point*** of my pencil is very sharp.
14. I ***enjoy*** playing soccer.
15. A pizza is usually ***round.***
16. They gave ***loud*** cheers as the band marched by.
17. The ***clown*** has a big red nose.
18. She lives in the ***town*** of Newton, Massachusetts.
19. Would you like to ***join*** our crafts class?
20. The ***crowd*** of happy fans cheered for their team.

Remind students to complete the Scoreboard and
write any misspelled words in their Word Locker.

★★ **All-Star Words**   You may want to point out
that the All-Star Words follow the spelling rule and
help students brainstorm ideas for their stories.

Lesson 27

Objective

To spell words with consonant digraphs *sh* and *th*

Correlated Phonics Lessons

MCP Phonics, Level C, Lessons 31–33
Silver Burdett Ginn *World of Reading,* 3/2, p. 353

Warm Up   **Page 109**

In this selection, students find out how Stanley Newman solved a puzzle to win a national championship. Ask students what skills and abilities they think are needed to solve crossword puzzles and whether or not they enjoy doing them.

Ask volunteers to say each word in dark print and name the pair of consonants that make one sound.

On Your Mark/Warm Up Test

1. The opposite of *tall* is *short.*
2. Did you *thaw* the chicken for dinner?
3. Your pencil should have a *sharp* point.
4. This book costs *thirty* dollars.
5. How many students are in the *fourth* row?
6. Gilberto lives on the *fifth* floor.
7. We had to *rush* to catch the bus.
8. Jason made a *dash* for the finish line.
9. Megan is two minutes older *than* her twin sister.
10. Now, *that* is a great idea!
11. I was *thinking* about buying a new bicycle.
12. Lean on the door and *push* hard.
13. Nick does push-ups to keep in *shape.*
14. *Thirteen* eggs is one more than a dozen.
15. Did you *finish* the book last night?
16. I got a splinter in my *thumb.*
17. Friday is the *sixth* day of the week.
18. Is a groundhog really afraid of its *shadow?*
19. If you use polish on the table, it will *shine.*
20. Get a *shovel* and help me dig in the garden.

Pep Talk/Game Plan   **Pages 110–111**

Introduce the spelling rule and have students read the List Words aloud. Encourage students to look back at their Warm Up Tests and apply the spelling rule to any misspelled words.

As students work through the **Spelling Lineup,** **Dictionary,** and **Synonyms** exercises, remind them to look back at their List Words or in their dictionaries if they need help. Before students begin the **Spelling Lineup,** explain that a consonant digraph may appear at the beginning, middle, or end of a word, as in *short, mushroom,* and *sixth.*

 See Rhymes and Songs, page 14

86

Name _____

/sh/, /th/, or /*th*/

LESSON **27**

Warm Up

What U.S. championship did Stanley Newman win?

The Crossword Kid

In a very **short** time, Stanley Newman won $1500 and a pencil six feet long. He won these prizes thanks to a lot of practice and a **sharp** mind. Stanley finished a crossword puzzle in **thirteen** minutes and twenty seconds. He won the first U.S. Open Crossword Puzzle Championship.

The 261 final players met at New York University in New York City. They were the best "puzzlers" in the country. Their hopes were high. They didn't want **fourth** or **fifth** place. Not even second or third place would do. Each one came to win first prize. When it came to the last and hardest puzzle, only a few players were left.

In the end, Stanley Newman was the big winner. He had to **rush** to **finish** in the fifteen-minute time limit. He completed the puzzle in time! He was able to **dash** off the answers faster and better **than** anyone. He did make one small mistake. That only proved that even the best player isn't always perfect.

 Look back at the words in dark print. Say each word. Can you find two consonants together in each word that make only one sound?

On Your Mark

Take your Warm Up Test. Then check your spelling with the List Words on the next page.

109

Pep Talk

The consonant pairs **sh** and **th** are called **consonant digraphs.** They spell the special sounds you hear in short, rush, thumb, and that. Listen for the sounds the letters **sh** and **th** spell in the List Words.

LIST WORDS

1. short
2. thaw
3. sharp
4. thirty
5. fourth
6. fifth
7. rush
8. dash
9. than
10. that
11. thinking
12. push
13. shape
14. thirteen
15. finish
16. thumb
17. sixth
18. shadow
19. shine
20. shovel

Game Plan

Spelling Lineup

Write the List Words that begin with **sh.**

1. short   4. shadow
2. sharp   5. shine
3. shape   6. shovel

Write the List Words that end with **sh.**

7. rush   9. push
8. dash   10. finish

Write the List Words that begin with **th.**

11. thaw   15. thinking
12. thirty   16. thirteen
13. than   17. thumb
14. that

Write the List Words that end with **th.**

18. fourth   20. sixth
19. fifth

110   Lesson 27 ▪ /sh/, /th/, or /*th*/

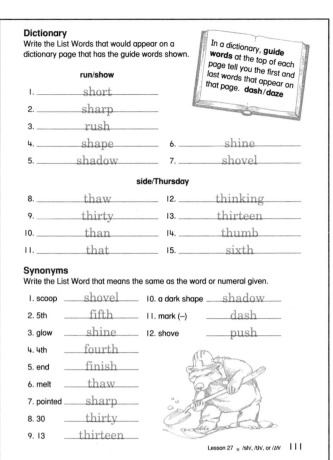

Dictionary

Write the List Words that would appear on a dictionary page that has the guide words shown.

> In a dictionary, **guide words** at the top of each page tell you the first and last words that appear on that page. **dash/daze**

run/show

1. _____ short _____
2. _____ sharp _____
3. _____ rush _____
4. _____ shape _____   6. _____ shine _____
5. _____ shadow _____   7. _____ shovel _____

side/Thursday

8. _____ thaw _____   12. _____ thinking _____
9. _____ thirty _____   13. _____ thirteen _____
10. _____ than _____   14. _____ thumb _____
11. _____ that _____   15. _____ sixth _____

Synonyms

Write the List Word that means the same as the word or numeral given.

1. scoop _____ shovel _____   10. a dark shape _____ shadow _____
2. 5th _____ fifth _____   11. mark (–) _____ dash _____
3. glow _____ shine _____   12. shove _____ push _____
4. 4th _____ fourth _____
5. end _____ finish _____
6. melt _____ thaw _____
7. pointed _____ sharp _____
8. 30 _____ thirty _____
9. 13 _____ thirteen _____

Lesson 27 ≡ /sh/, /th/, or /t͟h/   111

Flex Your Spelling Muscles

Writing

Puzzles are a lot of fun, and there are many kinds to choose from. There are crossword puzzles, word search puzzles, and jigsaw puzzles just to name a few. Use the List Words to describe your favorite puzzle. Tell why you like it.

Proofreading

The following article has eight mistakes. Use the proofreading marks to fix each mistake. Write the misspelled List Words on the lines.

arthur Wynne created the first crossword puzzle in 1913. His idea came from ⓐgame his grandfather had taught him called Magic Square. In a very (shorte) time, wynne's own puzzle began to take (shaip) When it was completed, he knew (thet) it would take a (sharpe) mind to solve it. Wynne's puzzle was so popular that soon people everywhere were in a (rushe) to buy crossword puzzle books.

Now proofread what you wrote about your favorite puzzle. Fix any mistakes.

Proofreading Marks	
◯	spelling mistake
≡	capital letter
∧	add something

1. _____ short _____
2. _____ shape _____
3. _____ that _____
4. _____ sharp _____
5. _____ rush _____

Go for the Goal

Take your Final Test. Then fill in your Scoreboard. Send your mistakes to the Word Locker.

SCOREBOARD

number correct	number wrong

★ ★ ★ ★ ★ ★ ★ **All-Star Words** ★ ★ ★ ★ ★ ★ ★

breathe   shoulder   shiver   thief   selfish

Try to use all five All-Star Words in a single sentence. Then get together with a partner and compare sentences.

⊙ Spelling Strategy   With a partner, students can take turns orally giving each other a List Word to spell. As one partner tells the other a word, he or she can stress the consonant digraph (ru*sh*, *th*umb). The partner who is spelling the word can also finger-write it in the air.

Flex Your Spelling Muscles   *Page 112*

As students complete the **Writing** activity, encourage them to brainstorm ideas, write a first draft, revise, and proofread their work. The **Proofreading** exercise will help them prepare to proofread their writing. To publish their work, students may want to read it aloud as they pass around examples of their favorite kind of puzzle.

✍ Writer's Corner

You may want to bring in a variety of children's word puzzles from newspapers and magazines. Photocopy the puzzles and distribute them to students, then invite the class to try to solve them.

Go for the Goal/Final Test

1. Did you bring a **shovel** to dig in the sand?
2. This is a **short** sentence.
3. I hope the sun will **shine** tomorrow.
4. In the spring, the ground will **thaw.**
5. The dog is chasing its own **shadow!**
6. That knife is **sharp,** so be careful.
7. Is your brother in the **sixth** grade?
8. I worked for the same company for **thirty** years.
9. Her garden shows that she has a green **thumb.**
10. This is the **fourth** time you've been late.
11. The people at the **finish** line cheered.
12. For the **fifth** and final time, go to bed!
13. You are a teenager when you are **thirteen.**
14. We must **rush** if we want to eat before the movie.
15. Do they lift weights to stay in **shape?**
16. Liz made a **dash** for shelter from the rain.
17. Help me **push** this bureau against the wall.
18. Kate runs faster **than** her brother Brian.
19. David is **thinking** about tomorrow's science test.
20. **That** is the prettiest painting I've ever seen!

Remind students to complete the Scoreboard and write any misspelled words in their Word Locker.

★★ **All-Star Words**   You may want to point out that the All-Star Words follow the spelling rule. Help students brainstorm ideas for including all the words in one sentence.

Lesson 28

Objective

To spell words containing the consonant digraphs *ch* and *wh*

Correlated Phonics Lessons

MCP Phonics, Level C, Lessons 31–33
Silver Burdett Ginn *World of Reading,* 3/2, p. 353

Warm Up   *Page 113*

In this selection, students read about a very special food called *nanomin.* Ask students which foods they consider special, and why.

Call on volunteers to say each word in dark print and identify the sound that *ch* or *wh* stands for.

On Your Mark/Warm Up Test

1. A tricycle has one more **wheel** than a bicycle.
2. The **whale** is a mammal that lives in the ocean.
3. We looked here, there, and **everywhere.**
4. I asked the policewoman **which** way I should go.
5. My friend and I **each** have three brothers.
6. Did you **check** the spelling in your report?
7. **While** Mom shops, I watch my little sister.
8. The crust on that bread is nice and **chewy.**
9. The soil in our garden is very **rich.**
10. Maria has one more **chapter** to read in her book.
11. They made a **chart** to show reading progress.
12. That was a great **catch!**
13. We have to **whisper** in the library.
14. Coretta asked **who** was going to the concert.
15. The **whole** class is going to the art show.
16. Is there room on the **bench** for me to sit, too?
17. The **whisk** broom is in the closet.
18. This batter can really **whack** the ball.
19. I asked **whether** I should call or write.
20. Do those new shoes **pinch** your feet?

Pep Talk/Game Plan   *Pages 114–115*

Introduce the spelling rule and have students read the List Words aloud. Discuss the meanings of unfamiliar words, such as *whisk* and *whack.* Then encourage students to look back at their Warm Up Tests and apply the spelling rule to any misspelled words.

As students work through the **Spelling Lineup,** **Dictionary,** and **Scrambled Letters** exercises, remind them to look back at their List Words or in their dictionaries if they need help. For the **Dictionary** exercise, explain that a schwa (ə) indicates an unstressed vowel sound.

 See **Categorizing,** page 15

88

Warm Up

What is *nanomin?*

Gift from the Creator

Each September, the Ojibwa Indians of Minnesota hold a very special harvest of a very special grain. They call it *nanomin,* **which** means "the gift from the creator." Nanomin is a grain not only **rich** in vitamins and nutrients, but it's also delicious. It's used in soups, salads, breads, cakes, and even as breakfast cereal. Also called wild rice, this wild grain from Minnesota is said to be the world's finest.

At daybreak, hundreds of canoes glide across the marshes among the tall green stalks. In each canoe there are two people. One partner pushes a pole against the pond's bottom to move the boat slowly through the marsh. The other partner uses a pair of slender sticks to bend the stalks of grain over the side of the canoe. The sticks are then used to **whack** the stalks, dislodging the rice into the canoe.

The harvesting of the wild rice is a cause for celebration of their Ojibwa's traditions. As one harvester said, "the sweet thing about the wild rice harvest is that it brings families together."

 Look back at the words in dark print. What sound does the consonant digraph **ch** make? What sounds does the consonant digraph **wh** make?

On Your Mark

Take your Warm Up Test. Then check your spelling with the List Words on the next page.

113

Pep Talk

Consonant digraphs are pairs of consonants, such as **ch** or **wh,** that make one sound when they are written together in a syllable. You can hear the /ch/ sound in <u>each</u> and the /hw/ sound in <u>whale.</u> In <u>who</u> and <u>whole,</u> the **w** is silent, but you hear the **h.**

LIST WORDS

1. wheel
2. whale
3. everywhere
4. which
5. each
6. check
7. while
8. chewy
9. rich
10. chapter
11. chart
12. catch
13. whisper
14. who
15. whole
16. bench
17. whisk
18. whack
19. whether
20. pinch

Game Plan

Spelling Lineup

Write each List Word under the correct sound of its consonant digraph. One word will be used twice.

/ch/

1. which   6. chapter
2. each   7. chart
3. check   8. catch
4. chewy   9. bench
5. rich   10. pinch

/hw/

11. which   15. while
12. wheel   16. whisper
13. whale   18. whisk
14. everywhere   19. whack

/h/

20. who   21. whole

114 Lesson 28 ■ /ch/, /hw/, or /h/

1. (chōō′ ē) _chewy_
2. (bench) _bench_
3. (hwisk) _whisk_
4. (chap′ tər) _chapter_
5. (kach) _catch_   7. (hwīl) _while_
6. (chärt) _chart_   8. (ev′rē hwer′) _everywhere_

Scrambled Letters
Unscramble the letters to make List Words.
Then use the number code to answer the riddle.

1. chawk w h a c k
               10
7. loweh w h o l e
               9 3

2. ohw w h o
            4
8. elehw w h e e l
               1   7

3. thewreh w h e t h e r
                        2

4. priwseh w h i s p e r
                           6

5. chinp p i n c h
                    5

6. hawel w h a l e
               8 11

Find the letter with the number 1 under it.
Print that letter on the line below that has
the number 1 under it. Do the same for
numbers 2 through 11.

Riddle: What do you say when you meet a three-headed monster?

Answer: h e l l o   h e l l o   h e l l o
         1 2 3 4   5 6 7 8 9   10 11 7 8 9

Flex Your Spelling Muscles

Writing
Many foods are made of rice. There are rice cakes, rice pudding, and rice cereal. Use the List Words to write a paragraph describing the rice foods you like.

Proofreading
This paragraph has nine mistakes. Use the proofreading marks to fix each mistake. Write the misspelled List Words on the lines.

Proofreading Marks
◯ spelling mistake
⊙ add period
⌐ take out something

In a Hopi family's cornfield, wich they have farmed for many years, plants are evreeware. The Hopi dig small holes in the ground and put kernels in in each hole They chek the plants daily to keep pests away If there is enough rain, the harvest will be be ritch.

1. _which_   4. _check_
2. _everywhere_   5. _rich_
3. _each_

Now proofread your paragraph. Fix any mistakes.

Go for the Goal
Take your Final Test. Then fill in your Scoreboard.
Send your mistakes to the Word Locker.

SCOREBOARD
number correct   number wrong

★ ★ ★ ★ ★ ★ ★ ★ *All-Star Words* ★ ★ ★ ★ ★ ★ ★ ★

whirl   whine   champion   witch   somewhat

Write a sentence for each word. Then scramble the letters in the All-Star Words. Trade papers with a partner. Unscramble the All-Star Word in each sentence and write it correctly.

◉ **Spelling Strategy**   Call out each List Word and invite the class to repeat it and spell it aloud. As students spell the word, write it on the board. Then ask a volunteer to come to the board and circle the consonant digraph *ch* or *wh*. (Note that *which* contains both digraphs.) Have the class pronounce the sound that *ch* or *wh* stands for in the word (/ch/, /hw/, or /h/).

Flex Your Spelling Muscles   *Page 116*
As students complete the **Writing** activity, encourage them to brainstorm ideas, write a first draft, revise, and proofread their work. The **Proofreading** exercise will help them prepare to proofread their paragraphs. To publish their writing, students may want to
• illustrate and display their paragraphs
• create a class book titled "Rice Is Nice."

✍ **Writer's Corner**

The class can receive the pamphlet *Facts about U.S. Rice* by writing to The Rice Council, P.O. Box 740121, Houston, TX 77274. Enclose a long, self-addressed stamped envelope.

Go for the Goal/Final Test
1. **Which** position does he play on the team?
2. Please finish this **chapter** before you leave.
3. His hard **whack** sent the ball over the fence.
4. Don't sit on the **bench** until the paint is dry.
5. People are studying, so we should **whisper.**
6. The cart won't go because the **wheel** is bent.
7. How is a **whale** different from a shark?
8. You may **each** have one apple and one orange.
9. Don't **pinch** your finger in the door!
10. Use a **whisk** broom to sweep off the workbench.
11. I don't know **whether** my mom will let me visit.
12. **Who** picked this beautiful bouquet?
13. Look on the **chart** to see what time gym starts.
14. Let me **check** my watch to see if it is right.
15. Do you like **chewy** brownies?
16. You throw the ball, and I'll **catch** it.
17. Are oranges **rich** in vitamin C?
18. I looked **everywhere** for my lost pen.
19. I'll try to finish the **whole** book tonight.
20. Please beat the eggs **while** I sift the flour.

Remind students to complete the Scoreboard and write any misspelled words in their Word Locker.

★★ **All-Star Words**   You may want to point out that the All-Star Words follow the spelling rule and model completing the activity with a List Word.

Lesson 29

Objective
To spell words with consonant clusters

Warm Up
Page 117

In "Mud Machines," students find out about an unusual race that began in Florida more than thirty years ago. After reading, invite students to discuss whether they would or wouldn't like to take part in a swamp buggy race.

Ask volunteers to say each word in dark print and name the three consonants that are together.

On Your Mark/Warm Up Test

1. What a **splash** I made when I jumped in!
2. Every **spring** we go to a baseball game.
3. What does the **patch** on your jacket say?
4. You must have **strong** legs to swim a mile.
5. Which rides give you the biggest **thrills?**
6. **Spray** from the fountain made my hair wet.
7. The children began to **scream** with delight.
8. Please **throw** me that ball.
9. Tie a long **string** to your kite.
10. The car **struck** the side of the building.
11. The **screen** will keep flies out of the house.
12. Mosquito bites often **itch.**
13. The umpire said the **pitch** was a strike.
14. **Spread** some peanut butter on these crackers.
15. My baby sister loves **strawberry** jam.
16. Let's go wading in the **stream.**
17. John and I **split** the last sandwich.
18. I hope the cat doesn't **scratch** me.
19. The workers dug a **ditch** for the water pipes.
20. Use strong **thread** to sew the button on.

Pep Talk/Game Plan
Pages 118–119

Introduce the spelling rule and have students read the List Words aloud. Encourage students to look back at their Warm Up Tests and apply the spelling rule to any misspelled words.

As students work through the **Spelling Lineup, Alphabetical Order, Puzzle,** and **Classification** exercises, remind them to look back at their List Words or in their dictionaries if they need help. For the **Spelling Lineup,** explain to students that some List Words have the same beginnings and endings.

 See Charades/Pantomime, page 15

90

Warm Up

Where was the first swamp buggy race held?

Mud Machines

Splash! It's another buggy in the mud. What do you think is going on? You could call it a mud rodeo. Some people say it's the dirtiest race on earth. It happens twice a year during Swamp Buggy Days in Naples, Florida. In late winter, just before **spring**, and again in the fall, the swamp buggies tune up for action.

Swamp buggies were once used for hunting in the swamps of Florida. Then over thirty years ago, a man named Ed Frank started the swamp buggy races. The first one was held in a muddy sweet potato **patch.** Through the years, the buggies got better and faster. They are all crazy-looking machines with big tires and **strong** engines.

Today the buggies race through "Mile-O-Mud" track. It runs through the swamps like a big figure eight. The drivers have to make sharp turns and look out for big holes. There are lots of spills and **thrills.** Mud sprays in all directions and the fans **scream.** It's quite a sight to see, and it's all good, but not clean, fun!

> Look back at the words in dark print. Say each word. Can you find the three consonants together in each word?

On Your Mark

Take your Warm Up Test. Then check your spelling with the List Words on the next page.

117

Pep Talk

Three consonants together in a word make a **consonant cluster.** In many List Words, **s** forms a cluster with two other letters. In some List Words, /ch/ or /th/ forms a cluster with another letter.

LIST WORDS

1. splash
2. spring
3. patch
4. strong
5. thrills
6. spray
7. scream
8. throw
9. string
10. struck
11. screen
12. itch
13. pitch
14. spread
15. strawberry
16. stream
17. split
18. scratch
19. ditch
20. thread

Game Plan

Spelling Lineup
Finish each List Word by writing a consonant cluster.

1. spl_ash_   13. _scr_atch
2. _spr_ead   14. _str_uck
3. _spr_ing   15. di_tch_
4. _str_ong   16. _i_tch
5. _spl_it   17. _s_tream
6. _str_awberry   18. _s_pray
7. _thr_ead   19. _s_creen
8. _thr_ills   20. _s_cream
9. _s_tring
10. _thr_ow
11. pi_tch_
12. pa_tch_

118   Lesson 29 ■ Consonant Clusters

Alphabetical Order

Write the List Words in alphabetical order.

spring	splash	spread	strong	scratch	spray

1. scratch   3. spray   5. spring

2. splash   4. spread   6. strong

Puzzle

Write a List Word to solve each clue. Then read down the shaded boxes to answer the riddle.

1. This word names a fruit.   s t r a w b e r r y

2. This will keep flies out of your home.   s c r e e n

3. This is a loud yell.   s c r e a m

4. This means "hit."   s t r u c k

5. This word names a deep hole.   d i t c h

Riddle: What did the strawberry patch say to the rain?

Answer: If you keep this up, my name will b e   m u d !

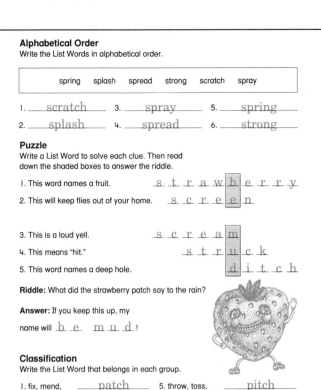

Classification

Write the List Word that belongs in each group.

1. fix, mend, ___ patch
2. skin, rash, ___ itch
3. fall, winter, ___ spring
4. share, divide, ___ split
5. throw, toss, ___ pitch
6. joy, excitement, ___ thrills
7. string, ribbon, ___ thread
8. brook, river, ___ stream

Lesson 29 ■ Consonant Clusters   119

Flex Your Spelling Muscles

Writing
Imagine that you just attended the races at Swamp Buggy Days. Write a brief news report about what you saw. Include lots of colorful details. Use as many List Words as you can.

Proofreading
The poster below has ten mistakes. Use the proofreading marks to fix each mistake. Write the misspelled List Words on the lines.

Proofreading Marks
◯ spelling mistake
∧ add something
/ make small letter

Where can you go to find (thrilz) and chills? Where else but (Strawbarry) (Pache) Beach for the annual (Spreeng) Fling. Watch the amazing dune buggy racers (splasch) through each wet, sandy (dicth). (Skream) for the winners when they reach the Finish line.
It all happens on June 23, beginning at 10 A.m.

1. thrills
2. Strawberry
3. Patch
4. Spring
5. splash
6. ditch
7. scream

Now proofread your news report. Fix any mistakes.

Go for the Goal
Take your Final Test. Then fill in your Scoreboard. Send your mistakes to the Word Locker.

SCOREBOARD

number correct	number wrong

★ ★ ★ ★ ★ ★ ★ **All-Star Words** ★ ★ ★ ★ ★ ★ ★

sprang   scramble   stranger   throne   hatch

With your partner, write a definition for each All-Star Word. Then look them up in the glossary. Do your meanings match? Now use each All-Star Word in a sentence.

120   Lesson 29 ■ Consonant Clusters

◎ **Spelling Strategy**   Write words on the board that contain consonant clusters found in the List Words (for example, *str*ange, *spl*endid, *thr*oat, *spr*ain, *scr*ub, ca*tch*). Say the words and have the class listen for the clusters. Then ask volunteers to come to the board, circle the consonant cluster in each word, and write a List Word that contains the same cluster.

Flex Your Spelling Muscles   *Page 120*

As students complete the **Writing** activity, encourage them to brainstorm ideas, write a first draft, revise, and proofread their work. The **Proofreading** exercise will help them prepare to proofread their news reports. To publish their writing, students may want to
• create a newspaper page
• read their news reports aloud as sportscasts.

✍ Writer's Corner

Students might enjoy reading a book about unusual contests, such as *Encyclopedia Brown's Book of Wacky Sports* by Donald J. Sobol. Invite students to write a brief summary of the competition they like the best and to post it in the school gymnasium.

Go for the Goal/Final Test

1. We had **strawberry** pie for dessert.
2. The **stream** flows into that big lake.
3. Luis will **pitch** for our baseball team this year.
4. Did you **spread** the jelly on the toast?
5. Sew up the hole with a needle and **thread.**
6. The car ran into a **ditch.**
7. The thorn gave Brandon a bad **scratch.**
8. Please **split** the banana in half and share it.
9. **Strong** winds blew many branches onto our lawn.
10. My dog likes to **splash** in puddles.
11. In what month does **spring** arrive?
12. A rabbit is in the cabbage **patch.**
13. We must fix the torn **screen** in your window.
14. Lightning **struck** the old barn last night.
15. Chicken pox can really make you **itch!**
16. The kitten played with a ball of **string.**
17. The pitcher will **throw** to the batter.
18. Riding a roller coaster really **thrills** me.
19. Let's **spray** the rose bushes with water.
20. Did you **scream** when the snake appeared?

Remind students to complete the Scoreboard and write any misspelled words in their Word Locker.

★★ **All-Star Words**   You may want to point out that the All-Star Words follow the spelling rule. Review with students how to use guide words to find entries in a glossary or a dictionary.

Lesson 30 • Instant Replay

Objective
To review spelling words with /ô/; /oi/ or /ou/; /sh/, /th/, or /*th*/; /ch/, /hw/, or /h/; and consonant clusters

Time Out
Pages 121–124
Check Your Word Locker Based on your observations, note which words are giving students the most difficulty and offer assistance for spelling them correctly. Here are some frequently misspelled words to watch for: *toys, which, while, whole,* and *whether.*

To give students extra help and practice in taking standardized tests, you may want to have them take the Review Test for this lesson on pages 94–95. After scoring the tests, return them to students so that they can record their misspelled words in their Word Locker.

After practicing their troublesome words, students can work through the exercises for **Lessons 25–29.** Before they begin each exercise, you may want to go over the spelling rule.

Take It Home With their families, students can brainstorm a list of hobbies they are interested in. Using List Words from **Lessons 25–29,** students can write questions they have about each hobby. For a complete list of the words, encourage them to take their *Spelling Workout* books home. Students can also use Take It Home Master 5 on pages 96–97 to help them do the activity. Invite them to try to answer one another's questions in class. Encourage students to consult an encyclopedia or other books to help them find answers.

Name _____

Instant Replay • Lessons 25–29

LESSON 30

Time Out
Take another look at the /ô/, /oi/, and /ou/ sounds, consonant digraphs, and consonant clusters.

Check Your Word Locker
Look at the words in your Word Locker. Write your most troublesome words for Lessons 25–29.

_____

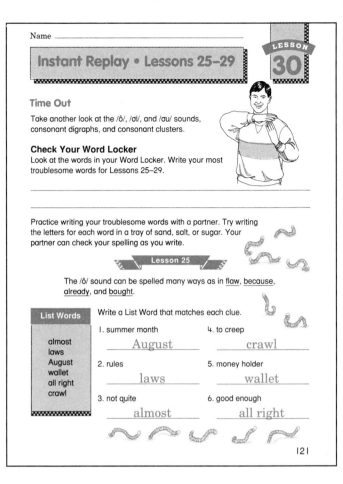

Practice writing your troublesome words with a partner. Try writing the letters for each word in a tray of sand, salt, or sugar. Your partner can check your spelling as you write.

Lesson 25

The /ô/ sound can be spelled many ways as in <u>flaw</u>, <u>because</u>, <u>already</u>, and <u>bought</u>.

List Words

almost
laws
August
wallet
all right
crawl

Write a List Word that matches each clue.

1. summer month   August
2. rules   laws
3. not quite   almost
4. to creep   crawl
5. money holder   wallet
6. good enough   all right

121

Lesson 26

Listen for the /oi/ sound in <u>join</u> and <u>toys</u>, and for the /ou/ sound in <u>loud</u> and <u>town</u>.

List Words

crowd
point
about
power
choice
loyal

Write each List Word under the correct heading.

one syllable
1. crowd
2. point
3. choice

two syllables
4. about
5. power
6. loyal

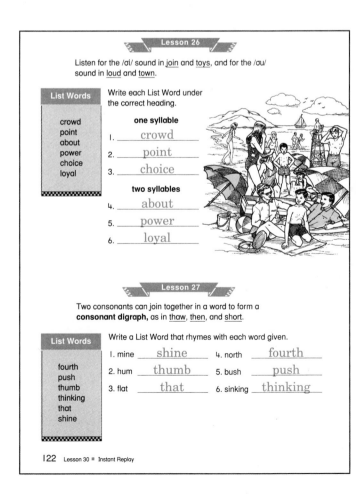

Lesson 27

Two consonants can join together in a word to form a **consonant digraph,** as in <u>thaw</u>, <u>then</u>, and <u>short</u>.

List Words

fourth
push
thumb
thinking
that
shine

Write a List Word that rhymes with each word given.

1. mine   shine
2. hum   thumb
3. flat   that
4. north   fourth
5. bush   push
6. sinking   thinking

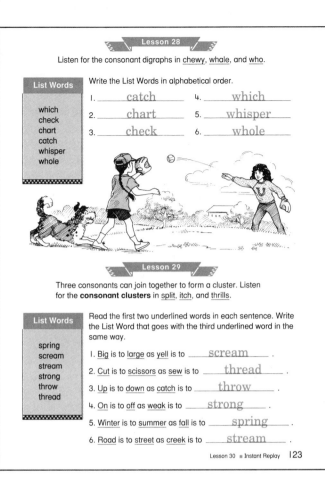

Lesson 28

Listen for the consonant digraphs in <u>chewy</u>, <u>whale</u>, and <u>who</u>.

List Words

which
check
chart
catch
whisper
whole

Write the List Words in alphabetical order.

1. catch
2. chart
3. check
4. which
5. whisper
6. whole

Lesson 29

Three consonants can join together to form a cluster. Listen for the **consonant clusters** in <u>split</u>, <u>itch</u>, and <u>thrills</u>.

List Words

spring
scream
stream
strong
throw
thread

Read the first two underlined words in each sentence. Write the List Word that goes with the third underlined word in the same way.

1. <u>Big</u> is to <u>large</u> as <u>yell</u> is to ___scream___ .
2. <u>Cut</u> is to <u>scissors</u> as <u>sew</u> is to ___thread___ .
3. <u>Up</u> is to <u>down</u> as <u>catch</u> is to ___throw___ .
4. <u>On</u> is to <u>off</u> as <u>weak</u> is to ___strong___ .
5. <u>Winter</u> is to <u>summer</u> as <u>fall</u> is to ___spring___ .
6. <u>Road</u> is to <u>street</u> as <u>creek</u> is to ___stream___ .

Lesson 30 ■ Instant Replay 123

Lessons 25–29

List Words

almost
shine
fourth
whisper
loyal
crowd
point
thumb
which
thread

Write a List Word to finish each sentence.

1. My mother says it's not polite to ___point___ at people.
2. Our baseball team took ___fourth___ place in the league.
3. You should always ___whisper___ quietly in a library.
4. The ___crowd___ was excited when the circus finally started.
5. ___Almost___ everyone likes to eat hamburgers.
6. I broke my ___thumb___ playing ball.
7. ___Which___ way does this bus go?
8. ___Loyal___ fans never miss a game.
9. May I borrow a needle and ___thread___ ?
10. I waxed my bicycle to make it ___shine___ .

Go for the Goal

Take your Final Replay Test. Then fill in your Scoreboard. Send any misspelled words to your Word Locker.

SCOREBOARD

number correct	number wrong

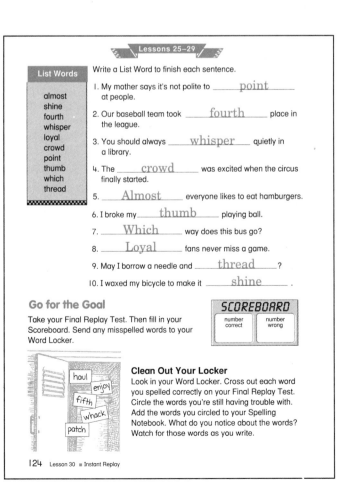

Clean Out Your Locker
Look in your Word Locker. Cross out each word you spelled correctly on your Final Replay Test. Circle the words you're still having trouble with. Add the words you circled to your Spelling Notebook. What do you notice about the words? Watch for those words as you write.

124   Lesson 30 ■ Instant Replay

Go for the Goal/*Final Replay Test*   *Page 124*

1. Now you throw and I'll *catch.*
2. Without your *thumb,* you could not grip a pencil.
3. The *crowd* waited to see the band after the show.
4. Help! They stole my *wallet!*
5. Use a *strong* bag to carry the groceries.
6. We recorded the daily temperatures on a *chart.*
7. The girl in the *fourth* row has her hand up.
8. Who makes our state's *laws?*
9. The book was *about* a dog named Lassie.
10. Each *spring* we plant a vegetable garden.
11. No one is allowed to fish in this *stream.*
12. Please do not *whisper* during the performance.
13. Are you *thinking* of getting a new skateboard?
14. I am *almost* as tall as my sister now.
15. It is not polite to *point* at people.
16. Just *push* those suitcases out of your way.
17. Please *check* to be sure everyone is here.
18. The star's fans began to *scream.*
19. Our new car has more *power* than our old one.
20. Is it *all right* if we watch another movie?
21. My birthday is in *August.*
22. The running shoes would be my first *choice.*
23. Did you eat that *whole* pizza by yourself?
24. If you move, the sun won't *shine* in your eyes.
25. Did you use blue *thread* to sew the button on?
26. Just *throw* your coats on the upstairs bed.
27. I love that book, *which* I've read twice.
28. Most dogs are *loyal* friends.
29. Is *that* your jacket on the floor?
30. Some snakes can *crawl* very quickly.

Clean Out Your Word Locker   For each word, students can identify the consonant cluster or the letter or letters that stand for the sounds they learned in **Lessons 25–29.**

Instant Replay Test

Side A

Read each set of phrases. Fill in the circle next to the phrase with an underlined word that is spelled wrong.

1. (a) his new <u>wallet</u>
   (b) without any <u>power</u>
   (c) will be <u>alrit</u>
   (d) state <u>laws</u>

2. (a) a quiet <u>whisper</u>
   (b) <u>thincking</u> hard
   (c) <u>almost</u> finished
   (d) an <u>awful</u> mess

3. (a) <u>push</u> the pedal
   (b) very <u>strict</u> laws
   (c) with blue <u>thred</u>
   (d) to <u>crawl</u> toward

4. (a) a <u>loyle</u> pet
   (b) <u>about</u> our vacation
   (c) next <u>spring</u>
   (d) its <u>strong</u> wings

5. (a) last <u>Awgust</u>
   (b) one <u>pound</u> of bananas
   (c) <u>that</u> clever idea
   (d) the second <u>chart</u>

6. (a) the only <u>choice</u>
   (b) <u>throw</u> the ball
   (c) <u>finish</u> the project
   (d) in <u>forth</u> grade

7. (a) a <u>chalk</u> line
   (b) <u>witch</u> answer
   (c) waves <u>splash</u>
   (d) count <u>each</u> correct answer

8. (a) the last <u>chapter</u>
   (b) the <u>hole</u> team
   (c) a red <u>strawberry</u>
   (d) her tiny <u>thumb</u>

9. (a) <u>catch</u> the flu
   (b) the pencil <u>point</u>
   (c) a long <u>string</u>
   (d) a large <u>croud</u>

10. (a) a silly <u>clown</u>
    (b) the <u>fifth</u> time
    (c) a rocky <u>streem</u>
    (d) by solar <u>power</u>

Name _____

Instant Replay Test

Side B

Read each set of phrases. Fill in the circle next to the phrase
with an underlined word that is spelled wrong.

11. ⓐ push the swing   ⓒ the log split
    ⓑ a restaurant check   ⓓ a loud screem

12. ⓐ that new computer   ⓒ a silver coin
    ⓑ to shien brightly   ⓓ push the pedal

13. ⓐ a dull poynt   ⓒ a terrible scream
    ⓑ a spring thaw   ⓓ her leather wallet

14. ⓐ catch a cold   ⓒ the hungry crowd
    ⓑ crawl away from   ⓓ her stong legs

15. ⓐ the fourth lesson   ⓒ to feel all right
    ⓑ his thum hurt   ⓓ a slim shape

16. ⓐ next August   ⓒ to keep thinking
    ⓑ about male geese   ⓓ fair lawes

17. ⓐ the king's power   ⓒ a soft wisper
    ⓑ a clear stream   ⓓ a quick check

18. ⓐ an excellent choise   ⓒ water the lawn
    ⓑ a sharp knife   ⓓ a rush job

19. ⓐ the pink thread   ⓒ the wooden bench
    ⓑ allmost ready   ⓓ a loyal friend

20. ⓐ thirty days and nights   ⓒ the letter charte
    ⓑ which teammate   ⓓ the whole sentence

5

TAKE IT HOME

Your child has learned to spell many new words in Lessons 25–29 and would like to share them with you and your family. Here are some ideas that will make reviewing those words fun for everyone.

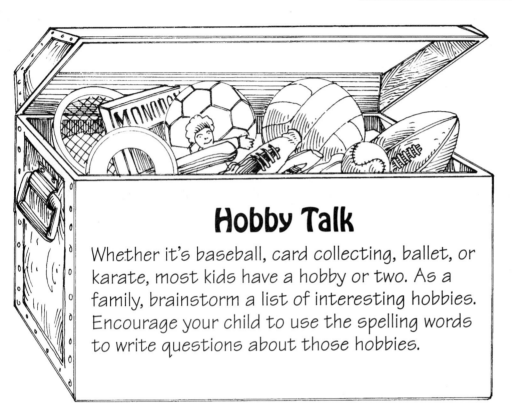

Hobby Talk

Whether it's baseball, card collecting, ballet, or karate, most kids have a hobby or two. As a family, brainstorm a list of interesting hobbies. Encourage your child to use the spelling words to write questions about those hobbies.

Scrambled Words

Uh-Oh! Somebody's stirred up the alphabet soup! Draw a line from each bowl of scrambled letters to the bowl with the correct spelling. Then, you and your child can mix up some spelling scrambles of your own.

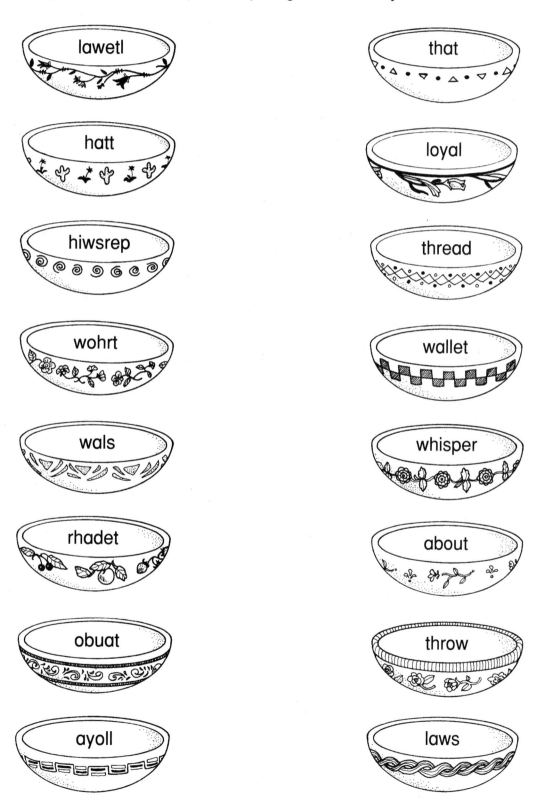

lawetl

that

hatt

loyal

hiwsrep

thread

wohrt

wallet

wals

whisper

rhadet

about

obuat

throw

ayoll

laws

Lesson 31

Objective
To spell words with consonant digraphs

Correlated Phonics Lesson
MCP Phonics, Level C, Lessons 31–32

Warm Up   **Page 125**

In this selection, students learn how the ancient Egyptians used hieroglyphs, or pictures, to write their language. After reading, invite students to create pictures to represent words such as *book, bicycle,* and *classroom.*

Encourage students to look back at the words in dark print. Ask volunteers to say each word and name the pair of consonants that makes one sound.

On Your Mark/Warm Up Test

1. My best friend goes to another **school.**
2. He **wrote** a letter to his grandparents.
3. Did Carmen **phone** you last night?
4. She **knew** how the magician did the trick.
5. There is a stop **sign** at the corner.
6. Can you get the **knots** out of your shoelaces?
7. The opposite of right is **wrong.**
8. Dad bounced the baby on his **knee.**
9. Be careful with that sharp **knife!**
10. Our house was a **wreck** after the family reunion.
11. Aaron used gold paper to **wrap** the present.
12. I heard someone **knock** on the door.
13. Julia used sandpaper to smooth the **rough** wood.
14. When Liang tells a joke, we all **laugh.**
15. The **elephant** took a mud bath to cool off.
16. Did your **cough** keep you awake last night?
17. The male **wren** helps raise its young.
18. The **writer** of this article spoke to our class.
19. The **graph** shows how many cans we recycled.
20. The race will begin at the **track** at noon.

Pep Talk/Game Plan   **Pages 126–127**

Introduce the spelling rule and have students read the List Words aloud, helping them identify the consonant digraph in each word. Then encourage students to look back at their Warm Up Tests and apply the spelling rule to any misspelled words.

As students work through the **Spelling Lineup, Puzzle,** and **Missing Words** exercises, remind them to look back at their List Words or in their dictionaries if they need help.

 See **Picture Clues,** page 15

Consonant Digraphs

Warm Up

What are hieroglyphs?

Hieroglyphs that spell the word <u>read</u>.

r

ea

d

The Art of Writing

Over 5,000 years ago, the Egyptians started to write their spoken language down. As with the beginnings of many written languages, the Egyptians **wrote** their language using pictures. These pictures are called hieroglyphs. Each hieroglyph stands for a different sound. Several hieroglyphs can stand for a letter, especially when it comes to vowels. That's because vowels have more than one sound.

Unlike English, hieroglyphs can be written in more than one direction. They can be written from left to right, like English, or right to left, like Arabic and Hebrew. They can also be written from top to bottom, like Chinese. You might ask how the ancient Egyptians kept **track** of which direction in which to read. They **knew** by the pictures themselves. If the sign for a letter faced left, they started reading from the left. If the **sign** faced right, they started reading from the right.

A **writer** using Egyptian hieroglyphs would probably have a **rough** time telling a story. You would not only have to know how to write, but also how to draw!

> Look back at the words in dark print. Say each word. Can you find two consonants together in each word that make only one sound?

On Your Mark

Take your Warm Up Test. Then check your spelling with the List Words on the next page.

125

Pep Talk

The /n/ can be spelled with **kn** or **gn**, as in <u>knew</u> and <u>sign</u>. The /r/ can be spelled with **wr**, as in <u>wrote</u>. The /f/ can be spelled with **gh** or **ph**, as in <u>rough</u> and <u>phone</u>. The /k/ can be spelled with **ch** or **ck**, as in <u>school</u> and <u>wreck</u>.

LIST WORDS

1. school
2. wrote
3. phone
4. knew
5. sign
6. knots
7. wrong
8. knee
9. knife
10. wreck
11. wrap
12. knock
13. rough
14. laugh
15. elephant
16. cough
17. wren
18. writer
19. graph
20. track

Game Plan

Spelling Lineup
Say each sound. Write the List Words that spell that sound with a digraph. Then circle the digraph in each word. Some words will be written more than once.

/n/	/f/
1. knew	13. phone
2. sign	14. rough
3. knots	15. laugh
4. knee	16. elephant
5. knife	17. cough
6. knock	18. graph
/r/	/k/
7. wrote	19. school
8. wrong	20. wreck
9. wreck	21. knock
10. wrap	22. track
11. wren	
12. writer	

126   Lesson 31 ■ Consonant Digraphs

98

Puzzle

Fill in the crossword puzzle by writing a List Word to answer each clue.

ACROSS

2. the bend in your leg
3. not correct
4. a person who writes
5. felt sure about
8. a place to learn
9. a chart

DOWN

1. used a pen and paper
2. rap on a door
3. a small bird
4. something that is a mess
6. to put a cover around
7. take medicine for this

Missing Words

Write a List Word from the box to finish each phrase.

1. as sharp as a _____ knife
2. as _ as sandpaper _____ rough
3. as big as an _____ elephant
4. the last _____ laugh
5. all tied up in _____ knots

Lesson 31 ■ Consonant Digraphs   127

Flex Your Spelling Muscles

Writing

Have you ever wanted to create your own secret language? If so, here's your chance. First, use the List Words to write a secret message. Then draw pictures or symbols to illustrate your message.

Proofreading

This diary entry has eleven mistakes. Use the proofreading marks to fix each mistake. Write the misspelled List Words on the lines.

Proofreading Marks
⬯ spelling mistake
⊙ add period
⤲ take out something

Dear Diary,

Last week, my teacher called me on the fone and asked me to to write an article for the sckool paper. I was so excited! First, I made an outline to keep trak of my ideas. Next, I wroat a ruff draft. Then, I proofread it it and fixed my mistakes. Finally, it was time to sine my name and turn it in. My teacher loved it! Well, Diary, today it appeared in the paper. Now I know what I want to be when I grow up—a riter.

Now proofread your secret message. Fix any mistakes.

1. _____ phone
2. _____ school
3. _____ track
4. _____ wrote
5. _____ rough
6. _____ sign
7. _____ writer

Go for the Goal

Take your Final Test. Then fill in your Scoreboard. Send your mistakes to the Word Locker.

SCOREBOARD

number correct	number wrong

★ ★ ★ ★ ★ ★ ★ ★ All-Star Words ★ ★ ★ ★ ★ ★ ★ ★

knit   wrinkle   tough   cricket   anchor

Write a story using all the words. Then scramble the letters in the All-Star Words. Trade papers with a partner. Unscramble the All-Star Words in the story.

128   Lesson 31 ■ Consonant Digraphs

○ **Spelling Strategy**   Divide the class into four groups and assign each group a consonant digraph or digraphs: *kn/gn, wr, gh/ph, ch/ck*. Encourage the groups to

• write List Words and other words that contain their assigned digraphs
• underline the digraphs
• share their lists with other groups.

Flex Your Spelling Muscles   *Page 128*

As students complete the **Writing** activity, encourage them to brainstorm ideas, write a first draft, revise, and proofread their work. The **Proofreading** exercise will help them prepare to proofread their messages. To publish their writing, students may want to try to decode a partner's message.

✍ **Writer's Corner** _____

You may want to bring in rebus puzzles to share with the class. Invite students to create some of their own and to try to solve one another's puzzles.

Go for the Goal/Final Test

1. Lionel has a bad ***cough.***
2. The train moved swiftly along the ***track.***
3. The car was a ***wreck*** after the accident.
4. Next Monday we don't have ***school.***
5. The ***sign*** said, "Puppies for sale."
6. This ***graph*** shows that the company lost money.
7. Dimitri ***wrote*** a limerick about an ostrich.
8. Have you read any other books by this ***writer?***
9. ***Phone*** home to let us know you arrived safely.
10. The ***wren*** flew to the birdhouse in the garden.
11. I ***knew*** everything would turn out all right.
12. How does an ***elephant*** defend its young?
13. I learned how to tie five kinds of ***knots.***
14. Don't ***laugh*** while eating!
15. These shoes are the ***wrong*** size.
16. The ship sailed on ***rough*** seas.
17. How did you get that cut on your ***knee?***
18. Please help me ***wrap*** Mom's present.
19. A sharp ***knife*** cuts better than a dull one.
20. ***Knock*** three times before you enter.

Remind students to complete the Scoreboard and write any misspelled words in their Word Locker.

★ ★ **All-Star Words**   You may want to point out that the All-Star Words follow the spelling rule and help students brainstorm ideas for their stories.

Lesson 32

Objective
To spell words with the prefixes *un* and *dis*

Correlated Phonics Lessons
MCP Phonics, Level C, Lesson 65
Silver Burdett Ginn *World of Reading*, 3/2, pp. 472–473

Warm Up   **Page 129**
In this selection, students discover that a shooting star is really a meteor. Afterward, invite students to read aloud the part of the selection they liked the best.

Encourage students to look back at the words in dark print. Ask volunteers to say each word and identify its prefix.

On Your Mark/Warm Up Test
1. The crickets chirped **unseen** in the high grass.
2. Were you **unable** to jump over the fence?
3. José was the first to **discover** an arrowhead.
4. My neighbor helped me **unload** the moving van.
5. **Unclean** hands may ruin the experiment.
6. I was **unsure** if I was going to the party.
7. It was hard to play soccer on an **uneven** field.
8. I **dislike** very hot days, but I love warm ones.
9. Your rudeness will surely **displease** your aunt.
10. The birds **distrust** the cat.
11. Hiro couldn't wait to **unwrap** his present.
12. The whole story is **untrue.**
13. What an **unlucky** day this has been!
14. Her old home was **unchanged.**
15. Was the kitten's food **untouched?**
16. Never **disobey** your parents.
17. **Disorder** in a room makes it hard to find things.
18. I cannot **unbutton** this cuff with my left hand.
19. My mother puts the **unpaid** bills in this pile.
20. The moon seems to **disappear** during an eclipse.

Pep Talk/Game Plan   **Pages 130–131**
Introduce the spelling rule and have students read the List Words aloud. Encourage students to look back at their Warm Up Tests and apply the spelling rule to any misspelled words.

As students work through the **Spelling Lineup, Synonyms,** and **Scrambled Letters** exercises, remind them to look back at their List Words or in their dictionaries if they need help.

 See **Comparing/Contrasting,** page 15

100

Prefixes <u>un</u>, <u>dis</u>   LESSON 32

Warm Up
What is the real name for a shooting star?

Shooting Stars?

Did you know that shooting stars aren't really stars at all? They start out as cold chunks of rock speeding through space. Often one will get caught in the air around the earth and start falling. As it races through the earth's air, it gets so hot it glows. Scientists call this shooting star a meteor.

Most of these glowing space rocks burn up in the air and **disappear.** The very few that ever reach the earth are called meteorites. These special rocks often go **unseen** on the ground. Wind and weather break them into smaller pieces. You would probably be **unable** to tell a meteorite from an ordinary earth rock.

Scientists have been able to **discover** many meteorites in Antarctica, near the South Pole. The dark rocks are easy to see on the empty ice fields. The cold, dry air has kept many meteorites **unchanged** for thousands of years. Unlike those in other places, the meteorites in Antarctica have been **untouched** by **unclean** air and by weather.

That shooting star you see may not make your wish come true. Don't be too **unhappy.** Scientists say it could unlock some secrets of the planets and outer space.

 Look back at the words in dark print. These words have word parts, or prefixes, added to the front of them to make new words. Name the two prefixes.

On Your Mark
Take your Warm Up Test. Then check your spelling with the List Words on the next page.

Pep Talk
A **prefix** is a word part added to the beginning of a **root word**. It changes the root's meaning. The prefixes **dis** and **un** mean <u>not</u> or the <u>opposite</u>, as in <u>unseen</u> and <u>dislike</u>. Think about the meaning of each List Word.

LIST WORDS

1. unseen
2. unable
3. discover
4. unload
5. unclean
6. unsure
7. uneven
8. dislike
9. displease
10. distrust
11. unwrap
12. untrue
13. unlucky
14. unchanged
15. untouched
16. disobey
17. disorder
18. unbutton
19. unpaid
20. disappear

Game Plan

Spelling Lineup
Write each List Word under the correct heading.

words with the prefix **dis**

1. discover   5. disobey
2. dislike   6. disorder
3. displease   7. disappear
4. distrust

words with the prefix **un**

8. unseen   15. untrue
9. unable   16. unlucky
10. unload   17. unchanged
11. unclean   18. untouched
12. unsure   19. unbutton
13. uneven   20. unpaid
14. unwrap

130   Lesson 32 ▪ Prefixes **un** and **dis**

Synonyms

Write the List Word that means the same as the word given.

1. find	discover	5. hate	dislike
2. false	untrue	6. dirty	unclean
3. mess	disorder	7. annoy	displease
4. vanish	disappear	8. uncertain	unsure

Scrambled Letters

Unscramble the letters to spell each root word. Write the List Word that contains it.

1. doutech	untouched	15. retu	untrue
2. aldo	unload	16. dorer	disorder
3. praw	unwrap	17. leapse	displease
4. hangced	unchanged	18. rapepa	disappear
5. boye	disobey	19. ruse	unsure
6. neev	uneven	20. eikl	dislike
7. surtt	distrust		
8. tunobt	unbutton		
9. nese	unseen		
10. apid	unpaid		
11. culky	unlucky		
12. bale	unable		
13. nalec	unclean		
14. rocev	discover		

THE GREAT DISAPPEARING ACT

Flex Your Spelling Muscles

Writing

Have you ever wished on a star? What did you wish for? Write a few sentences telling about your wish. Use as many List Words as you can.

Proofreading

This diary entry below has nine mistakes. Use the proofreading marks to fix the mistakes. Then write the misspelled List Words on the lines.

last night I was unabel to sleep so I sat up and watched the stars. Suddenly I saw something streak through the sky and then disappeer. I was surprised and a little unshure of what Id seen. So, I listened to the news this morning hoping to diskover the answer. sure enough, the news reported the sighting of a meteor last night. what a relief! Now I know I wasnt seeing things.

Proofreading Marks
- ◯ spelling mistake
- ≡ capital letter
- ⌄ add apostrophe

1.	unable	3. unsure
2.	disappear	4. discover

Now proofread your sentences. Fix any mistakes.

Go for the Goal

Take your Final Test. Then fill in your Scoreboard. Send your mistakes to the Word Locker.

SCOREBOARD

number correct	number wrong

★ ★ ★ ★ ★ ★ ★ **All-Star Words** ★ ★ ★ ★ ★ ★ ★

unusual   uneasy   unprepared   disrespect   distaste

Write a sentence for each All-Star Word. Trade sentences with a partner. Circle the prefixes in the All-Star Words and tell their meanings.

⊙ **Spelling Strategy**   With a partner, students can take turns telling each other a root word contained in a List Word. The partner who is listening adds the prefix *dis* or *un* to the root word, saying the complete word aloud, and then finger-writes the word as he or she spells it aloud.

Flex Your Spelling Muscles   *Page 132*

As students complete the **Writing** activity, encourage them to brainstorm ideas, write a first draft, revise, and proofread their work. The **Proofreading** exercise will help them prepare to proofread their sentences. To publish their writing, students may want to

- trade sentences with a partner and illustrate each other's wish come true
- combine their work into a "Wish Book."

✍ Writer's Corner

Students might be interested in reading a book such as *Comets, Meteors, and Asteroids: Rocks in Space* by David J. Darling. Encourage them to take notes and share what they learned with a classmate.

Go for the Goal/Final Test

1. Please help me **unbutton** the costume.
2. Was your pie **untouched** when you returned?
3. It is easy to **displease** a cranky person.
4. Microscopes show previously **unseen** germs.
5. I would like to **discover** buried treasure.
6. Put all the **unclean** glasses in the sink.
7. The magician made a car **disappear!**
8. Please don't **disobey** the camp rules.
9. The story wasn't **untrue,** but it was mixed up.
10. I'm sorry I'll be **unable** to go to your party.
11. Would you please **unload** the dishwasher?
12. I'm **unsure** which road goes to the park.
13. Don't **unwrap** your present before your birthday!
14. I will write checks for those **unpaid** bills.
15. Dirt bothers me, but **disorder** doesn't.
16. The patient's condition remained **unchanged.**
17. Watch your step on that **uneven** path.
18. I **distrust** people who make wild promises.
19. I was **unlucky** because my name was last.
20. Dogs **dislike** the smell of smoke.

Remind students to complete the Scoreboard and write any misspelled words in their Word Locker.

★★ **All-Star Words**   You may want to point out that the All-Star Words follow the spelling rule and model writing a sentence with a List Word.

Lesson 33

Objective
To spell words with the prefix *re*

Correlated Phonics Lesson
MCP Phonics, Level C, Lesson 66

Warm Up   **Page 133**
In "Bigger Than Life," students read about the painstaking process involved in creating the Statue of Liberty. Afterward, invite students to suggest ideas for huge statues they would like to see in their community.

    Encourage students to look back at the words in dark print. Ask volunteers to say the words and suggest how the prefix *re* changes the meanings of the root words.

On Your Mark/Warm Up Test
1. They decided to **rename** the ship *Hope*.
2. Please **remind** me to bring the music.
3. A quiet walk might **refresh** me.
4. Can you **retell** the story in just a few words?
5. Yasmine decided to **rewrite** her poem.
6. Let's **replay** the tape.
7. George will **repay** the money he owes.
8. Please **refill** the pitcher with orange juice.
9. I need to **reload** my stapler.
10. We watched a **rerun** of a television show.
11. Domingo will **replace** the broken window.
12. Will you **redo** the decorations on the window?
13. The gardener will **replant** the daisies.
14. John has to **renew** his library book.
15. Tomorrow we will **rebuild** the old fence.
16. Kim needs to **recopy** her homework assignment.
17. After lunch, the committee will **regroup**.
18. We'll have to **rethink** our plans if it rains.
19. Did you **rework** the problem to find your mistake?
20. "We must **reform** the government!" she shouted.

Pep Talk/Game Plan   **Pages 134–135**
Introduce the spelling rule and have students read the List Words aloud. Encourage students to look back at their Warm Up Tests and apply the spelling rule to any misspelled words.

    As students work through the **Spelling Lineup, Scrambled Letters Puzzle,** and **Rhyming** exercises, remind them to look back at their List Words or in their dictionaries if they need help.

 See **Student Dictation**, page 14

Prefix re

Warm Up
Why did it take so long for Bartholdi to finish the statue?

Bigger Than Life

She stands in New York Harbor. She is more than twenty times larger than life. One of her fingers is taller than a person, and one fingernail is 13 inches wide! She's the Statue of Liberty! Her full name is "Liberty Enlightening the World." People often **rename** her "Miss Liberty."

The statue was a gift to the United States from France. In the 1700's both countries had fought to free themselves from the rule of kings. The French people wanted to **remind** Americans of the friendship and freedom they now shared.

The artist, Frederic Auguste Bartholdi, took nearly ten years to finish the statue. He had to make and remake his plan on paper. Then he had to build and **rebuild** models until the statue pleased him. First, he made a small clay model in Paris. Then he built one 36 feet tall and marked it off into 300 pieces. Each piece was then made in a larger size and sent to America. In 1886, on an island in New York Harbor, the giant puzzle was put together.

Even today the Statue of Liberty stands proudly to **retell** the world that America is free. No other statue could ever **replace** it.

> Take a look at the words in dark print in the selection. How does the prefix **re** change the meaning of each root word?

On Your Mark
Take your Warm Up Test. Then check your spelling with the List Words on the next page.

Pep Talk
The prefix **re** can mean <u>again</u> or <u>back</u>.
re + tell = <u>retell</u>, meaning "tell again"
re + pay = <u>repay</u>, meaning "pay back"

Think about the meaning of **re** in each of the List Words.

LIST WORDS
1. rename
2. remind
3. refresh
4. retell
5. rewrite
6. replay
7. repay
8. refill
9. reload
10. rerun
11. replace
12. redo
13. replant
14. renew
15. rebuild
16. recopy
17. regroup
18. rethink
19. rework
20. reform

Game Plan
Spelling Lineup
Add the prefix re to each of these roots to form a List Word. Write the List Words.

1. form	reform	14. new	renew
2. build	rebuild	15. pay	repay
3. load	reload	16. fill	refill
4. mind	remind	17. run	rerun
5. place	replace	18. work	rework
6. think	rethink	19. play	replay
7. group	regroup	20. name	rename
8. plant	replant		
9. write	rewrite		
10. fresh	refresh		
11. copy	recopy		
12. do	redo		
13. tell	retell		

134   Lesson 33 ▪ Prefix re

102

Scrambled Letters Puzzle

Fill in the crossword puzzle by unscrambling each set of letters to write a List Word.

ACROSS
3. RETWIRE
6. RECLEAP
7. DORE
8. YAPER

DOWN
1. GROPURE
2. EMANER
3. PRAYLE
4. PORCEY
5. KREROW

Rhyming

The root of a List Word rhymes with each of these words. Write the complete List Word.

1. can't _____ replant
2. floppy _____ recopy
3. sun _____ rerun
4. ink _____ rethink
5. face _____ replace
6. sell _____ retell
7. toad _____ reload

8. warm _____ reform
9. flight _____ rewrite
10. loop _____ regroup
11. hill _____ refill
12. kind _____ remind
13. mesh _____ refresh
14. filled _____ rebuild

Lesson 33 ■ Prefix re   135

Flex Your Spelling Muscles

Writing

There are many monuments and statues that honor people or events in our history. Write a paragraph about one you have visited or know about. Use as many List Words as you can.

Proofreading

This article has nine mistakes. Use the proofreading marks to fix the mistakes. Then write the misspelled List Words on the lines.

Proofreading Marks
◯ spelling mistake
^ add something
/ make small letter

Can a mountain be made into a Monument? Of course it can! Mount Rushmore, on which the faces of four American presidents are carved, should reemind you of that fact. Nearby, another mountain will someday retel the story of Crazy Horse, a Sioux warrior. The image of this famous warrior and his horse will eventually replase an ordinary mountain. Unfortunately, the Artist died before he could complete his sculpture. The artist's wife and family plan to reneu and complete this incredible work of art.

1. _____ remind
2. _____ retell
3. _____ replace
4. _____ renew

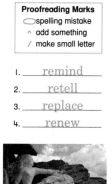

Now proofread your paragraph. Fix any mistakes.

Go for the Goal

Take your Final Test. Then fill in your Scoreboard. Send your mistakes to the Word Locker.

SCOREBOARD
| number correct | number wrong |

★ ★ ★ ★ ★ ★ ★ All-Star Words ★ ★ ★ ★ ★ ★ ★

reappear   rewire   reapply   reassign   reorder

Use the All-Star Words to create a crossword puzzle. Make a grid and then write a clue for each word. Swap papers with a partner. Can you fill in the puzzle with the correct All-Star Words?

136   Lesson 33 ■ Prefix re

◉ **Spelling Strategy**   With a partner, students can take turns saying the List Words aloud. The partner who is listening
• repeats the word
• writes it while spelling it aloud
• circles the prefix
• gives the meaning of the word.

Flex Your Spelling Muscles   *Page 136*

As students complete the **Writing** activity, encourage them to brainstorm ideas, write a first draft, revise, and proofread their work. The **Proofreading** exercise will help them prepare to proofread their paragraphs. To publish their writing, students may want to read their work aloud, displaying pictures of the places they are describing.

✍ Writer's Corner

To learn more about the Statue of Liberty, students can read *Lady with a Torch: How the Statue of Liberty Was Born* by Eleanor Coerr, or a similar book. They might enjoy using what they learn to write a radio script about the construction of the statue.

Go for the Goal/Final Test

1. Let's plan to **redo** the kitchen next year.
2. Will you help me **reload** the wheelbarrow?
3. I watched a **rerun** of my favorite movie.
4. You must **replace** the book that you lost!
5. Tasha will **recopy** the poem in ink.
6. Let's **replant** the tree in the back yard.
7. Did you **renew** your magazine subscription?
8. LaToya will help me **rebuild** the doghouse.
9. Most authors **rewrite** their work.
10. Don't forget to **repay** the money that you owe me.
11. Did you **refill** the tank with gas?
12. I listened to the **replay** of my recorded speech.
13. Does he think we should **reform** our tax laws?
14. Let's **rework** our dance and add some new steps.
15. The players agreed to **regroup** after lunch.
16. I think you need to **rethink** your plan, Jeff.
17. These photos **remind** me of our vacation.
18. Please **retell** that story.
19. I will **rename** my cat Whiskers.
20. A shower will **refresh** the tired soccer player.

Remind students to complete the Scoreboard and write any misspelled words in their Word Locker.

★★ **All-Star Words**   Point out that the All-Star Words follow the spelling rule. Suggest that students first arrange the All-Star Words, then draw their grids based on that arrangement.

103

Lesson 34

Objective
To spell contractions

Correlated Phonics Lessons
MCP Phonics, Level C, Lessons 40–41
Silver Burdett Ginn *World of Reading*, 3/3, p. 845

Warm Up
Page 137

In this selection, students discover the identity of "Ursus horribilis." After reading, invite students to discuss wild animals that they have seen.

Encourage students to look back at the words in dark print. Ask volunteers to say each word and tell which letters were left out.

On Your Mark/Warm Up Test
1. **There's** a robin hopping around on the lawn.
2. I **haven't** played the new video game.
3. Tim is here, and **he's** fixing your bike.
4. **Couldn't** you see the ball coming?
5. **That's** the best song I ever heard!
6. **I'll** meet you after school.
7. **Isn't** Chris home from school yet?
8. We **didn't** go to the movie last night.
9. **They're** going on a vacation to the beach.
10. **We'll** see you at the bicycle race.
11. You **mustn't** open your eyes until I tell you.
12. **Shouldn't** you call your mother now?
13. Marco **wasn't** in school yesterday.
14. They **won't** be able to come to the party.
15. **I'd** like to borrow your book about dinosaurs.
16. She **wouldn't** tell us who won the contest.
17. I **don't** want to practice the piano.
18. **I've** got a wonderful idea for your project.
19. **You've** been out of town for a long time.
20. **Doesn't** your brother want to come, too?

Pep Talk/Game Plan
Pages 138–139

Introduce the spelling rule and have students read the List Words aloud, helping students identify the two words that each contraction represents. Then encourage students to look back at their Warm Up Tests and apply the spelling rule to any misspelled words.

As students work through the **Spelling Lineup, Contractions, Alphabetical Order,** and **Rhyming** exercises, remind them to look back at their List Words or in their dictionaries if they need help. For the **Spelling Lineup,** you may want to work through the first item with students.

 See **Questions/Answers,** page 15

104

Warm Up
Who or what is Ursus horribilis?

Ursus Horribilis
One night not too long ago, a group of campers at Yellowstone National Park had an unwelcome visitor to their barbecue—a yearling grizzly bear. A yearling is a grizzly **that's** about 1 year old. This 170 pound youngster walked into the picnic area, and calmly roamed from table to table, enjoying the feast. Of course, the terrified picnickers **didn't** stay around to watch the grizzly help himself to 180 steaks, rice, coleslaw, baked beans, and watermelon!

Park rangers have nicknamed this grizzly Ursus horribilis Number 181. Rangers have captured him, and moved him to another area of the park. It is the park's policy to relocate bears, so that they **won't** become dependent on human food. Rangers try to keep human contact to a minimum, so that the bears will stick to natural foods like berries and rodents, and stay away from the things they **shouldn't** eat, like steaks!

Yellowstone's bear expert says that **there's** a "good possibility" Number 181 will return to the scene of his crime. He claims that bears never forget where there's a good meal, and 181's last picnic was probably the best he'll ever have.

 Look back at the words in dark print. What do you notice about their spelling?

On Your Mark
Take your Warm Up Test. Then check your spelling with the List Words on the next page.

Pep Talk
All the List Words are **contractions.** A contraction is a short way to write two words. Use an **apostrophe** (') to show where letters have been left out of a contraction. I'd is a contraction for I would. He's is a contraction for he is.

LIST WORDS
1. there's
2. haven't
3. he's
4. couldn't
5. that's
6. I'll
7. isn't
8. didn't
9. they're
10. we'll
11. mustn't
12. shouldn't
13. wasn't
14. won't
15. I'd
16. wouldn't
17. don't
18. I've
19. you've
20. doesn't

Game Plan
Spelling Lineup
Write the List Words. Remember to include the apostrophe in each word.

1. there's
2. haven't
3. he's
4. couldn't
5. that's
6. I'll
7. isn't
8. didn't
9. they're
10. we'll
11. mustn't
12. shouldn't
13. wasn't
14. won't
15. I'd
16. wouldn't
17. don't
18. I've
19. you've
20. doesn't

there's = there is
don't = do not
I've = I have

Contractions

Circle the two words in each sentence that can be shortened into a contraction to make a List Word. Then write the List Words.

1. You (must not) tell my secret. _____ musn't _____
2. We (have not) seen Bill all day. _____ haven't _____
3. Pedro (is not) feeling well. _____ isn't _____
4. (You have) made me happy. _____ You've _____
5. (That is) a pretty dress you're wearing. _____ That's _____
6. (They are) all going to a party. _____ They're _____
7. (I have) never been to the zoo. _____ I've _____

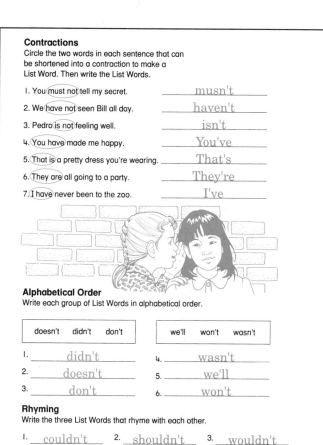

Alphabetical Order

Write each group of List Words in alphabetical order.

doesn't	didn't	don't		we'll	won't	wasn't

1. _____ didn't _____   4. _____ wasn't _____
2. _____ doesn't _____   5. _____ we'll _____
3. _____ don't _____   6. _____ won't _____

Rhyming

Write the three List Words that rhyme with each other.

1. _____ couldn't _____   2. _____ shouldn't _____   3. _____ wouldn't _____

Lesson 34 ■ Contractions   139

Flex Your Spelling Muscles

Writing

Imagine that you are the bear that raided the picnic area. Write a paragraph telling your side of the story. Use as many List Words as you can.

Proofreading

This poem has eight mistakes. Use the proofreading marks to fix each mistake. Circle the List Words that are incorrect, then write them correctly on the lines.

Proofreading Marks
⌄ add apostrophe
℀ take out something

(Theres) a bear in in the woods I know for sure.
(Hes) black and covered with fuzzy fur.
(Youve) never seen such a great, big beast.
(Id) say he's ten feet tall at at the very least.
Now, I think that bear is is chasing me.
So (Ill) have to run and climb a tree.

1. _____ There's _____
2. _____ He's _____
3. _____ You've _____
4. _____ I'd _____
5. _____ I'll _____

Now proofread your paragraph. Fix any mistakes.

Go for the Goal

Take your Final Test. Then fill in your Scoreboard. Send your mistakes to the Word Locker.

SCOREBOARD

number correct	number wrong

★ ★ ★ ★ ★ ★ ★ ★ *All-Star Words* ★ ★ ★ ★ ★ ★ ★ ★

hasn't   they'll   where's   how's   would've

With a partner, write a paragraph using each All-Star Word in its two-word form. Trade papers with other students. Rewrite their paragraph with the correct All-Star Word contractions.

140   Lesson 34 ■ Contractions

⊙ **Spelling Strategy**   To help students understand that every contraction is a short way of writing two words, invite them to
• listen carefully as you say each List Word
• write the two words that form the contraction
• circle the letter or letters that are left out when the contraction is formed
• write the contraction.

Flex Your Spelling Muscles   *Page 140*

As students complete the **Writing** activity, encourage them to brainstorm ideas, write a first draft, revise, and proofread their work. The **Proofreading** exercise will help them prepare to proofread their paragraphs. To publish their writing, students may want to
• present a dramatic reading of their work
• create humorous drawings to accompany their paragraphs.

✐ **Writer's Corner**

You may want to bring a map of your state to class and read information about parks and other recreational areas. Invite students to write a few sentences about a place they would like to visit or have visited.

Go for the Goal/Final Test

1. *We'll* find out soon who has the lead in the play.
2. *They're* not arriving until noon.
3. I really *mustn't* be late for the ceremony.
4. *Didn't* she take pictures of the race?
5. "This *shouldn't* hurt," the nurse told me.
6. Justin *isn't* as tall as Jason.
7. The singer *wasn't* able to perform.
8. If you'll wash the dishes, *I'll* wipe them.
9. I *won't* be going to the same school next year.
10. *That's* the weirdest sound I've ever heard!
11. *I'd* rather go to bed early and get up early.
12. Ashley *couldn't* find her wallet anywhere.
13. I *wouldn't* go near that alligator if I were you.
14. *He's* the boy who scored the winning goal.
15. The stores *don't* open until ten o'clock.
16. *Haven't* you eaten lunch yet?
17. *I've* moved to a new apartment in the city.
18. *There's* more soup in the bowl.
19. *You've* been chosen as the Student of the Year.
20. *Doesn't* that dog look like a small bear?

Remind students to complete the Scoreboard and write any misspelled words in their Word Locker.

★★ **All-Star Words**   You may want to point out that the All-Star Words follow the spelling rule and help students figure out the two-word forms, if necessary.

Lesson 35

Objective
To spell homonyms

Correlated Phonics Lessons
MCP Phonics, Level C, Lesson 82
Silver Burdett Ginn *World of Reading,* 3/2, p. 358

Warm Up   **Page 141**
In this selection, students find out how Dr. Edward Hunter accidentally invented a knot called "Hunter's Bend." Ask whether anyone knows how to tie the "Hunter's Bend" or other kinds of knots, and invite them to demonstrate with a piece of cord or twine.

Ask a volunteer to say the words in dark print and identify the pair that sounds the same but has different spellings. Ask other volunteers to find words in the selection that sound the same as *here, grate, tide,* and *maid.*

On Your Mark/Warm Up Test
1. I *hear* that Tomiko will be arriving tomorrow.
2. You can wait for the bus *here.*
3. There is a knot *tied* in my shoelace.
4. We can swim here at high *tide.*
5. Bring *your* papers in tomorrow.
6. *You're* sure to win first prize!
7. The train leaves in an *hour.*
8. Can you come to *our* house for dinner?
9. This boat needs a new *sail.*
10. These sneakers were on *sale* at the shoe store.
11. *Two* teams are needed for tug-of-war.
12. Let's go *to* the movies later.
13. Wait a minute! I need my science books, *too.*
14. Do you have an extra *pair* of running shoes?
15. The *pear* tasted delicious in the fruit salad.
16. Should I *pare* the cucumber before I cut it up?
17. A *maid* will bring towels to your hotel room.
18. I love that skirt you *made* in sewing class.
19. Pablo looks as if he's having a *great* time.
20. Broil the hamburgers on the *grate* over the fire.

Pep Talk/Game Plan   **Pages 142–143**
Introduce the spelling rule and have students read the List Words aloud. Encourage students to look back at their Warm Up Tests and apply the spelling rule to any misspelled words.

As students work through the **Spelling Lineup, Definitions,** and **Homonyms** exercises, remind them to look back at their List Words or in their dictionaries if they need help.

 See **Words in Context,** page 14

106

Homonyms

Warm Up
What is the "Hunter's Bend"?

New Knot

Girl Scouts! Boy Scouts! Now **hear** this! Let me tell you about a **great** knot. It was invented in England by Dr. Edward Hunter. Years ago, he was playing with some string and **tied** it by accident.

"I put two ends opposite each other," he said. "I made loops on each end and pulled them through one another. It was very even and easy **to** tie."

The doctor thought someone must have **made** such a knot before. After many years, he took his knot to the Maritime Museum in London. There he found books filled with pictures of **too** many knots to count. A man helped him look back over 300 years of sailors' knots. They did not see any knot exactly like Dr. Hunter's. In fact, no one anywhere knew of a knot like his.

This knot has a shape all its own. It is very useful. It can be used both on land and sea. The knot went into the books. Dr. Hunter can be proud. The knot was named the "Hunter's Bend."

> Look back at the words in dark print. Which words sound the same but have different spellings? Which words sound the same as <u>here</u>, <u>grate</u>, <u>tide</u>, and <u>maid</u>?

On Your Mark
Take your Warm Up Test. Then check your spelling with the List Words on the next page.

141

Pep Talk
Homonyms are words that sound alike but have different meanings and different spellings. The words *two, to,* and *too* are homonyms. Find the pairs or groups of homonyms in the List Words.

LIST WORDS

1. hear
2. here
3. tied
4. tide
5. your
6. you're
7. hour
8. our
9. sail
10. sale
11. two
12. to
13. too
14. pair
15. pear
16. pare
17. maid
18. made
19. great
20. grate

Game Plan

Spelling Lineup
Write the List Words that contain the vowel sounds given.

/ā/ as in <u>say</u>		/er/ as in <u>care</u>	
1. sail		12. pair	
2. sale		13. pear	
3. maid		14. pare	
4. made		/ôr/ as in <u>for</u>	
5. great		15. your	
6. grate		16. you're	

/ir/ as in <u>year</u>		/ī/ as in <u>side</u>	
7. hear		17. tied	
8. here		18. tide	

/o͞o/ as in <u>food</u>		/ou/ as in <u>found</u>	
9. two		19. hour	
10. to		20. our	
11. too			

142   Lesson 35 ■ Homonyms

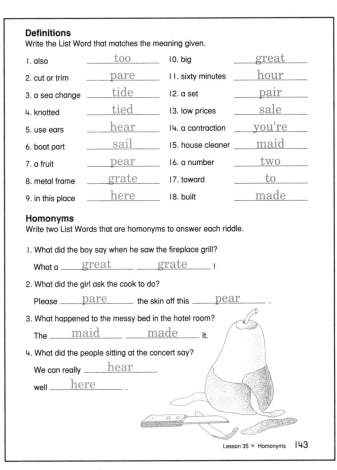

Definitions

Write the List Word that matches the meaning given.

1. also	too	10. big	great
2. cut or trim	pare	11. sixty minutes	hour
3. a sea change	tide	12. a set	pair
4. knotted	tied	13. low prices	sale
5. use ears	hear	14. a contraction	you're
6. boat part	sail	15. house cleaner	maid
7. a fruit	pear	16. a number	two
8. metal frame	grate	17. toward	to
9. in this place	here	18. built	made

Homonyms

Write two List Words that are homonyms to answer each riddle.

1. What did the boy say when he saw the fireplace grill?

What a ___great___ ___grate___ !

2. What did the girl ask the cook to do?

Please ___pare___ the skin off this ___pear___ .

3. What happened to the messy bed in the hotel room?

The ___maid___ ___made___ it.

4. What did the people sitting at the concert say?

We can really ___hear___

well ___here___

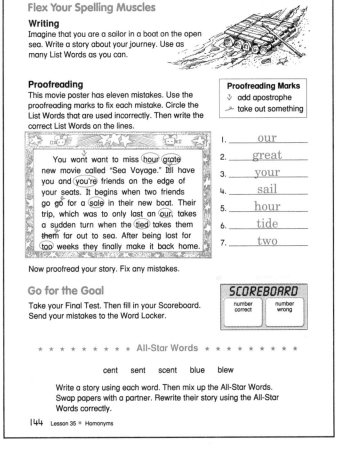

Flex Your Spelling Muscles

Writing

Imagine that you are a sailor in a boat on the open sea. Write a story about your journey. Use as many List Words as you can.

Proofreading

This movie poster has eleven mistakes. Use the proofreading marks to fix each mistake. Circle the List Words that are used incorrectly. Then write the correct List Words on the lines.

Proofreading Marks
ᨆ add apostrophe
⟋ take out something

You wont want to miss hour grate new movie called "Sea Voyage." Itll have you and you're friends on the edge of your seats. It begins when two friends go go for a sale in their new boat. Their trip, which was to only last an our, takes a sudden turn when the tied takes them them far out to sea. After being lost for too weeks they finally make it back home.

1.	our
2.	great
3.	your
4.	sail
5.	hour
6.	tide
7.	two

Now proofread your story. Fix any mistakes.

Go for the Goal

Take your Final Test. Then fill in your Scoreboard. Send your mistakes to the Word Locker.

SCOREBOARD
number correct
number wrong

★ ★ ★ ★ ★ ★ ★ **All-Star Words** ★ ★ ★ ★ ★ ★ ★

cent   sent   scent   blue   blew

Write a story using each word. Then mix up the All-Star Words. Swap papers with a partner. Rewrite their story using the All-Star Words correctly.

⊙ **Spelling Strategy**   Write cloze sentences on the board for pairs of List Words, adding letters as a clue next to each sentence. For example:
• "The book is __ on the table." (er)
• "Did you __ what I said?" (ea)
Invite the class to read each pair of sentences and to decide which List Words go in the blanks. Call on a volunteer to fill in the words. You may also want to tell students that mnemonic tricks can help them remember which spelling goes with which meaning (i.e., There's an *ear* in *hear*).

Flex Your Spelling Muscles   *Page 144*

As students complete the **Writing** activity, encourage them to brainstorm ideas, write a first draft, revise, and proofread their work. The **Proofreading** exercise will help them prepare to proofread their stories. To publish their writing, students may want to
• perform their stories as skits or plays
• illustrate each other's stories.

✑ Writer's Corner

Students might enjoy reading books such as *Sailing Ships* by Chris Chant. Encourage them to write brief reports, telling why they would or wouldn't like to sail on a ship.

Go for the Goal/Final Test

1. Look at the terrific model boat we **made!**
2. I want to **hear** the President's speech.
3. Wait for a **sale** before you buy the television.
4. The seaweed floats in with the **tide.**
5. Clean the **grate** before you cook the steaks on it.
6. I like your new **pair** of boots.
7. The bus stop is just a short walk from **our** house.
8. Are you going to be **here** after five o'clock?
9. Give me a knife and I'll **pare** the apple for you.
10. I am **two** years older than my sister.
11. My uncle is a **great** big man.
12. The riders **tied** their horses to the fence.
13. Does this bus go **to** the museum?
14. My aunt works as a **maid** in a big hotel.
15. This **pear** is nice and juicy!
16. Tell us when **you're** going to leave.
17. Many boats **sail** on this lake.
18. The roast has to cook for one **hour.**
19. Yes, your friends can come, **too.**
20. Will you have **your** report done by Monday?

Remind students to complete the Scoreboard and write any misspelled words in their Word Locker.

★★ **All-Star Words**   You may want to point out that the All-Star Words follow the spelling rule and help students brainstorm ideas for their stories.

Lesson 36 • Instant Replay

Objective

To review spelling words with consonant digraphs; the prefixes *un, dis, re;* contractions; and homonyms

Time Out   *Pages 145–148*

Check Your Word Locker Based on your observations, note which words are giving students the most difficulty and offer assistance for spelling them correctly. Here are some frequently misspelled words to watch for: *knew, rough, haven't, your, you're,* and *hour.*

To give students extra help and practice in taking standardized tests, you may want to have them take the Review Test for this lesson on pages 110–111. After scoring the tests, return them to students so that they can record their misspelled words in their Word Locker.

After practicing their troublesome words, students can work through the exercises for **Lessons 31–35.** Before they begin each exercise, you may want to go over the spelling rule.

Take It Home Invite students to use List Words in **Lessons 31–35** in telephone conversations at home with friends. For a complete list of the words, encourage them to take their *Spelling Workout* books home. Students can also use Take It Home Master 6 on pages 112–113 to help them do the activity. Invite students to discuss the words they used with the class.

Name _____

Time Out

Take another look at consonant digraphs, prefixes, contractions, and homonyms.

Check Your Word Locker
Look at the words in your Word Locker. Write your troublesome words for Lessons 31 through 35.

_____

Practice writing your troublesome words with a partner. Take turns dividing the words into syllables as your partner spells them aloud.

Lesson 31

A **consonant digraph** is two consonants together that make one sound, as in <u>kn</u>ot, <u>wr</u>ote, cou<u>gh</u>, and <u>ph</u>one.

List Words	Write a List Word that means the opposite of each word given.
knew	1. fix _____ wreck
wreck	2. right _____ wrong
rough	3. forgot _____ knew
wrong	4. smooth _____ rough
wrap	5. unwrap _____ wrap
laugh	6. cry _____ laugh

145

Lesson 32

A **prefix** is a word part that is added to the beginning of a root word, as in <u>unable</u> and <u>discover</u>.

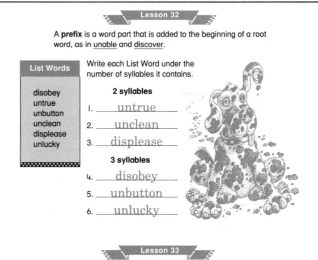

List Words	Write each List Word under the number of syllables it contains.
disobey	**2 syllables**
untrue	1. _____ untrue
unbutton	2. _____ unclean
unclean	3. _____ displease
displease	**3 syllables**
unlucky	4. _____ disobey
	5. _____ unbutton
	6. _____ unlucky

Lesson 33

The **prefix re** can mean <u>again</u> or <u>back</u>, as in <u>retell</u> and <u>repay</u>.

List Words	Look at each set of guide words. Decide which List Words go between each set. Then write them in alphabetical order.
rename	**rebuild/regroup** **remind/replant**
redo	1. _____ redo 4. _____ rename
replace	2. _____ refill 5. _____ renew
reform	3. _____ reform 6. _____ replace
refill	
renew	

Lesson 34

A **contraction** is a word made by writing two words together and leaving out one or more letters. An **apostrophe** shows where letters are missing, as in I'll.

List Words

there's
couldn't
doesn't
he's
they're
I'd

Write a List Word that rhymes with each word given.

1. wasn't _____doesn't_____
2. bears _____there's_____
3. hair _____they're_____
4. wide _____I'd_____
5. bees _____he's_____
6. wouldn't _____couldn't_____

Lesson 35

Homonyms are words that sound alike, but have different meanings and spellings, such as <u>sale</u> and <u>sail</u>.

List Words

your
to
here
you're
too
hear

Write a List Word to complete each sentence.

1. When you whisper, I can't _____hear_____ .
2. Each person must walk _____to_____ the exit.
3. It is getting _____too_____ dark to read.
4. Please hang _____your_____ coat in the hall.
5. We will be _____here_____ when you return.
6. I see that _____you're_____ on my bus now.

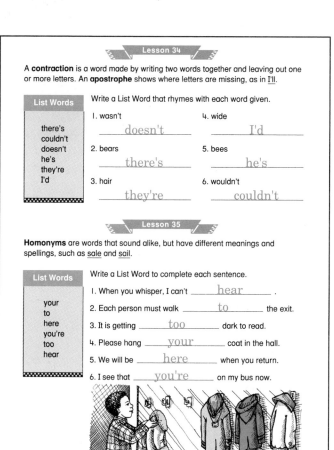

Lesson 36 ■ Instant Replay 147

Lessons 31–35

List Words

knew
rough
unbutton
reform
couldn't
redo
wreck
disobey
refill
there's
hear
you're

In each set of List Words, one word is misspelled. Circle the List Word that is wrong. Then write it correctly on the line.

1. unbutton / you're / (disobay) — disobey
2. (redoo) / rough / refill — redo
3. reform / wreck / (knoo) — knew
4. (your'e) / couldn't / there's — you're
5. knew / (reck) / hear — wreck
6. couldn't / reform / (ther'es) — there's
7. redo / (refil) / rough — refill
8. (unbuton) / disobey / refill — unbutton
9. redo / knew / (heer) — hear
10. wreck / (rouph) / you're — rough
11. disobey / (refform) / unbutton — reform
12. there's / you're / (coudn't) — couldn't

Go for the Goal

Take your Final Replay Test. Then fill in your Scoreboard. Send any misspelled words to your Word Locker.

SCOREBOARD

number correct	number wrong

Clean Out Your Word Locker

Look in your Word Locker. Cross out each word you spelled correctly on your Final Replay Test. Circle the words you're still having trouble with. Add the words you circled to your Spelling Notebook. What do you notice about the words? Watch for those words as you write.

Go for the Goal/Final Replay Test   *Page 148*

1. Let's go **to** the Science Museum today.
2. If **there's** a breeze, you can go sailing.
3. Ramon **knew** the answer to every question.
4. Did he **disobey** his mother and go to the movie?
5. Ask Vladimir whether **he's** driving to the game.
6. Bring a swimsuit if **you're** planning to swim.
7. That board is **rough,** so watch out for splinters.
8. Please **refill** the hamster's water bottle.
9. You can **hear** the bus come before you see it.
10. The car looked like a **wreck,** but it ran well.
11. Can you **redo** the party invitation?
12. I cannot **unbutton** the last two buttons.
13. The senator promised to **reform** the tax laws.
14. She **couldn't** remember Alan's last name.
15. Pigs are not really **unclean** animals.
16. **Doesn't** the bus stop in front of the library?
17. Did Sir Walter's manners **displease** the queen?
18. Circle every word that is spelled **wrong.**
19. You may keep **your** books on the top shelf.
20. Sadako has lived **here** all her life.
21. I am **unlucky** when it comes to winning contests.
22. My parents always **laugh** at that woman's jokes.
23. Shall we **renew** the magazine subscription?
24. Her story sounds **untrue,** but it really happened.
25. If I can buy another ticket, you can come, **too.**
26. Before we eat, **I'd** like to wash my hands.
27. We should **replace** that bulb with a brighter one.
28. Did you **wrap** Pedro's birthday gift yet?
29. Why do you want to **rename** your dog?
30. **They're** planning a surprise for Grandmother.

Clean Out Your Word Locker   After writing each word, students can point to the consonant digraph or the prefix, or tell whether the word is a contraction or a homonym.

109

Instant Replay Test

Side A

Read each set of words. Fill in the circle next to the word that
is spelled wrong.

1. ⓐ our   ⓒ hear
   ⓑ regroup   ⓓ wrapp

2. ⓐ they're   ⓒ two
   ⓑ laugh   ⓓ reforem

3. ⓐ dissplease   ⓒ unclean
   ⓑ redo   ⓓ wrong

4. ⓐ here   ⓒ doesnt
   ⓑ you're   ⓓ rename

5. ⓐ reck   ⓒ that's
   ⓑ knew   ⓓ there's

6. ⓐ youre   ⓒ he's
   ⓑ untrue   ⓓ replant

7. ⓐ replay   ⓒ disobay
   ⓑ disappear   ⓓ retell

8. ⓐ unlucky   ⓒ cough
   ⓑ he's   ⓓ her're

9. ⓐ rerun   ⓒ to
   ⓑ reknewe   ⓓ refill

10. ⓐ unseen   ⓒ I'd
    ⓑ couldnt   ⓓ hear

LESSON 36

Name _____

Instant Replay Test

Side B

Read each set of words. Fill in the circle next to the word that
is spelled wrong.

11. ⓐ rough ⓒ knots
    ⓑ wren   ⓓ tou

12. ⓐ laugh ⓒ replase
    ⓑ untrue ⓓ your

13. ⓐ unbutten ⓒ knew
    ⓑ doesn't ⓓ redo

14. ⓐ rename ⓒ unclean
    ⓑ I'ld   ⓓ hour

15. ⓐ he's   ⓒ too
    ⓑ your'e ⓓ discover

16. ⓐ to   ⓒ unload
    ⓑ here   ⓓ rouff

17. ⓐ retell ⓒ theres'
    ⓑ knee   ⓓ hear

18. ⓐ unluckey ⓒ disobey
    ⓑ couldn't ⓓ cough

19. ⓐ disappear ⓒ refil
    ⓑ unable   ⓓ unseen

20. ⓐ I've   ⓒ remind
    ⓑ rong   ⓓ wreck

TAKE IT HOME

Your child has learned to spell many new words in Lessons 31–35 and would enjoy sharing them with you and your family. Be sure to check out these activities for ways to make spelling review F-U-N!

Calling All Spellers!

You've heard of "call waiting"—now try "call spelling"! Here's how it works. Your child can call up another classmate or a friend. As they enjoy a friendly chat, have your child use some of the spelling words.

Crossword Puzzle

Here's a crossword puzzle for you and your child to solve. Encourage your child to print the correct spelling word for each clue.

rerun	rename	hear	couldn't	too	I'll	here
wreck	replace	redo	you're	your	to	

ACROSS

2. belonging to you
4. From me _____ you.
5. Wouldn't, shouldn't, _____!
8. do it again
9. Name it again, Sam!
10. Did you _____ that big noise?
11. Wish you were _____!

DOWN

1. That smashed-up car is one.
2. One word for "you are"
3. _____ go! Will you?
6. also
7. I've seen it! It's a _____ .
8. Let's _____ the broken vase.

Writing and Proofreading Guide

1. Choose a topic to write about.
2. Write your ideas. Don't worry about mistakes.
3. Now organize your writing so that it makes sense.
4. Proofread your work.
   Use these proofreading marks to make changes.

Proofreading Marks

⬭	spelling mistake
≡	capital letter
⊙	add period
∧	add something
✓	add apostrophe
⟋	take out something
¶	indent paragraph
/	make small letter

did you see the ~~the~~ spider (makeng) a web?

5. Write your final copy.

   Did you see the spider making a web?

6. Share your writing.

Using Your Dictionary

The Spelling Workout Dictionary shows you many things about your spelling words.

The **entry word** listed in alphabetical order is the word you are looking up.

The **sound-spelling** or **respelling** tells how to pronounce the word.

The **part of speech** is given as an abbreviation.

> **im·prove** (im pro͞ov′) **v.** 1 to make or become better [Business has *improved*.] 2 to make good use of [She *improved* her spare time by reading.] — **im·proved′**, **im·prov′ing**

Sample sentences or phrases show how to use the work.

Other **forms** of the word are given.

The **definition** tells what the word means. There may be more than one definition.

Pronunciation Key

SYMBOL	KEY WORDS	SYMBOL	KEY WORDS	SYMBOL	KEY WORDS	SYMBOL	KEY WORDS
a	ask, fat	o͝o	look, pull	b	bed, dub	t	top, hat
ā	ape, date	o͞o	ooze, tool	d	did, had	v	vat, have
ä	car, lot	ou	out, crowd	f	fall, off	w	will, always
				g	get, dog	y	yet, yard
e	elf, ten	u	up, cut	h	he, ahead	z	zebra, haze
ē	even, meet	ʉ	fur, fern	j	joy, jump		
				k	kill, bake	ch	chin, arch
i	is, hit	ə	a in ago	l	let, ball	ŋ	ring, singer
i	ice, fire		e in agent	m	met, trim	sh	she, dash
			e in father	n	not, ton	th	thin, truth
ō	open, go		i in unity	p	put, tap	*th*	then, father
ô	law, horn		o in collect	r	red, dear	zh	s in pleasure
oi	oil, point		u in focus	s	sell, pass		

An Americanism is a word or usage of a word that was born in this country. An open star before an entry word or definition means that the word or definition is an Americanism

These dictionary entries are taken, by permission, in abridged or modified form from *Webster's New World Dictionary.* Copyright © 1992 by Simon & Schuster Inc.

Aa

a·bout (ə bout′) *adv.* **1** on every side; all around [Look *about*.] **2** nearly; more or less [*about* ten years old]. ◆*adj.* active; awake or recovered [At dawn I was up and *about*.] ◆*prep.* **1** almost ready [I am *about* to cry.] **2** having to do with [a book *about* ships].

ac·ro·bat (ak′rə bat) *n.* a performer who does tricks in tumbling or on the trapeze, tightrope, etc.

a·cross (ə krôs′) *adv.* from one side to the other [The new bridge makes it easy to get *across* in a car.] ◆*prep.* **1** from one side to the other of [We swam *across* the river.] **2** on the other side of [They live *across* the street.]

act (akt) *n.* **1** a thing done; deed [an *act* of bravery]. **2** one of the main divisions of a play, opera, etc. [The first *act* takes place in a palace.] ◆*v.* **1** to play the part of, as on a stage [She *acted* Juliet.] **2** to behave like [Don't *act* the fool.]

add (ad) *v.* **1** to put or join something to another thing so that there will be more or so as to mix into one thing [We *added* some books to our library. *Add* two cups of sugar to the batter.] **2** to join numbers so as to get a total, or sum [*Add* 3 and 5.]

ad·mit (əd mit′) *v.* **1** to permit or give the right to enter [One ticket *admits* two persons.] **2** to take or accept as being true; confess [Lucy will not *admit* her mistake.] —**ad·mit′ted, ad·mit′ting**

ad·ver·tise (ad′vər tīz) *v.* **1** to tell about a product in public and in such a way as to make people want to buy it [to *advertise* cars on television]. **2** to announce or ask for publicly, as in a newspaper [to *advertise* a house for rent; to *advertise* for a cook]. —**ad′ver·tised, ad′ver·tis·ing** —**ad′ver·tis′er** *n.*

af·ford (ə fôrd′) *v.* to have money enough to spare for [Can we *afford* a new car?]

af·ter·noon (af tər nōōn′) *n.* the time of day from noon to evening.

a·gain (ə gen′) *adv.* once more; a second time [If you don't understand the sentence, read it *again*.]

age (āj) *n.* **1** the time that a person or thing has existed from birth or beginning [He left school at the *age* of fourteen.] **2** the fact of being old [Gray hair comes with *age*.]

air·plane (er′plān) *n.* an aircraft that is kept up by the force of air upon its wings and driven forward by a jet engine or propeller.

air·port (er′pôrt) *n.* a place where aircraft can take off and land, get fuel, or take on passengers.

a·live (ə līv′) *adj.* **1** having life; living. **2** going on; in action; not ended or destroyed [to keep old memories *alive*]. **3** lively; alert.

☆**al·ler·gy** (al′ər jē) *n.* a condition in which one becomes sick, gets a rash, etc., by breathing in, touching, eating, or drinking something that is not harmful to most people [Hay fever is usually caused by an *allergy* to certain pollens.] —*pl.* **al′ler·gies**

al·low (ə lou′) *v.* **1** to let be done; permit; let [*Allow* us to pay. No smoking *allowed*.] **2** to give or keep an extra amount so as to have enough [*Allow* an inch for shrinkage.]

all right 1 good enough; satisfactory; adequate [Your work is *all right*.] **2** yes; very well [*All right*, I'll do it.]

acrobat

a	ask, fat
ā	ape, date
ä	car, lot
e	elf, ten
ē	even, meet
i	is, hit
ī	ice, fire
ō	open, go
ô	law, horn
oi	oil, point
ॡ	look, pull
ōō	ooze, tool
ou	out, crowd
u	up, cut
u	fur, fern
ə	a in ago
	e in agent
	e in father
	i in unity
	o in collect
	u in focus
ch	chin, arch
ŋ	ring, singer
sh	she, dash
th	thin, truth
th	then, father
zh	s in pleasure

al·most (ôl′mōst) *adv.* not completely but very nearly [He tripped and *almost* fell. Sue is *almost* ten.]

al·read·y (ôl red′ē) *adv.* **1** by or before this time [When we arrived, dinner had *already* begun.] **2** even now [I am *already* ten minutes late.]

al·though (ôl *thō*′) *conj.* in spite of the fact that; even if; though [*Although* the book was very long, he enjoyed it.]

al·to·geth·er (ôl′tōo geth*thər)* *adv.* to the full extent; wholly; completely [You're not *altogether* wrong.]

al·ways (ôl′wāz) *adv.* at all times; at every time [*Always* be courteous.]

an·chor (aŋ′kər) *n.* a heavy object let down into the water by a chain or rope to keep a ship or boat from drifting. ◆ *v.* to keep from drifting by using an anchor [to *anchor* the boat and go ashore].

an·gry (aŋ′grē) *adj.* **1** feeling or showing anger [*angry* words; an *angry* crowd]. **2** wild and stormy [an *angry* sea]. —**an′gri·er, an′gri·est**

an·y (en′ē) *adj.* **1** one, no matter which one, of more than two [*Any* pupil may answer.] **2** some, no matter how much, how many, or what kind [Do you have *any* apples?] ◆ *pron.* any one or ones; any amount or number [I lost my pencils; do you have *any*?]

an·y·how (en′ē hou′) *adv.* **1** no matter what else may be true; in any case [I don't like the color, and *anyhow* it's not my size.] **2** no matter in what way [That's a fine report *anyhow* you look at it.]

an·y·one (en′ē wun′) *pron.* any person; anybody [Does *anyone* know where the house is?]

an·y·way (en′ē wā′) *adv.* nevertheless; anyhow.

Atlanta

ap·pear (ə pir′) *v.* to come into sight or into being [A ship *appeared* on the horizon. Leaves *appear* on the tree every spring.]

ar·my (är′mē) *n.* **1** a large group of soldiers trained for war, especially on land; also, all the soldiers of a country. **2** any large group of persons or animals [An *army* of workers was building the bridge.] —*pl.* **ar′mies**

ash·es (ash′əz) *pl.n.* the grayish powder or fine dust that is left after something has been burned.

At·lan·ta (at lan′tə) the capital of Georgia, in the northern part.

Au·gust (ô′gəst) *n.* the eighth month of the year, which has 31 days: abbreviated **Aug.**

a·void (ə void′) *v.* to keep away from; get out of the way of; shun [to *avoid* crowds].

aw·ful (ô′fəl) *adj.* **1** making one feel awe or dread; causing fear [an *awful* scene of destruction]. **2** very bad, ugly, great, etc.: *used only in everyday talk* [an *awful* joke; an *awful* fool].

awk·ward (ôk′wərd *or* äk′wərd) *adj.* not having grace or skill; clumsy; bungling [an *awkward* dancer].

aye or **ay** (ī) *adv.* yes. ◆ *n.* a vote of "yes."

ba·by (bā′bē) *n.* **1** a very young child; infant. **2** a person who seems helpless, cries easily, etc., like a baby. **3** the youngest or smallest in a group. —*pl.* **ba′bies**

bam·boo (bam bōo′) *n.* a tropical plant with woody stems that are hollow and jointed.

base·ment (bās′mənt) *n.* the cellar or lowest rooms of a building, below the main floor and at least partly below the surface of the ground.

be·cause (bē kôz′) *conj.* for the reason that; since [I'm late *because* I overslept.]

bed·room (bed′rōōm) *n.* a room with a bed, for sleeping in.

be·fore (bē fôr′) *prep.* earlier than; previous to [Will you finish *before* noon?] ◆*adv.* in the past; earlier [I've heard that song *before*.] ◆*conj.* earlier than the time that [Think *before* you speak.]

be·gin·ning (bē gin′iŋ) *n.* a start or starting; first part or first action [We came in just after the *beginning* of the movie. Going to the dance together was the *beginning* of our friendship.]

be·half (bē haf′) *n.* support for someone; interest [Many of his friends spoke in his *behalf*.]

be·long (bē lôŋ′) *v.* **1** to have its proper place [This chair *belongs* in the corner.] **2** to be owned by someone [This book *belongs* to you.]

be·low (bē lō′) *adv., adj.* in or to a lower place; beneath [I'll take the upper bunk and you can sleep *below*.] ◆*prep.* lower than in place, position, price, rank, etc. [the people living *below* us; a price *below* $25].

bench (bench) *n.* a long, hard seat for several persons, with or without a back.

be·neath (bē nēth′) *adv.* in a lower place; below or just below; underneath [Look *beneath* the table.] ◆*prep.* lower than; below or just below; under [the ground *beneath* my feet].

ber·ry (ber′ē) *n.* any small, juicy fruit with seeds and a soft pulp, as a strawberry, blackberry, or blueberry. In scientific use, many fleshy fruits having a skin are classed as berries, for example, the tomato, banana, and grape. —*pl.* **ber′ries**

be·side (bē sīd′) *prep.* by or at the side of; close to [The garage is *beside* the house.]

best (best) *adj.* above all others in worth or ability; most excellent, most fit, most desirable, etc. [Joan is the *best* player on the team. When is the *best* time to plant tulips?] ◆*adv.* **1** in a way that is best or most excellent, fit, etc. [Which choir sang *best*?] **2** more than any other; most [Of all your books, I like that one *best*.] ◆*n.* **1** a person or thing that is most excellent, most fit, etc. [That doctor is among the *best* in the profession. When I buy shoes, I buy the *best*.] **2** the most that can be done; utmost [We did our *best* to win.]

bet·ter (bet′ər) *adj.* **1** above another, as in worth or ability; more excellent, more fit, more desirable, etc. [Grace is a *better* player than Chris. I have a *better* idea.] **2** not so sick; more healthy than before. ◆*adv.* **1** in a way that is better or more excellent, fit, etc. [They will sing *better* with more practice.] **2** more [I like the orange drink *better* than the lime.]

big (big) *adj.* of great size; large [a *big* cake; a *big* city]. —**big′ger, big′gest** —**big′ness** *n.*

bird (burd) *n.* a warmblooded animal that has a backbone, two feet, and wings, and is covered with feathers. Birds lay eggs and can usually fly.

bi·son (bī′sən) *n.* a wild animal that is related to the ox, with a shaggy mane, short, curved horns, and a humped back. The American bison is often called a *buffalo*. —*pl.* **bi′son**

blame (blām) *v.* to say or think that someone or something is the cause of what is wrong or bad [Don't *blame* others for your own mistakes.] —**blamed, blam′ing** ◆*n.* the fact of being the cause of what is wrong or bad [I will take the *blame* for the broken window.]

a	ask, fat
ā	ape, date
ä	car, lot
e	elf, ten
ē	even, meet
i	is, hit
ī	ice, fire
ō	open, go
ô	law, horn
oi	oil, point
ōō	look, pull
ōō	ooze, tool
ou	out, crowd
u	up, cut
ʉ	fur, fern
ə	a in ago
	e in agent
	e in father
	i in unity
	o in collect
	u in focus
ch	chin, arch
ŋ	ring, singer
sh	she, dash
th	thin, truth
th	then, father
zh	s in pleasure

blast (blast) *n.* a strong rush of air or gust of wind. ◆ *v.* to blow up with an explosive [to *blast* rock].

blaze (blāz) *n.* a bright flame or fire. ◆ *v.* to burn brightly. —**blazed, blaz′ing**

blew (bloo) *past tense of* **blow.**

blind (blīnd) *adj.* not able to see; having no sight. ◆ *v.* to make blind; make unable to see. ◆ *n.* a window shade of stiffened cloth, metal slats, etc.

blood (blud) *n.* the red liquid that is pumped through the arteries and veins by the heart. The blood carries oxygen and cell-building material to the body tissues and carries carbon dioxide and waste material away from them.

blouse (blous) *n.* a loose outer garment like a shirt, worn by women and children.

blow (blō) *v.* **1** to move with some force [There is a wind *blowing.*] **2** to force air out from the mouth [*Blow* on your hands to warm them.] —**blew, blow′ing** ◆ *n.* **1** the act of blowing. **2** a strong wind; gale.

blue (bloo) *adj.* having the color of the clear sky or the deep sea. —**blu′er, blu′est**

bod·y (bäd′ē) *n.* the whole physical part of a person or animal [Athletes have strong *bodies.*]

bot·tom (bät′əm) *n.* the lowest part [Sign your name at the *bottom* of this paper.] ◆ *adj.* of or at the bottom; lowest [the *bottom* shelf].

bought (bôt) *past tense and past participle of* **buy.**

bou·quet (boo kā′ *or* bō kā′) *n.* **1** a bunch of cut flowers [a *bouquet* of roses].

branch (branch) *n.* any part of a tree growing from the trunk or from a main limb. —*pl.* **branch′es** ◆ *v.* to divide into branches [The road *branches* two miles east of town.]

break (brāk) *v.* **1** to come or make come apart by force; split or crack sharply into pieces [*Break* an egg into the bowl. The rusty hinge *broke.*] **2** to do better than; outdo [He *broke* the record for running the mile.] ◆ *n.* **1** a broken place [The X ray showed a *break* in the bone.] **2** an interruption [Recess is a relaxing *break* in our school day.]

breathe (brē*th*) *v.* to take air into the lungs and then let it out [to *breathe* deeply]. —**breathed, breath′ing**

bright (brīt) *adj.* **1** shining; giving light; full of light [a *bright* star; a *bright* day]. **2** having a quick mind; clever [a *bright* child]. —**bright′ly** *adv.* —**bright′ness** *n.*

bring (briŋ) *v.* to carry or lead here or to the place where the speaker will be [*Bring* it to my house tomorrow.] —**brought, bring′ing**

bro·ken (brō′kən) *past participle of* **break.** ◆ *adj.* **1** split or cracked into pieces [a *broken* dish; a *broken* leg]. **2** not in working condition [a *broken* watch].

brook (brook) *n.* a small stream.

broom (broom) *n.* a brush with a long handle, used for sweeping.

brought (brôt *or* brät) *past tense and past participle of* **bring.**

brush (brush) *n.* a bunch of bristles, hairs, or wires fastened into a hard back or handle. Brushes are used for cleaning, polishing, grooming, painting, etc. —*pl.* **brush′es** ◆ *v.* **1** to use a brush on; clean, polish, paint, smooth, etc., with a brush [*Brush* your shoes. *Brush* the paint on evenly.] **2** to touch or graze in passing [The tire of the car *brushed* against the curb.]

buf·fa·lo (buf′ə lō) *n.* **1** a wild ox of Africa and Asia that is sometimes used as a work animal. **2** *another name for* the North American **bison.** —*pl.* —**buf′fa·loes** or **buf′fa·los** or **buf′fa·lo**

bunch (bunch) *n.* a group of things of the same kind growing or placed together [a *bunch* of bananas; a *bunch* of keys]. —*pl.* **bunch'es**

bush (boosh) *n.* a woody plant, smaller than a tree and having many stems branching out low instead of one main stem or trunk; shrub. —*pl.* **bush'es**

busi·ness (biz'nəs) *n.* **1** what a person does for a living; a person's work or occupation [Her *business* was writing plays.] **2** a place where things are made or sold; store or factory [Raul owns three *businesses.* — *pl.* **bus'i·ness·es**

butterfly (but'ər flī) *n.* an insect with a slender body and four broad, usually brightly colored wings. —*pl.* —**but'ter·flies**

buy (bī) *v.* to get by paying money or something else [The Dutch *bought* Manhattan Island for about $24.] —**bought, buy'ing** ◆*n.* the value of a thing compared with its price [Turnips are your best *buy* in January vegetables.]

Cc

cage (kāj) *n.* a box or closed-off space with wires or bars on the sides, in which to keep birds or animals. ◆*v.* to shut up in a cage. —**caged, cag'ing**

calf¹ (kaf) *n.* **1** a young cow or bull. **2** a young elephant, whale, hippopotamus, seal, etc. —*pl.* **calves**

calf² (kaf) *n.* the fleshy back part of the leg between the knee and the ankle. —*pl.* **calves**

camp (kamp) *n.* a place in the country where people, especially children, can have an outdoor vacation. ◆*v.* to live in a camp or in the outdoors for a time [We'll be *camping* in Michigan this summer.]

can·dy (kan'dē) *n.* a sweet food made from sugar or syrup, with flavor, coloring, fruits, nuts, etc., added. —*pl.* **can'dies**

can·not (kan'ät *or* kə nät') *the usual way of writing* can not.

can·vas (kan'vəs) *n.* **1** a strong, heavy cloth of hemp, cotton, or linen, used for tents, sails, or oil paintings. —*pl.* **can'vas·es**

care (ker) *n.* a watching over or tending; protection [The books were left in my *care.*] ◆*v.* **1** to watch over or take charge of something [Will you *care* for my canary while I'm gone?] **2** to feel a liking [I don't *care* for dancing.] —**cared, car'ing**

car·go (kär'gō) *n.* the load of goods carried by a ship, airplane, or truck. —*pl.* —**car'goes** or **car'gos**

car·pet (kär'pət) *n.* a thick, heavy fabric used to cover floors. ◆ *v.* to cover with a carpet or with something like a carpet [The lawn was *carpeted* with snow.]

car·ry (kar'ē) *v.* to take from one place to another; transport or conduct [Please help me *carry* these books home. The large pipe *carries* water. Air *carries* sounds.] —**car'ried, car'ry·ing**

case (kās) *n.* a container for holding and protecting something [a watch*case*; a seed*case*; a violin *case*].

catch (kach) *v.* **1** to stop by grasping with the hands or arms [to *catch* a ball]. **2** to become sick or infected with [to *catch* the flu]. —**caught, catch'ing** ◆*n.* **1** the act of catching a ball, etc. [The outfielder made a running *catch*.] **2** anything that is caught [a *catch* of 14 fish].

cat·tle (kat'l) *n.pl.* animals of the cow family that are raised on farms and ranches, as cows, bulls, steers, and oxen.

calf

a	ask, fat
ā	ape, date
ä	car, lot
e	elf, ten
ē	even, meet
i	is, hit
ī	ice, fire
ō	open, go
ô	law, horn
oi	oil, point
oo	look, pull
ōo	ooze, tool
ou	out, crowd
u	up, cut
u	fur, fern
ə	a in ago
	e in agent
	e in father
	i in unity
	o in collect
	u in focus
ch	chin, arch
ŋ	ring, singer
sh	she, dash
th	thin, truth
th	then, father
zh	s in pleasure

155

caught (kôt) *past tense and past participle of* **catch**.

cent (sent) *n.* a coin worth 100th part of a dollar; penny.

chair (cher) *n.* a piece of furniture that has a back and is a seat for one person.

chalk (chôk) *n.* **1** a whitish limestone that is soft and easily crushed into a powder. It is made up mainly of tiny sea shells. **2** a piece of chalk or material like it, for writing on chalkboards.

cham·pi·on (cham′pē ən) *n.* a person, animal, or thing that wins first place or is judged to be best in a contest or sport [a spelling *champion*].

change (chānj) *v.* **1** to make or become different in some way; alter [Time *changes* all things. His voice began to *change* at the age of thirteen.] **2** to put or take one thing in place of another; substitute [to *change* one's clothes; to *change* jobs]. —**changed, chang′ing** ◆*n.* **1** the act of changing in some way [There will be a *change* in the weather tomorrow.] **2** something put in place of something else [a fresh *change* of clothing]. **3** the money returned when one has paid more than the amount owed [If it costs 70 cents and you pay with a dollar, you get back 30 cents as *change*.]

chap·ter (chap′tər) *n.* any of the main parts into which a book is divided.

chart

chart (chärt) *n.* **1** a map, especially one for use in steering a ship or guiding an aircraft [A sailor's *chart* shows coastlines, depths, currents, etc.] **2** a group of facts about something set up in the form of a diagram, graph, table, etc. ◆*v.* to make a map of.

chase (chās) *v.* to go after or keep following in order to catch or harm [The fox was *chasing* a rabbit.] —**chased, chas′ing**

chimney

cheap (chēp) *adj.* low in price [Vegetables are *cheaper* in summer than in winter.] ◆*adv.* at a low cost [I bought these shoes *cheap* at a sale.] —**cheap′ly** *adv.* —**cheap′ness** *n.*

check (chek) *n.* **1** the mark ✓, used to show that something is right or to call attention to something. **2** a written order to a bank to pay a certain amount of money from one's account to a certain person. ◆*v.* ☆to prove to be right or find what is wanted by examining, comparing, etc. [These figures *check* with mine. *Check* the records for this information.]

cheer (chir) *n.* **1** a glad, excited shout of welcome, joy, or approval [The crowd gave the team three *cheers*.] **2** good or glad feelings; joy, hope, etc. [a visit that brought *cheer* to the invalid]. ◆*v.* **1** to make or become glad or hopeful [Things are getting better, so *cheer* up!] **2** to urge on or applaud with cheers.

chew·y (choo′ē) *adj.* needing much chewing [*chewy* candy]. —**chew′i·er, chew′i·est**

child (chīld) *n.* **1** a baby; infant. **2** a young boy or girl. **3** a son or daughter [Their *children* are all grown up.] —*pl.* **chil′dren**

chil·dren (chil′drən) *n. plural of* **child**.

chim·ney (chim′nē) *n.* a pipe or shaft going up through a roof to carry off smoke from a furnace, fireplace, or stove. Chimneys are usually enclosed with brick or stone. —*pl.* **chim′neys**

choice (chois) *n.* **1** the act of choosing or picking; selection [You may have a dessert of your own *choice*.] **2** a person or thing chosen [Green is my *choice* for mayor.] —**choic′er, choic′est**

choose (cho͞oz) *v.* to pick out one or more from a number or group [*Choose* a subject from this list.] —**chose, cho′sen, choos′ing**

chop (chäp) *v.* **1** to cut by strokes with a sharp tool [to *chop* down a tree]. —**chopped, chop′ping**

churn (chʉrn) *n.* a container in which milk or cream is stirred hard or shaken to make butter. ◆ *v.* to use a churn to make butter [to *churn* milk or cream].

cir·cus (sʉr′kəs) *n.* a traveling show held in tents or in a hall, with clowns, trained animals, acrobats, etc.

clap (klap) *v.* to make a sudden, loud sound like that of two flat surfaces being struck together [I *clapped* my hands.] —**clapped, clap′ping**

class (klas) *n.* ☆a group of students meeting together to be taught; also, a meeting of this kind [My English *class* is held at 9 o'clock.] —*pl.* **class′es**

clean (klēn) *adj.* **1** without dirt or impure matter [*clean* dishes; *clean* oil]. **2** neat and tidy [to keep a *clean* desk]. ◆ *v.* to make clean. [Please *clean* the oven.]

clear (klir) *adj.* **1** bright or sunny; without clouds or mist [a *clear* day]. **2** that can be seen through; transparent [*clear* glass]. **3** without anything in the way; not blocked; open [a *clear* view; a *clear* passage]. ◆ *adv.* in a clear manner; clearly [The bells rang out *clear.*] ◆ *v.* to empty or remove [*Clear* the snow from the sidewalk. Help me *clear* the table of dishes.] —**clear′ly** *adv.* —**clear′ness** *n.*

climb (klīm) *v.* to go up, or sometimes down, by using the feet and often the hands [to *climb* the stairs; to *climb* up or down a tree]. ◆ *n.* the act of climbing; rise; ascent [a tiring *climb*]. —**climb′er** *n.*

close (klōs) *adj.* **1** with not much space between; near [The old houses are too *close* to each other.] **2** thorough or careful [Pay *close* attention.] —**clos′er, clos′est** ◆ *adv.* so as to be close or near; closely [Follow *close* behind the leader.] —**close′ly** *adv.* —**close′ness** *n.*

clown (kloun) *n.* **1** a person who entertains, as in a circus, by doing comical tricks and silly stunts; jester; buffoon. **2** a person who likes to make jokes or act in a comical way [the *clown* of our family].

clue (klo͞o) *n.* a fact or thing that helps to solve a puzzle or mystery [Muddy footprints were a *clue* to the man's guilt.]

coach (kōch) *n.* **1** a large, closed carriage drawn by horses, with the driver's seat outside. **2** a person who teaches and trains students, athletes, singers, and so on. ◆ *v.* to teach, train, or tutor [Will you *coach* me for the test in history?]

cock·er spaniel (käk′ər) a small dog with long, drooping ears, long, silky hair, and short legs.

coin (koin) *n.* a piece of metal money having a certain value.

col·lar (käl′ər) *n.* **1** the part of a garment that fits around the neck. It is sometimes a separate piece or a band that is folded over. **2** the part of a horse's harness that fits around its neck.

com·ma (käm′ə) *n.* a punctuation mark (,) used to show a pause that is shorter than the pause at the end of a sentence [The *comma* is often used between clauses or after the opening phrase of a sentence. Words, numbers, or phrases in a series are separated by *commas*.]

a	ask, fat
ā	ape, date
ä	car, lot
e	elf, ten
ē	even, meet
i	is, hit
ī	ice, fire
ō	open, go
ô	law, horn
oi	oil, point
o͝o	look, pull
o͞o	ooze, tool
ou	out, crowd
u	up, cut
ʉ	fur, fern
ə	a in ago
	e in agent
	e in father
	i in unity
	o in collect
	u in focus
ch	chin, arch
ŋ	ring, singer
sh	she, dash
th	thin, truth
th	then, father
zh	s in pleasure

com·pare (kəm per′) **v. 1** to describe as being the same; liken [The sound of thunder can be *compared* to the roll of drums.] **2** to examine certain things in order to find out how they are alike or different [How do the two cars *compare* in size and price?] —**com·pared′, com·par′ing**

cone (kōn) **n. 1** a solid object that narrows evenly from a flat circle at one end to a point at the other. **2** anything shaped like this, as a shell of pastry for holding ice cream. **3** the fruit of some evergreen trees, containing the seeds.

con·tain (kən tān′) **v.** to have in it; hold; enclose or include [This bottle *contains* cream. Your list *contains* 25 names.]

cook·ie or **cook·y** (kook′ē) **n.** ☆a small, flat, sweet cake. —*pl.* **cook′ies**

cool·er (kool′ər) **n.** a container or room in which things are cooled or kept cool.

cop·y (käp′ē) **n. 1** a thing made just like another; imitation or likeness [four carbon *copies* of a letter]. **2** any one of a number of books, magazines, pictures, etc., with the same printed matter [a library with six *copies* of *Tom Sawyer*]. —*pl.* **cop′ies** ◆ **v. 1** to make a copy or copies of [*Copy* the questions that are on the chalkboard.] **2** to act or be the same as; imitate. —**cop′ied, cop′y·ing**

cor·ne·a (kôr′nē ə) **n.** the clear outer layer of the eyeball, covering the iris and the pupil.

cost (kôst) **v.** to be priced at; be sold for [It *costs* a dime.] —**cost, cost′ing** ◆ **n.** amount of money, time, work, etc., asked or paid for something; price [the high *cost* of meat].

cough (kôf) **v. 1** to force air from the lungs with a sudden, loud noise, as to clear the throat.

2 to get out of the throat by coughing [to *cough* up phlegm]. ◆ **n.** a condition of coughing often [I have a bad *cough*.]

could·n't (kood′nt) could not.

coun·try (kun′trē) **n. 1** an area of land; region [wooded *country*]. **2** the whole land of a nation [The *country* of Japan is made up of islands.] **3** land with farms and small towns; land outside of cities [Let's drive out to the *country*.] —*pl.* **coun′tries**

crack (krak) **v.** to break or split, with or without the parts falling apart [The snowball *cracked* the window.] ◆ **n.** a break, usually with the parts stilll holding together [a *crack* in a cup].

crawl (krôl) **v.** to move slowly by dragging the body along the ground as a worm does. ◆ **n.** a crawling; slow, creeping movement.

cra·zy (krā′zē) **adj. 1** mentally ill; insane. **2** very foolish or mad [a *crazy* idea]. —**cra′zi·er, cra′zi·est** —**cra′zi·ly adv.** —**cra′zi·ness n.**

creek (krēk *or* krik) **n.** a small stream, a little larger than a brook.

crib (krib) **n.** a small bed with high sides, for a baby.

cricket (krik′it) **n.** a leaping insect related to the grasshopper.

crook·ed (krook′əd) **adj. 1** not straight; bent, curved, or twisted [a *crooked* road]. **2** not honest; cheating.

crowd (kroud) **n.** a large group of people together [*crowds* of Christmas shoppers]. ◆ **v.** to push or squeeze [Can we all *crowd* into one car?]

crown (kroun) **n.** a headdress of gold, jewels, etc., worn by a king or queen. ◆ **v.** to make a king or queen by putting a crown on [Elizabeth I was *crowned* in 1558.]

cooler

crown

cut (kut) **v.** **1** to make an opening in with a knife or other sharp tool; pierce; gash [Andy *cut* his chin while shaving.] **2** to divide into parts with such a tool; sever [Will you *cut* the cake?] **3** to make shorter by trimming [to *cut* one's hair]. **4** to go through or across, usually to make a shorter way [The path *cuts* across the meadow. The tunnel *cuts* through the mountain.] —**cut, cut′ting**

Dd

Dal·las (dal′əs) a city in northeastern Texas.

Dal·ma·tian (dal mā′shən) **n.** a large dog with short hair and a black-and-white coat.

dance (dans) **v.** to move the body and feet in some kind of rhythm, usually to music [to *dance* a waltz or a minuet]. —**danced, danc′ing**

dan·ger (dān′jər) **n.** **1** a condition in which there could be harm, trouble, loss, etc.; risk; peril [to live in constant *danger*].

dark (därk) **adj.** having little or no light [a *dark* night]. — **dark′ness n.**

dash (dash) **v.** to move quickly; rush [The thief *dashed* down the alley.] ◆**n.** **1** a little bit; pinch [Put a *dash* of salt in the salad.] ☆**2** a short, fast run or race [a 100-yard *dash*]. **3** the mark (—), used in printing or writing.

dead (ded) **adj.** no longer living; without life [Throw out those *dead* flowers.] ◆**adv.** completely; entirely [I am *dead* tired from running.] ◆**n.** the time of most cold, most darkness, etc. [the *dead* of winter; the *dead* of night].

deer (dir) **n.** a swift-running, hoofed animal that chews its cud. The male usually has antlers that are shed every year. —*pl.* **deer.**

de·pend (dē pend′) **v.** **1** to be controlled or decided by [The attendance at the game *depends* on the weather.] **2** to put one's trust in; be sure of [You can't *depend* on this weather.] **3** to rely on for help or support [They *depend* on their parents for money.]

desk (desk) **n.** a piece of furniture with a smooth top at which one can write, draw, or read. It often has drawers for storing things.

des·sert (də zurt′) **n.** something sweet served at the end of a meal.

de·stroy (dē stroi′) **v.** to put an end to by breaking up, tearing down, ruining, or spoiling [The flood *destroyed* 300 homes.]

de·vice (dē vīs′) **n.** something made or invented for some special use. [A windmill is a *device* for putting wind power to work.]

did·n't (did′nt) did not.

dig (dig) **v.** **1** to turn up or remove ground with a spade, the hands, claws, etc. [The children are *digging* in the sand.] **2** to make by digging [to *dig* a well]. —**dug** *or in older use* **digged, dig′ging**

dim (dim) **adj.** not bright or clear; somewhat dark; shadowy; gloomy [the *dim* twilight]. — **dim′mer, dim′mest**

dis·ap·pear (dis ə pir′) **v.** to stop being seen or to stop existing; vanish [The car *disappeared* around a curve. Dinosaurs *disappeared* millions of years ago.] —**dis′ap·pear′ance n.**

dis·cov·er (dis kuv′ər) **v.** to be the first to find, see, or learn about [Marie and Pierre Curie *discovered* radium.]

dish (dish) **n.** any of the plates, bowls, saucers, etc., used to serve food at the table. —*pl.* **dish′es** ◆ **v.** to serve in a dish [*Dish* up the beans.] —**dish′ful adj.**

desk

a	ask, fat
ā	ape, date
ä	car, lot
e	elf, ten
ē	even, meet
i	is, hit
ī	ice, fire
ō	open, go
ô	law, horn
oi	oil, point
ͻͻ	look, pull
o͞o	ooze, tool
ou	out, crowd
u	up, cut
u	fur, fern
ə	a in ago
	e in agent
	e in father
	i in unity
	o in collect
	u in focus
ch	chin, arch
ŋ	ring, singer
sh	she, dash
th	thin, truth
th	then, father
zh	s in pleasure

ditch

dis·like (dis līk′) **v.** to have a feeling of not liking; be opposed to [I *dislike* people I can't trust.] —**dis·liked′, dis·lik′ing** ◆**n.** a feeling of not liking; distaste [The gardener felt a strong *dislike* for toads.]

dis·o·bey (dis′ ō bā′) **v.** to fail to obey or refuse to obey.

dis·or·der (dis ôr′dər) **n.** lack of order; jumble; confusion [The troops retreated in *disorder*.]

dis·please (dis plēz′) **v.** to make angry or not satisfied; annoy. —**dis·pleased′, dis·pleas′ing**

dis·re·spect (dis′rē spekt′) **n.** lack of respect or politeness; rudeness.—**dis′re·spect′ful adj.** —**dis′re·spect′ful·ly adv.**

dis·taste (dis tast′) **n.** dislike; aversion [a *distaste* for worms].

dis·trust (dis trust′) **n.** a lack of trust; doubt; suspicion. ◆**v.** to have no trust in; doubt. —**dis·trust′ful adj.**

ditch (dich) **n.** a long, narrow opening dug in the earth, as for carrying off water; trench [a *ditch* along the road].

do (do̅o̅) **v.** **1** to work at or carry out an action; perform [What do you *do* for a living? I'll *do* the job.] **2** to bring about; cause [The storm *did* a lot of damage.] **3** to put forth; exert [She *did* her best.] **4** to take care of; attend to [Who will *do* the dishes?] —**did, done, do′ing**

does (duz) *the form of the verb* **do** *showing the present time with singular nouns and with* he, she, *or* it.

does·n't (duz′nt) does not.

don't (dōnt) do not.

doubt (dout) **v.** **1** to think that something may not be true or right; be unsure of; question [I *doubt* that this is the correct answer.] **2** to consider unlikely [I *doubt* it will snow today.] ′ **n.** a feeling of not being sure or certain of [I have no *doubt* that you will return safely.]

drain (drān) **v.** to make flow away [*Drain* the water from the potatoes.] ′ **n.** a pipe or channel for carrying off water [a bathtub *drain*].

dress·ing (dres′iŋ) **n.** **1** a bandage or medicine for a wound or sore. **2** a sauce, as of oil, vinegar, and seasoning, added to salads and other dishes. **3** a stuffing, as of bread and seasoning, for roast chicken, turkey, etc.

drive (drīv) **v.** to control the movement of an automobile, horse and wagon, bus, etc. —**drove, driv′en, driv′ing** ◆**n.** **1** a trip in an automobile, etc. **2** a street, road, or driveway.

drove (drōv) *past tense of* **drive.**

drown (droun) **v.** to die from being under water, where the lungs can get no air [to fall overboard and *drown*].

dry (drī) **adj.** **1** not wet or damp; without moisture. **2** having little or no rain or water [a *dry* summer]. **3** thirsty. —**dri′er, dri′est** ◆**v.** to make or become dry. —**dried, dry′ing** —**dry′ly adv.** —**dry′ness n.**

dug (dug) *past tense and past participle of* **dig.**

each (ēch) **adj., pron.** every one of two or more, thought of separately [*Each* pupil will receive a book. *Each* of the books is numbered.] ◆**adv.** for each; apiece [Tickets cost $5.00 *each*.]

ea·ger (ē′gər) **adj.** wanting very much; anxious to do or get [*eager* to win; *eager* for praise]. —**ea′ger·ly adv.** —**ea′ger·ness n.**

ear·ly (ur′lē) **adv., adj.** **1** near the beginning; soon after the start [in the *early* afternoon; *early* in his career]. **2** before the usual or expected time [The bus arrived *early.*] —**ear′li·er, ear′li·est** —**ear′li·ness n.**

earn (urn) **v.** **1** to get as pay for work done [She *earns* $10 an hour.] **2** to get or deserve because of something one has done [At the Olympics she *earned* a gold medal for swimming.]

earth (urth) **n.** **1** the planet that we live on. It is the fifth largest planet and the third in distance away from the sun. **2** the dry part of the earth's surface, that is not the sea. **3** soil or ground [a flowerpot filled with good, rich *earth*].

east (ēst) **n.** **1** the direction toward the point where the sun rises. **2** a place or region in or toward this direction. ◆**adj.** in, of, to, or toward the east [the *east* bank of the river]. ◆**adv.** in or toward the east [Go *east* ten miles.]

eas·y (ē′zē) **adj.** not hard to do, learn or get [an *easy* job]. —′**eas′i·er, eas′i·est**

egg (eg) **n.** the oval or round body that is laid by a female bird, fish, reptile, insect, etc., and from which a young bird, fish, etc., is later hatched. It has a brittle shell or tough outer skin.

eight (āt) **n., adj.** one more thn seven; the number 8.

el·e·phant (el′ə fənt) **n.** a huge animal with a thick skin, two ivory tusks, and a long snout, or trunk. It is found in Africa and India and is the largest of the four-legged animals.

else (els) **adj.** **1** not the same; different; other [I thought you were someone *else*.] **2** that may be added; more [Do you want anything *else*?] ◆**adv.** in a different time, place, or way [Where *else* did you go?]

emp·ty (emp′tē) **adj.** having nothing or no one in it; not occupied; vacant [an *empty* jar; an *empty* house]. —**emp′ti·er, emp′ti·est** ◆**v.** to take out or pour out [*Empty* the dirty water in the sink.] —**emp′tied, emp′ty·ing** —*pl.* **emp′ties** —**emp′ti·ly adv.** —**emp′ti·ness n.**

en·joy (en joi′) **v.** to get joy or pleasure from [We *enjoyed* the baseball game.]

e·rase (ē rās′) **v.** to rub out; scrape away [to *erase* writing].

ev·er·y (ev′rē) **adj.** **1** all the group of which the thing named is one; each [*Every* student must take the test. She has read *every* book on the list.] **2** all that there could be [You've been given *every* chance.]

ev·er·y·bod·y (ev′rē bäd′e *or* ev′rē bud′ē) **pron.** every person; everyone [*Everybody* loves a good story.]

ev·er·y·where (ev′rē hwer) **adv.** in or to every place [*Everywhere* I go I meet friends.]

ex·er·cise (ek′sər sīz) **n.** the active use of the body in order to make it stronger or healthier [Long walks are good outdoor *exercise*.] ◆**v.** to put into use or do certain regular movements, in order to develop or train [I *exercise* every morning.]

eye (ī) **n.** the part of the body with which a human being or animal sees. ◆**v.** to look at; observe [We *eyed* the stranger suspiciously.] —**eyed, ey′ing**

face (fās) **n.** the front part of the head, including the eyes, nose, and mouth. ◆**v.** to turn toward or have the face turned toward [Please *face* the class. Our house *faces* a park.] —**faced, fac′ing**

elephant

a	ask, fat
ā	ape, date
ä	car, lot
e	elf, ten
ē	even, meet
i	is, hit
ī	ice, fire
ō	open, go
ô	law, horn
oi	oil, point
ᴏᴏ	look, pull
o͞o	ooze, tool
ou	out, crowd
u	up, cut
u	fur, fern
ə	a in ago
	e in agent
	e in father
	i in unity
	o in collect
	u in focus
ch	chin, arch
ŋ	ring, singer
sh	she, dash
th	thin, truth
th	then, father
zh	s in pleasure

fail (fāl) **v. 1** to not do what one tried to do or what one should have done; not succeed; miss or neglect [She *failed* as a singer. He *failed* to keep his promise.] **2** to give or get a grade that shows one has not passed a test, a school course, etc.

fam·i·ly (fam′ə lē) **n. 1** a group made up of two parents and all of their children. **2** a group of people who are related by marriage or a common ancestor; relatives; clan. —*pl.* **fam′i·lies**

farm·er (fär′mər) **n.** a person who owns or works on a farm.

fast¹ (fast) **adj.** moving, working, etc., at high speed; rapid; quick; swift [a *fast* pace; a *fast* reader]. ◆*adv.* **1** at a high speed; swiftly; rapidly [arrested for driving too *fast*]. **2** in a complete way; soundly; thoroughly [*fast* asleep].

fast² (fast) **v.** to go without any food or certain foods, as in following the rules of one's religion.

fear (fir) **n.** the feeling one has when danger, pain, or trouble is near; feeling of being worried or excited or of wanting to run and hide [Jungle animals have a natural *fear* of lions.] ◆*v.* to feel fear of; be afraid of; dread [Even brave people can *fear* real danger.]

feast (fēst) **n.** a large meal with many courses; banquet. ◆*v.* to eat a big or rich meal.

feel (fēl) **v. 1** to touch in order to find out something [*Feel* the baby's bottle to see if the milk is warm.] **2** to be aware of through the senses or the mind [He *felt* rain on his face. Do you *feel* pain in this tooth?] **3** to think or believe [She *feels* that we should go.] —**felt, feel′ing** ◆*n.* the way a thing feels to the touch [It seems to be all wool by the *feel* of it.]

felt¹ (felt) **n.** a heavy material made of wool, fur, or hair pressed together under heat. ◆*adj.* made of felt [a *felt* hat].

felt² (felt) *past tense and past participle of* **feel.**

fifth (fifth) **adj.** coming after four others; 5th in order. ◆*n.* one of five equal parts of something; 1/5.

fight (fīt) **v.** to use fists, weapons, or other force in trying to beat or overcome someone or something; battle; struggle [to *fight* hand to hand; to *fight* a war]. —**fought, fight′ing** ◆*n.* the use of force to beat or overcome someone or something; battle.

fin·ish (fin′ish) **v.** to bring or come to an end; complete or become completed [Did you *finish* your work? The game *finished* early.] ◆*n.* **1** the last part; end [The audience stayed to the *finish*.] **2** the kind of surface a thing has [an oil *finish* on wood]. —**fin′ished adj.**

first (furst) **adj.** before another or before all others in time, order, quality, etc.; earliest, foremost, etc. [the *first* snow of winter; the *first* door to the right; *first* prize]. ◆*adv.* before anything or anyone else [*First* we had soup. Guests are served *first*.] ◆*n.* **1** the one that is first [to be the *first* to succeed]. **2** the beginning; start [At *first*, I believed him.]

fish (fish) **n.** an animal that lives in water and has a backbone, fins, and gills for breathing. Most fish are covered with scales. —*pl.* **fish** (or when different kinds are meant, **fishes**) [She caught three *fish*. The aquarium exhibits many *fishes*.] ◆*v.* to catch or try to catch fish.

flaw (flô) **n.** a break, scratch, crack, etc., that spoils something; blemish [There is a *flaw* in this diamond.] —**flaw′less adj.** —**flaw′less·ly adv.**

flex (fleks) **v. 1** to bend [to *flex* an arm]. **2** to make tighter and harder; contract [to *flex* a muscle].

flight (flīt) *n.* **1** the act or way of flying or moving through space [the swift *flight* of birds]. **2** a trip through the air [a long *flight* from Los Angeles to New York].

float (flōt) *v.* **1** to rest on top of water or other liquid and not sink [Ice *floats.*] **2** to move or drift slowly, as on a liquid or through the air [Clouds *floated* overhead.] ◆*n.* a platform on wheels that carries a display or exhibit in a parade. —**float′er** *n.*

flood (flud) *n.* an overflowing of water onto a place that is usually dry. ◆*v.* to flow over its banks onto nearby land [The river *floods* every spring.]

floor (flôr) *n.* the bottom part of a room, hall, etc., on which to walk.

flow·er (flou′ər) *n.* the part of a plant that bears the seed and usually has brightly colored petals; blossom or bloom. ◆*v.* to come into bloom; bear flowers.

fly[1] (flī) *v.* **1** to move through the air by using wings, as a bird. **2** to travel or carry through the air, as in an aircraft. —**flew, flown, fly′ing**

fly[2] (flī) *n.* **1** a flying insect having one pair of wings, as the housefly and gnat. —*pl.* **flies**

fog (fôg *or* fäg) *n.* **1** a large mass of tiny drops of water, near the earth's surface; thick mist that makes it hard to see. **2** a condition of being confused or bewildered. —**fogged, fog′ging**

fog·gy (fôg′ē *or* fäg′ē) *adj.* **1** having fog [a *foggy* day]. **2** mixed up; confused [a *foggy* idea]. —**fog′gi·er, fog′gi·est** —**fog′gi·ly adv.** —**fog′gi·ness** *n.*

foil[1] (foil) *v.* to keep from doing something; thwart; stop [Their evil plans were *foiled* again.]

foil[2] (foil) *n.* a very thin sheet of metal [aluminum *foil*].

fold (fōld) *v.* to bend something over upon itself so that one part is on top of another [You *fold* a letter before putting it in an envelope.]

for·est (fôr′əst) *n.* many trees growing closely together over a large piece of land; large woods. ◆*v.* to plant with trees.

fork (fôrk) *n.* **1** a tool with a handle at one end and two or more points or prongs at the other, used to pick up something. Small forks are used in eating, and large forks, as pitchforks, are used for tossing hay and manure on a farm. ☆**2** the point where something divides into two or more branches [the *fork* of a road or of a tree]. ◆*v.* to divide into branches [Go left where the road *forks.*]

for·ward (fôr′wərd) *adj.* at, toward, or of the front [the *forward* part]. ◆*adv.* to the front; ahead [We moved slowly *forward* in the ticket line.]

fought (fôt) *past tense and past participle of* **fight**.

four (fôr) *n., adj.* one more than three; the number 4.

fourth (fôrth) *adj.* coming after three others; 4th in order. ◆*n.* one of four equal parts of something; 1/4.

frame (frām) *n.* **1** the support or skeleton around which a thing is built and that gives the thing its shape; framework [the *frame* of a house]. **2** the border or case into which a window, door, picture, etc., is set. ◆*v.* **1** to put a frame, or border, around [to *frame* a picture]. ☆**2** to make an innocent person seem guilty by a plot: *used only in everyday talk*. —**framed, fram′ing**

frame

a	ask, fat
ā	ape, date
ä	car, lot
e	elf, ten
ē	even, meet
i	is, hit
ī	ice, fire
ō	open, go
ô	law, horn
oi	oil, point
ၾ	look, pull
ၾၾ	ooze, tool
ou	out, crowd
u	up, cut
u	fur, fern
ə	a in ago
	e in agent
	e in father
	i in unity
	o in collect
	u in focus
ch	chin, arch
ŋ	ring, singer
sh	she, dash
th	thin, truth
th	then, father
zh	s in pleasure

163

free (frē) *adj.* **1** not under the control of another; not a slave or not in prison. **2** able to vote and to speak, write, meet, and worship as one pleases; having political and civil liberty. **3** not tied up, fastened, or shut in; loose [As soon as the bird was *free*, it flew away.] **4** with no charge; without cost [*free* tickets to the ball game]. —**fre′er, fre′est** ◆ *v.* to make free [The governor *freed* five prisoners by granting pardons.] —**freed, free′ing.**

freeze (frēz) *v.* to harden into ice; make or become solid because of cold [Water *freezes* at 0°C or 32°F.] —**froze, freez′ing**

freight (frāt) *n.* a load of goods shipped by train, truck, ship, or airplane.

fresh (fresh) *adj.* **1** newly made, got, or grown; not spoiled, stale, etc. [*fresh* coffee; *fresh* eggs]. **2** cool and clean [*fresh* air].
—**fresh′ly** *adv.* —**fresh′ness** *n.*

Fri·day frī′dā) *n.* the sixth day of the week.

friend (frend) *n.* a person whom one knows well and likes.

fright (frīt) *n.* **1** sudden fear; alarm. **2** something that looks so strange or ugly as to startle one [That old fur coat is a perfect *fright*.]

frost (frôst) *n.* **1** frozen dew or vapor in the form of white crystals [the *frost* on the ground]. **2** cold weather that can freeze things [*Frost* in the spring may damage fruit trees.]

frown (froun) *v.* to wrinkle the forehead and draw the eyebrows together in anger, worry, or deep thought. ◆*n.* a frowning or the look one has in frowning.

fro·zen (frōz′ən) *past participle of* **freeze.** ◆*adj.* turned into or covered with ice [a *frozen* pond].

fry (frī) *v.* to cook in hot fat over direct heat [to *fry* eggs]. —**fried, fry′ing**

fume (fyōōm) *n.* *often* **fumes,** *pl.* a gas, smoke, or vapor, especially if harmful or bad-smelling. ◆*v.* **1** to give off fumes. **2** to show that one is angry or irritated [He *fumed* at the long delay.]
—**fumed, fum′ing**

Gg

garage (gər äzh′ *or* gər äj′′) *n.* **1** a closed place where automobiles are sheltered. **2** a place where automobiles are repaired.

gar·den (gärd′n) *n.* a piece of ground where flowers, vegetables, etc., are grown. ◆*v.* to take care of a garden. —**gar·den·er** (gärd′nər) *n.*

gaze (gāz) *v.* to look in a steady way; stare [The crowd *gazed* in wonder at the spaceship.] —**gazed, gaz′ing**

geese (gēs) *n.* *plural of* **goose.**

gi·ant (jī′ənt) *n.* **1** an imaginary being that looks like a person but is many times larger and stronger. **2** a person or thing that is especially large, strong, etc. [Einstein was a mental *giant*.]

give (giv) *v.* **1** to pass or hand over to another [*Give* me your coat and I'll hang it up.] **2** to hand over to another to keep; make a gift of [My uncle *gave* a book to me for my birthday.] —**gave, giv′en, giv′ing** —**giv′er** *n.*

glaze (glāz) *v.* **1** to give a hard, shiny finish to [to *glaze* pottery]. **2** to cover with a sugar coating [to *glaze* doughnuts]. —**glazed, glaz′ing**

glide (glīd) *v.* to move along in a smooth and easy way [Skaters *glided* across the ice.] —**glid′ed, glid′ing**

glis·ten (glis′ən) *v.* to shine or sparkle with reflected light [The snow *glistened* in the sunlight.]

gloom·y (glōōm′ē) *adj.* **1** dark or dim [a *gloomy* dungeon]. **2** having or giving a feeling of deep sadness [a *gloomy* story]. — **gloom′i·er, gloom′i·est**

glue (glōō) *n.* **1** a thick, sticky substance made by boiling animal hoofs and bones, used for sticking things together. **2** any sticky substance like this. ◆*v.* to stick together with glue. —**glued, glu′ing** —**glue′y** *adj.*

gob·ble[1] (gäb′əl) *n.* the throaty sound made by a male turkey. ◆*v.* to make this sound. —**gob′bled, gob′bling**

gob·ble[2] (gäb′əl) *v.* to eat quickly and greedily. —**gob′bled, gob′bling**

gone (gôn) *past participle of* **go**. ◆*adj.* **1** moved away; departed. **2** used up.

good·bye or **good-bye** (good bī′) *interj., n.* a word said when leaving someone; farewell [We said our *goodbyes* quickly and left.] —*pl.* **good·byes′** or **good-byes′**

good·ness (good′nəs) *n.* the condition of being good. ◆*interj.* an exclamation showing surprise [My *goodness! Goodness* me!]

goose (gōōs) *n.* a swimming bird that is like a duck but has a larger body and a longer neck; especially, the female of this bird.— *pl.* **geese**

graph (graf) *n.* a chart or diagram that shows the changes taking place in something, by the use of connected lines, a curve, etc. [a *graph* showing how sales figures vary during the year].

grate[1] (grāt) *v.* to grind into small bits or shreds by rubbing against a rough surface [to *grate* cabbage]. —**grat′ed, grat′ing**

grate[2] (grāt) *n.* **1** a frame of metal bars for holding fuel, as in a fireplace or furnace. **2** a framework of bars set in a window or door; grating.

great (grāt) *adj.* **1** much above the average in size, degree, power, etc.; big or very big; much or very much [the *Great* Lakes; a *great* distance; *great* pain]. **2** very important; noted; remarkable [a *great* composer; a *great* discovery]. **3** older or younger by a generation: *used in words formed with a hyphen* [my *great*-aunt; my *great*-niece]. —**great′ly** *adv.* —**great′ness** *n.*

grind (grīnd) *v.* **1** to crush into tiny bits or into powder [The miller *grinds* grain between millstones.] **2** to sharpen or smooth by rubbing against a rough surface [to *grind* a knife]. **3** to press down or rub together harshly or with a grating sound [She *ground* her teeth in anger.] —**ground, grind′ing**

ground[1] (ground) *n.* the solid part of the earth's surface; land; earth. ◆*adj.* of, on, or near the ground [the *ground* floor of a building].

ground[2] (ground) *past tense and past participle of* **grind**.

group (grōōp) *n.* a number of persons or things gathered together. ◆*v.* to gather together into a group [*Group* yourselves in a circle.]

Monthly Sales (in thousands of dollars)

graph

Hh

half (haf) *n.* either of the two equal parts of something [Five is *half* of ten.] —*pl.* **halves** ◆*adj.* being either of the two equal parts [a *half* gallon].

harm (härm) *n.* **1** damage or hurt [Too much rain can do *harm* to crops.] **2** wrong; evil [I meant no *harm* by my remark.] ◆*v.* to do harm to; hurt or damage [Some cleaning fluids can *harm* the skin.]

a	ask, fat
ā	ape, date
ä	car, lot
e	elf, ten
ē	even, meet
i	is, hit
ī	ice, fire
ō	open, go
ô	law, horn
oi	oil, point
ᴏᴏ	look, pull
ōō	ooze, tool
ou	out, crowd
u	up, cut
ʉ	fur, fern
ə	a in ago
	e in agent
	e in father
	i in unity
	o in collect
	u in focus
ch	chin, arch
ŋ	ring, singer
sh	she, dash
th	thin, truth
th	then, father
zh	s in pleasure

has·n't (haz′ənt) has not.

hatch (hach) *v.* to come forth from the egg [Our chicks *hatched* this morning.]

haul (hôl) *v.* **1** to move by pulling; drag or tug [We *hauled* the boat up on the beach.] **2** to carry by wagon, truck, etc. [He *hauls* steel for a large company.] ◆*n.* the distance that something is hauled [It's a long *haul* to town.]

have·n't (hav′ənt) have not.

health (helth) *n.* the condition of being well in body and mind; freedom from sickness.

hear (hir) *v.* **1** to receive sound through the ears [I *hear* music. Pat doesn't *hear* well.] **2** to listen to; pay attention [*Hear* what I tell you.] —**heard** (hʉrd), **hear′ing**

heav·y (hev′ē) *adj.* hard to lift or move because of its weight; weighing very much [a *heavy* load]. —**heav′i·er, heav′i·est** —**heav′i·ly** *adv.* —**heav′i·ness** *n.*

hel·lo (he lō′) *interj.* a word used in greeting someone or in answering the telephone. ◆*n.* a saying or calling of "hello." —*pl.* **hel·los′** ◆*v.* to say or call "hello." —**hel·loed′, hel·lo′ing**

help (help) *v.* **1** to give or do something that is needed or useful; make things easier for; aid; assist [We *helped* our poor relatives. *Help* me lift this.] **2** to make better; give relief to; remedy [This medicine will *help* your cold.] ◆*n.* the act of helping or a thing that helps; aid; assistance [Your advice was a great *help*.] —**help′er** *n.*

here (hir) *adv.* at or in this place [Who lives *here*?] ◆*interj.* a word called out to get attention, answer a roll call, etc. ◆*n.* this place [Let's get out of *here*.]

he·ro (hir′ō) *n.* **1** a person, especially a man or boy, who is looked up to for having done something brave or noble [He became a *hero* when he saved his family from a burning house. Washington was the *hero* of the American Revolution.] **2** the most important man in a novel, play, etc., especially if he is good or noble. —*pl.* **he′roes**

he's (hēz) **1** he is. **2** he has.

high·way (hī′wā) *n.* a main road.

hock·ey (häk′ē) *n.* a game played on ice, in which the players wear ice skates and use curved sticks to try to drive or push a rubber disk into the other team's goal.

hol·i·day (häl′ə dā) *n.* a day on which most people do not have to work, often one set aside by law [Thanksgiving is a *holiday* in all States.]

hon·est (än′əst) *adj.* **1** capable of being trusted; not stealing, cheating, or lying [an *honest* person].

hon·ey (hun′ē) *n.* **1** a thick, sweet, yellow syrup that bees make from the nectar of flowers and store in honeycombs. **2** sweet one; darling: used in talking to someone dear to one [How are you, *honey*?]

hon·or (än′ər) *n.* **1** great respect given because of worth, noble deeds, high rank, etc. [to pay *honor* to the geniuses of science]. **2** something done or given as a sign of respect [Madame Curie received many *honors* for her work.] **3** good name or reputation [You must uphold the *honor* of the family.] **4** a being true to what is right, honest, etc. [Her sense of *honor* kept her from cheating.] ◆*v.* to have or show great respect for [America *honors* the memory of Lincoln. *Honor* your father and your mother.] ◆*adj.* of or showing honor [an *honor* roll].

hope (hōp) *n.* a feeling that what one wants will happen [We gave up *hope* of being rescued.] ◆*v.* **1** to have hope; want and expect [I *hope* to see you soon.] **2** to want to believe [I *hope* I didn't overlook anybody.] —**hoped, hop′ing**

hour (our) *n.* **1** any of the 24 equal parts of a day; 60 minutes. **2** a particular time [At what *hour* shall we meet?]

how's (houz) **1** how is. **2** how has. **3** how does.

huge (hyōōj) *adj.* very large; immense [the *huge* trunk of the redwood tree]. —**huge′ly** *adv.* —**huge′ness** *n.*

hu·man (hyōō′mən) *adj.* that is a person or that has to do with people in general [a *human* being; *human* affairs]. ◆*n.* a person: *some people still prefer the full phrase* **human being.**

hum·ble (hum′bəl) *adj.* knowing one's own weaknesses and faults; not proud or bold; modest or meek [He became *humble* and asked her to forgive him.] —**hum′bler, hum′blest**

hun·gry (hun grē) *adj.* **1** wanting or needing food [Cold weather makes me *hungry*.] **2** having a strong desire; eager [*hungry* for praise]. —**hun′gri·er, hun′gri·est** —**hun′gri·ly** *adv.* —**hun′gri·ness** *n.*

hunt·er (hunt′ər) *n.* a person who hunts.

hur·ried (hur′ēd) *adj.* done or acting in a hurry; hasty [We ate a *hurried* lunch.] —**hur′ried·ly** *adv.*

hurt (hurt) *v.* **1** to cause pain or injury to; wound [The fall *hurt* my leg.] **2** to have pain [My head *hurts*.] **3** to harm or damage in some way [Water won't *hurt* this table top.] —**hurt, hurt′ing** ◆*n.* pain, injury, or harm [Warm water will ease the *hurt*.]

ice (īs) *n.* water frozen solid by cold [Water turns to *ice* at 0°C.] ◆*v.* **1** to change into ice; freeze [The lake *iced* over.] **2** to cover with icing, or frosting [to *ice* a cake]. —**iced, ic′ing**

i·cy (ī′sē) *adj.* **1** full of or covered with ice [*icy* streets]. **2** like ice; slippery or very cold [*icy* fingers]. —**i′ci·er, i′ci·est** —**i′ci·ly** *adv.* —**i′ci·ness** *n.*

I'd (īd) **1** I had. **2** I would. **3** I should.

I'll (īl) **1** I shall. **2** I will.

inch (inch) *n.* a unit for measuring length, equal to 1/12 foot. One inch equals 2.54 centimeters. —*pl.* **inch′es** ◆*v.* to move a little at a time [Lou *inched* along the narrow ledge.]

in·side (in′sīd′) *n.* the side or part that is within; interior [Wash the windows on the *inside*.] ◆*adj.* on or in the inside; internal; indoor [*inside* work; an *inside* page].

in·stead (in sted′) *adv.* in place of the other; as a substitute [If you have no cream, use milk *instead*.]

in·to (in′tōō *or* in′tə) *prep.* **1** to the inside of [to go *into* the house]. **2** to the form, condition, etc., of [The farm has been turned *into* a park. They got *into* trouble.]

is·n't (iz′ənt) is not.

itch (ich) *v.* to have a tickling feeling on the skin that makes one want to scratch; also, to cause to have this feeling [The wool shirt *itches* my skin.] ◆*n.* an itching feeling on the skin.

its (its) *pron.* of it or done by it: *the possessive form of* **it,** *thought of as an adjective* [Give the cat *its* dinner. The frost had done *its* damage.]

I've (īv) I have.

a	ask, fat
ā	ape, date
ä	car, lot
e	elf, ten
ē	even, meet
i	is, hit
ī	ice, fire
ō	open, go
ô	law, horn
oi	oil, point
oo	look, pull
ōō	ooze, tool
ou	out, crowd
u	up, cut
u	fur, fern
ə	a in ago
	e in agent
	e in father
	i in unity
	o in collect
	u in focus
ch	chin, arch
ŋ	ring, singer
sh	she, dash
th	thin, truth
th	then, father
zh	s in pleasure

167

Jj

jog (jäg) **v.** to move along slowly or steadily, but with a jolting motion. —**jogged, jog′ging** ◆**n.** a jogging pace; trot. —**jog′ger n.**

join (join) **v.** **1** to bring together; connect; fasten [We *joined* hands and stood in a circle.] **2** to become a part or member of [Paula has *joined* our club.] **3** to take part along with others [*Join* in the game.]

joke (jōk) **n.** anything said or done to get a laugh, as a funny story. ◆**v.** to tell or play jokes. —**joked, jok′ing** —**jok′ing·ly adv.**

knight

Kk

keep (kēp) **v.** **1** to have or hold and not let go [He was *kept* after school. She kept her trim figure. Can you *keep* a secret?] **2** to hold for a later time; save [I *kept* the cake to eat later.] **3** to take care of; look after [He *keeps* house for himself.] **4** to stay or make stay as it is; last; continue [The fish will *keep* a while if you pack it in ice. *Keep* your engine running. *Keep* on walking.] —**kept, keep′ing**

kept (kept) *past tense and past participle of* **keep**.

kill (kil) **v.** **1** to cause the death of; make die; slay. **2** to put an end to; destroy or ruin [Her defeat *killed* all our hopes.] **3** to make time pass in doing unimportant things [an hour to *kill* before my train leaves]. ◆**n.** **1** the act of killing [to be in at the *kill*]. **2** an animal or animals killed [the lion's *kill*]. —**kill′er n.**

kind¹ (kīnd) **n.** sort or variety [all *kinds* of books].

kind² (kīnd) **adj.** **1** always ready to help others and do good; friendly, gentle, generous, sympathetic, etc. **2** showing goodness, generosity, sympathy, etc. [*kind* deeds; *kind* regards].

knee (nē) **n.** the joint between the thigh and the lower leg.

knew (nōō *or* nyōō) *past tense of* **know**.

knife (nīf) **n.** a tool having a flat, sharp blade set in a handle, used for cutting. —*pl.* **knives** ◆**v.** to cut or stab with a knife. —**knifed, knif′ing**

knight (nīt) **n.** a man in the Middle Ages who was given a military rank of honor after serving as a page and squire. Knights were supposed to be gallant and brave. ◆**v.** to give the rank of knight to.

knit (nit) **v.** **1** to make by looping yarn or thread together with special needles [to *knit* a scarf]. —**knit′ted** or **knit, knit′ting**

knives (nīvz) **n.** *plural of* **knife**.

knock (näk) **v.** **1** to hit as with the fist; especially, to rap on a door [Who is *knocking*?] **2** to hit and cause to fall [The dog *knocked* down the papergirl.] ◆**n.** a hard, loud blow, as with the fist; rap, as on a door.

knot (nät) **n.** **1** a lump, as in a string or ribbon, formed by a loop or a tangle drawn tight. **2** a fastening made by tying together parts or pieces of string, rope, etc. [Sailors make a variety of *knots*.] ◆**v.** **1** to tie or fasten with a knot; make a knot in. **2** to become tangled. —**knot′ted, knot′ting**

know (nō) **v.** **1** to be sure of or have the facts about [Do you *know* why grass is green? She *knows* the law.] **2** to have in one's mind or memory [The actress *knows* her lines.] **3** to be acquainted with [I *know* your brother well.] —**knew, known, know′ing**

lack (lak) **n.** **1** the condition of not having enough; shortage [*Lack* of money forced him to return home.] **2** the thing that is needed [Our most serious *lack* was fresh water.] ◆**v.** to be without or not have enough; need [The soil *lacks* nitrogen.]

la·dy (lā′dē) **n.** a woman, especially one who is polite and refined and has a sense of honor. —*pl.* **la′dies** ◆**adj.** that is a woman; female [a *lady* barber].

large (lärj) **adj.** of great size or amount; big [a *large* house; a *large* sum of money]. —**larg′er, larg′est** ◆**adv.** in a large way [Don't write so *large*.] — **large′ness n.**

late·ly (lāt′lē) **adv.** just before this time; not long ago; recently.

laugh (laf) **v.** to make a series of quick sounds with the voice that show one is amused or happy or, sometimes, that show scorn. One usually smiles or grins when laughing. ◆**n.** the act or sound of laughing.

law (lô) **n.** all the rules that tell people what they must or must not do, made by the government of a city, state, nation, etc. [the *law* of the land].

lawn (lôn) **n.** ground covered with grass that is cut short, as around a house.

leaf (lēf) **n.** **1** any of the flat, green parts growing from the stem of a plant or tree. **2** a sheet of paper in a book [Each side of a *leaf* is a page.] —*pl.* **leaves** —**leaf′less adj.**

learn (lurn) **v.** **1** to get some knowledge or skill, as by studying or being taught [I have *learned* to knit. Some people never *learn* from experience.] **2** to find out about something; come to know [When did you *learn* of his illness?] **3** to fix in the mind; memorize [*Learn* this poem by tomorrow.] —**learned** (lurnd) or **learnt** (lurnt), **learn′ing**

least (lēst) **adj.** smallest in size, amount, or importance [I haven't the *least* interest in the matter.] ◆**adv.** in the smallest amount or degree [I was *least* impressed by the music.] ◆**n.** the smallest in amount, degree, etc. [The *least* you can do is apologize. I'm not in the *least* interested.]

leave (lēv) v. to go away or go from [Rosa *left* early. Jose *leaves* the house at 8:00.] —**left, leav′ing**

leaves (lēvz) **n.** *plural of* **leaf.**

left¹ (left) **adj.** on or to the side that is toward the west when one faces north [the *left* hand; a *left* turn]. ◆**n.** the left side [Forks are placed at the *left* of the plate.] ◆**adv.** on or toward the left hand or side [Turn *left* here.]

left² (left) *past tense and past participle of* **leave.**

lev·el (lev′əl) **adj.** with no part higher than any other part; flat and even [a *level* plain]. ◆**n.** a small tube of liquid in a frame that is placed on a surface to see if the surface is level. A bubble in the liquid moves to the center of the tube when the frame is level. ◆**v.** to make level or flat [to *level* ground with a bulldozer]. —**lev′eled** or **lev′elled, lev′el·ing** or **lev′el·ling**

lie¹ (lī) **v.** **1** to stretch one's body in a flat position along the ground, a bed, etc. **2** to be in a flat position; rest [A book is *lying* on the table.] —**lay, lain, ly′ing**

lie² (lī) **n.** something said that is not true, especially if it is said on purpose to fool or trick someone. ◆**v.** to tell a lie; say what is not true. —**lied, ly′ing**

a	ask, fat
ā	ape, date
ä	car, lot
e	elf, ten
ē	even, meet
i	is, hit
ī	ice, fire
ō	open, go
ô	law, horn
oi	oil, point
o͞o	look, pull
o͞o	ooze, tool
ou	out, crowd
u	up, cut
u	fur, fern
ə	a in ago
	e in agent
	e in father
	i in unity
	o in collect
	u in focus
ch	chin, arch
ŋ	ring, singer
sh	she, dash
th	thin, truth
th	then, father
zh	s in pleasure

169

life (līf) *n.* **1** the quality of plants and animals that makes it possible for them to take in food, grow, produce others of their kind, etc., and that makes them different from rocks, water, etc. [Death is the loss of *life*.] **2** a living thing; especially, a human being [The crash took six *lives*.] **3** the time that a person or thing is alive or lasts [Her *life* has just begun. What is the *life* of a battery?] —*pl.* **lives**

light[1] (līt) *n.* **1** brightness or radiance [the *light* of a candle; the *light* of love in his eyes]. **2** something that gives light, as a lamp [Turn off the *light*.] **3** a flame or spark to start something burning [a *light* for a pipe]. ◆*adj.* **1** having light; not dark [It's getting *light* outside.] **2** having a pale color; fair [*light* hair]. ◆*adv.* not brightly; in a pale way [a *light* green dress]. ◆*v.* to set on fire or catch fire; burn [to *light* a match; the candle *lighted* at once].
—**light′ed** or **lit, light′ing**
—**light′ness** *n.*

light[2] (līt) *adj.* having little weight, especially for its size; not heavy [a *light* cargo; a *light* suit].

line (līn) *n.* **1** a cord, rope, string, etc. [a fishing *line*; a clothes*line*]. **2** a long, thin mark [*lines* made by a pen or pencil; *lines* formed in the face by wrinkles]. **3** a row of persons or things [a *line* of people waiting to get in; a *line* of words across a page]. ◆*v.* to form a line along [Elms *line* the streets.] —**lined, lin′ing**

lit·tle (lit′l) *adj.* small in size; not large or big [a *little* house].
—**lit′tler** or **less** or **less′er, lit′tlest** or **least** ◆*adv.* to a small degree; not very much [She is a *little* better.] —**less, least** ◆*n.* a small amount [Have a *little* of this cake.] —**lit′tle·ness** *n.*

live[1] (liv) *v.* **1** to have life; be alive [No one *lives* forever.] **2** to make one's home; reside [We *live* on a farm.] —**lived, liv′ing**

live[2] (līv) *adj.* **1** having life; not dead. **2** that is broadcast while it is taking place; not photographed or recorded [a *live* television or radio program].

liv·ing (liv′iŋ) *adj.* having life; alive; not dead. ◆*n.* **1** the fact of being alive. **2** the means of supporting oneself or one's family [He makes a *living* selling shoes.]

load (lōd) *n.* something that is carried or to be carried at one time [a heavy *load* on his back]. ◆*v.* to put something to be carried into or upon a carrier [to *load* a bus with passengers; to *load* groceries into a cart].
—**load′er** *n.*

loaf (lōf) *n.* **1.** a portion of bread baked in one piece, usually oblong in shape. **2.** any food baked in this shape [a meat *loaf*].
—*pl.* **loaves**

long[1] (lôŋ) *adj.* **1** measuring much from end to end or from beginning to end; not short [a *long* board; a *long* trip; a *long* wait]. **2** taking a longer time to say than other sounds [The "a" in "cave" and the "i" in "hide" are *long*.] ◆*adv.* for a long time [Don't be gone *long*.]

long[2] (lôŋ) *v.* to want very much; feel a strong desire for [We *long* to go home.]

loose (loōs) *adj.* **1** not tied or held back; free [a *loose* end of wire]. **2** not tight or firmly fastened on or in something [*loose* clothing; a *loose* table leg]. ◆*adv.* in a loose way [My coat hangs *loose*.] —**loose′ly** *adv.*
—**loose′ness** *n.*

lose (loōz) *v.* **1** to put, leave, or drop, so as to be unable to find; misplace; mislay [He *lost* his keys somewhere.] **2** to fail to win; be defeated [We *lost* the football game.] —**lost, los′ing**

lost (lôst) *past tense and past participle of* **lose.** ◆*adj.* that is mislaid, missing, destroyed, defeated, wasted, etc. [a *lost* hat; a *lost* child; a *lost* ship; a *lost* cause; *lost* time].

loud (loud) *adj.* **1** strong in sound; not soft or quiet [a *loud* noise; a *loud* bell]. **2** noisy [a *loud* party]. ◆*adv.* in a loud way. —**loud′ly** *adv.* —**loud′ness** *n.*

love·ly (luv′lē) *adj.* **1** very pleasing in looks or character; beautiful [a *lovely* person]. **2** very enjoyable: *used only in everyday talk* [We had a *lovely* time.] —**love′li·er, love′li·est** —**love′li·ness** *n.*

loy·al (loi′əl) *adj.* **1** faithful to one's country [a *loyal* citizen]. **2** faithful to one's family, duty, beliefs, etc. [a *loyal* friend; a *loyal* member]. —**loy′al·ly** *adv.*

Mm

mad (mad) *adj.* **1** angry [Don't be *mad* at us for leaving.] **2** crazy; insane. —**mad′der, mad′dest**

made (mād) *past tense and past participle of* **make.** ◆*adj.* built; put together; formed [a well-*made* house].

mag·ic (maj′ik) *n.* **1** the use of charms, spells, and rituals that are supposed to make things happen in an unnatural way [In fairy tales, *magic* is used to work miracles.] **2** the skill of doing puzzling tricks by moving the hands so fast as to fool those watching and by using boxes with false bottoms, hidden strings, etc.; sleight of hand. ◆*adj.* of or as if by magic.

maid (mād) *n.* **1** a maiden. **2** a girl or woman servant.

mail (māl) *n.* **1** letters, packages, etc., carried and delivered by a post office. **2** the system of picking up and delivering letters, papers, etc.; postal system [Send it by *mail*.] ◆*adj.* having to do with or carrying mail [a *mail* truck]. ◆*v.* ☆to send by mail; place in a mailbox. —**mail′a·ble** *adj.*

Maine (mān) a New England state of the U.S.: abbreviated **Me., ME**

make (māk) *v.* **1** to bring into being; build, create, produce, put together, etc. [to *make* a dress; to *make* a fire; to *make* plans; to *make* noise]. **2** to do, perform, carry on, etc. [to *make* a right turn; to *make* a speech]. —**made, mak′ing**

man (man) *n.* **1** an adult male human being. **2** any human being; person ["that all *men* are created equal"]. **3** the human race; mankind [*man's* conquest of space]. —*pl.* **men**

mark (märk) *n.* **1** a spot, stain, scratch, dent, etc., made on a surface. **2** a printed or written sign or label [punctuation *marks*; a trade*mark*]. **3** a grade or rating [a *mark* of B in spelling]. ◆*v.* **1** to make a mark or marks on. **2** to draw or write [*Mark* your name on your gym shoes.] **3** to give a grade to [to *mark* test papers].

mar·ry (mer′ē) *v.* **1** to join a man and a woman as husband and wife [A ship's captain may *marry* people at sea.] **2** to take as one's husband or wife [John Alden *married* Priscilla.] —**mar′ried, mar′ry·ing**

may (mā) *a helping verb used with other verbs and meaning:* **1** to be possible or likely [It *may* rain.] **2** to be allowed or have permission [You *may* go.] **3** to be able to as a result [Be quiet so that we *may* hear.] *May* is also used in exclamations to mean "I or we hope or wish" [*May* you win!] —The past tense is **might.**

may·be (mā′bē) *adv.* it may be; perhaps.

a	ask, fat
ā	ape, date
ä	car, lot
e	elf, ten
ē	even, meet
i	is, hit
ī	ice, fire
ō	open, go
ô	law, horn
oi	oil, point
σο	look, pull
ōο	ooze, tool
ou	out, crowd
u	up, cut
ʉ	fur, fern
ə	a in ago
	e in agent
	e in father
	i in unity
	o in collect
	u in focus
ch	chin, arch
ŋ	ring, singer
sh	she, dash
th	thin, truth
th	then, father
zh	s in pleasure

money

mel·o·dy (mel′ə dē) **n. 1** an arrangement of musical tones in a series so as to form a tune; often, the main tune in the harmony of a musical piece [The *melody* is played by the oboes.] **2** any pleasing series of sounds [a *melody* sung by birds]. —*pl.* **mel′o·dies**

melt (melt) **v. 1** to change from a solid to a liquid, as by heat [The bacon fat *melted* in the frying pan.] **2** to dissolve [The candy *melted* in my mouth.]

men (men) **n.** *plural of* **man**.

mice (mīs) **n.** *plural of* **mouse**.

might¹ (mīt) *past tense of* **may**.

might² (mīt) **n.** great strength, force, or power [Pull with all your *might*.]

mile (mīl) **n.** a standard measure of length, equal to 5,280 feet or 1,760 yards or 1.6093 kilometers.

mix (miks) **v.** to put, stir, or come together to form a single, blended thing [*Mix* red and yellow paint to get orange.] — **mixed** or **mixt** (mikst), **mix′ing ◆ n.** a mixture. —*pl.* **mix′es**

Monday (mun′dā) **n.** the second day of the week.

mon·ey (mun′ē) **n.** coins of gold, silver, or other metal, or paper bills to take the place of these, issued by a government for use in buying and selling. —*pl.* **mon′eys** or **mon′ies**

mood (mōod) **n.** the way one feels; frame of mind [She's in a happy *mood* today.]

moon·light (mōon′līt) **n.** the light of the moon.

morn·ing (môrn′iŋ) **n.** the early part of the day, from midnight to noon or, especially, from dawn to noon.

most·ly (mōst′lē) **adv.** mainly; chiefly.

☆**mo·tel** (mō tel′) **n.** a hotel for those traveling by car, usually with a parking area easily reached from each room.

mouse

moth (môth *or* mäth) **n.** an insect similar to the butterfly, but usually smaller and less brightly colored and flying mostly at night —*pl.* **moths** (mothz *or* mäths)

mouse (mous) **n. 1** a small, gnawing animal found in houses and fields throughout the world. **2** a timid person. ☆**3** a small device moved by hand, as on a flat surface, so as to make the cursor move on a computer terminal screen. —*pl.* **mice** (mīs)

muf·fler (muf′lər) **n. 1** a scarf worn around the throat for warmth. **2** a thing used to deaden noise, as ☆a part fastened to the exhaust pipe of an automobile engine.

mul·ti·ply (mul′tə plī) **v. 1** to become more, greater, etc.; increase [Our troubles *multiplied*.] **2** to repeat a certain figure a certain number of times [If you *multiply* 10 by 4, or repeat 10 four times, you get the product 40.] —**mul′ti·plied, mul′ti·ply·ing**

mu·sic (myōo′zik) **n. 1** the art of putting tones together in various melodies, rhythms, and harmonies to form compositions for singing or playing on instruments [She teaches *music*.] **2** any series of pleasing sounds [the *music* of birds].

must·n't (mus′ənt) must not.

my·self (mī self′) **pron. 1** my own self. *This form of* **I** *is used when the object is the same as the subject of the verb* [I hurt *myself*.] **2** my usual or true self [I'm not *myself* today.] *Myself* is also used to give force to the subject [I'll do it *myself*.]

nee·dle (nēd′əl) *n.* **1** a small, slender piece of steel with a sharp point and a hole for thread, used for sewing. **2** a short, slender piece of metal, often tipped with diamond, that moves in the grooves of a phonograph record to pick up the vibrations. **3** the thin, pointed leaf of a pine, spruce, etc. **4** the sharp, very slender metal tube at the end of a hypodermic syringe.

New York (yôrk) **1** a state in the northeastern part of the U.S.: abbreviated **N.Y.**, **NY** **2** a seaport in southeastern New York State, on the Atlantic Ocean; the largest city in the U.S.: *often called* **New York City.**

next (nekst) *adj.* coming just before or just after; nearest or closest [the *next* person in line; the *next* room; *next* Monday]. ◆*adv.* **1** in the nearest place, time, etc. [She sits *next* to me in school. Please wait on me *next*.] **2** at the first chance after this [What should I do *next*?]

nice (nīs) *adj.* good, pleasant, agreeable, pretty, kind, polite, etc.: *used as a general word showing that one likes something* [a *nice* time; a *nice* dress; a *nice* neighbor]. —**nic′er, nic′est** —**nice′ly** *adv.*

night (nīt) *n.* the time of darkness between sunset and sunrise. ◆*adj.* of, for, or at night [*night* school].

nine (nīn) *n., adj.* one more than eight; the number 9.

ninth (nīnth) *adj.* coming after eight others; 9th in order. ◆*n.* one of nine equal parts of something; 1/9.

noise (noiz) *n.* sound, especially a loud, harsh, or confused sound [the *noise* of fireworks; *noises* of a city street]. ◆*v.* to make public by telling; spread [to *noise* a rumor about]. —**noised, nois′ing**

nois·y (noi′zē) *adj.* **1** making noise [a *noisy* bell]. **2** full of noise [a *noisy* theater]. —**nois′i·er, nois′i·est** —**nois′i·ly** *adv.* —**nois′i·ness** *n.*

note (nōt) *n.* **1** a word, phrase, or sentence written down to help one remember something one has heard, read, thought, etc. [The students kept *notes* on the lecture.] **2** a short letter. **3** close attention; notice [Take *note* of what I say.] **4** a musical tone; also, the symbol for such a tone, showing how long it is to be sounded. Where it is placed on the staff tells how high or low it is.

noun (noun) *n.* a word that is the name of a person, thing, action, quality, etc. A phrase or a clause can be used in a sentence as a noun ["Boy," "water," and "truth" are *nouns*.]

No·vem·ber (nō vem′bər) *n.* the eleventh month of the year, which has 30 days: abbreviated **Nov.**

nurse (nʉrs) *n.* a person who has been trained to take care of sick people, help doctors, etc. ◆*v.* to take care of sick people, as a nurse does. —**nursed, nurs′ing**

ob·ject (äb′jekt) *n.* **1** a thing that can be seen or touched; something that takes up space [That brown *object* is a purse.] **2** a person or thing toward which one turns one's thoughts, feelings, or actions [the *object* of my affection].

needle

a	ask, fat
ā	ape, date
ä	car, lot
e	elf, ten
ē	even, meet
i	is, hit
ī	ice, fire
ō	open, go
ô	law, horn
oi	oil, point
o͞o	look, pull
o͞o	ooze, tool
ou	out, crowd
u	up, cut
ʉ	fur, fern
ə	a in ago
	e in agent
	e in father
	i in unity
	o in collect
	u in focus
ch	chin, arch
ŋ	ring, singer
sh	she, dash
th	thin, truth
th	then, father
zh	s in pleasure

Oc·to·ber (äk tō′bər) **n.** the tenth month of the year, which has 31 days: abbreviated **Oct.**

O·hi·o (ō hī′ō) **1** a state in the north central part of the U.S.: abbreviated **O., OH 2** a river that flows along the southern borders of Ohio, Indiana, and Illinois to the Mississippi. —**O·hi′o·an adj., n.**

oint·ment (oint′mənt) **n.** an oily cream rubbed on the skin to heal it or make it soft and smooth; salve.

once (wuns) **adv. 1** one time [We eat together *once* a week.] **2** at some time in the past; formerly [They were rich *once*.] ◆**conj.** as soon as; whenever [*Once* the horse tires, it will quit.] ◆**n.** one time [I'll go this *once*.]

on·ly (ōn′lē) **adj.** without any other or others of the same kind; sole [the *only* suit I own; their *only* friends]. ◆**adv.** and no other; and no more; just; merely [I have *only* fifty cents. Bite off *only* what you can chew.]

or·der (ôr′dər) **n. 1** the way in which things are placed or follow one another; arrangement [The entries in this dictionary are in alphabetical *order*.] **2** a direction telling someone what to do, given by a person with authority; command [The general's *orders* were quickly obeyed.] **3** a request for something that one wants to buy or receive [Mail your *order* for flower seeds today.] ◆**v. 1** to tell what to do; give an order to [The captain *ordered* the troops to charge.] **2** to ask for something one wants to buy or receive [Please *order* some art supplies for the class.]

our (our) **pron.** of us or done by us. *This possessive form of* **we** *is used before a noun and thought of as an adjective* [*our* car; *our* work].

OX

oxford

our·selves (our selvz′) **pron. 1** our own selves. *This form of* **we** *is used when the object is the same as the subject of the verb* [We hurt *ourselves*.] **2** our usual or true selves [We are not *ourselves* today.] *Ourselves is also used to give force to the subject* [We built it *ourselves*.]

ox (äks) **n.** any animal of a group that chew their cud and have cloven hoofs, including the buffalo, bison, etc. —*pl.* **ox·en** (äks′ən)

ox·ford (äks′fərd) **n.** a low shoe that is laced over the instep: *also called* **oxford shoe.**

pack (pak) **n.** a bundle of things that is tied or wrapped [a hiker's *pack*]. ◆**v. 1** to tie or wrap together in a bundle [I *packed* books at the book sale.] **2** to put things together in a box, trunk, or suitcase for carrying or storing [to *pack* a suitcase].

page¹ (pāj) **n.** one side of a leaf of paper in a book, newspaper, letter, etc. ◆**v.** to turn pages in looking quickly [to *page* through a book]. —**paged, pag′ing**

page² (pāj) **n.** a boy, or sometimes a girl, who runs errands and carries messages in a hotel, office building, or legislature. ◆**v.** ☆to try to find a person by calling out the name, as a hotel page does. —**paged, pag′ing**

pair (per) **n. 1** two things of the same kind that are used together; set of two [a *pair* of skates]. **2** a single thing with two parts that are used together [a *pair* of eyeglasses; a *pair* of pants]. ◆**v.** to arrange in or form a pair or pairs; match.

pa·per (pā′pər) **n.** **1** a thin material in sheets, made from wood pulp, rags, etc., and used to write or print on, to wrap or decorate with, etc. **2** a single sheet of this material. **3** something written or printed on paper, as an essay, report, etc. [The teacher is grading a set of *papers*.]

pa·rade (pə rād′) **n.** any march or procession, as to celebrate a holiday [a Fourth of July *parade*]. ◆*v.* to march in a parade. —**pa·rad′ed, pa·rad′ing**

pare (per) **v.** to cut or trim away the rind or covering of something; peel [to *pare* a potato; to *pare* the bark from a tree]. —**pared, par′ing**

par·ty (pär′tē) **n.** **1** a gathering of people to have a good time [a birthday *party*]. **2** a group of people working or acting together [a hunting *party*]. —*pl.* **par′ties**

past (past) **adj.** gone by; ended; over [What is *past* is finished.] ◆*n.* the time that has gone by [That's all in the *past*.] ◆*prep.* later than or farther than; beyond [ten minutes *past* two; *past* the city limits].

patch (pach) **n.** **1** a piece of cloth, metal, etc., put on to mend a hole, tear, or worn spot. **2** a bandage put on a wound or a pad worn over an injured eye. **3** an area or spot [*patches* of blue sky]. ◆*v.* to put a patch or patches on [to *patch* the worn elbows of a coat].

pear (per) **n.** a soft, juicy fruit, often yellow or green, that is round at one end and narrows toward the stem.

peo·ple (pē′pəl) **n.** human beings; persons.

per·haps (pər haps′) **adv.** possibly; maybe [*Perhaps* it will rain. Did you, *perhaps*, lose it?]

pe·ri·od (pir′ē əd) **n.** **1** the time that goes by during which something goes on, a cycle is repeated, etc. [the medieval *period*; a *period* of hot weather]. **2** the mark of punctuation (.) used at the end of most sentences or often after abbreviations.

per·son (pur′sən) **n.** a human being; man, woman, or child [every *person* in this room].

☆**phone** (fōn) **n., v.** *a shorter word for* **telephone**: *used only in everyday talk.* —**phoned, phon′ing**

pick[1] (pik) **n.** a heavy metal tool with a pointed head, used for breaking up rock, soil, etc.

pick[2] (pik) **v.** **1** to choose or select [The judges *picked* the winner.] **2** to scratch or dig at with the fingers or with something pointed [to *pick* the teeth with a toothpick]. **3** to pluck or gather with the fingers or hands [to *pick* flowers]. ◆*n.* the act of choosing or the thing chosen; choice [Take your *pick* of these books.] —**pick′er n.**

pinch (pinch) **v.** to squeeze between a finger and the thumb or between two surfaces [He gently *pinched* the baby's cheek. She *pinched* her finger in the door.] ◆*n.* **1** a pinching; squeeze; nip [a *pinch* on the arm]. **2** the amount that can be picked up between the finger and thumb [a *pinch* of salt].

pi·rate (pī′rət) **n.** **1** a person who attacks and robs ships on the ocean. **2** a person who uses copyrighted or patented work without permission.

pitch (pich) **v.** **1** to throw or toss [*Pitch* the newspaper on the porch.] **2** to set up; make ready for use [to *pitch* a tent]. **3** to slope downward [The roof *pitches* sharply.] ◆*n.* **1** anything pitched or thrown [The wild *pitch* hit the batter.] **2** the highness or lowness of a musical sound.

pick

a	ask, fat
ā	ape, date
ä	car, lot
e	elf, ten
ē	even, meet
i	is, hit
ī	ice, fire
ō	open, go
ô	law, horn
oi	oil, point
oo	look, pull
ōō	ooze, tool
ou	out, crowd
u	up, cut
ʉ	fur, fern
ə	a in ago
	e in agent
	e in father
	i in unity
	o in collect
	u in focus
ch	chin, arch
ŋ	ring, singer
sh	she, dash
th	thin, truth
th	then, father
zh	s in pleasure

175

place (plās) *n.* **1** a space taken up or used by a person or thing [Please take your *places*.] **2** a house, apartment, etc., where one lives [Visit me at my *place*.] **3** rank or position, especially in a series [I finished the race in fifth *place*.] ◆*v.* **1** to put in a certain place, position, etc. [*Place* the pencil on the desk.] **2** to finish in a certain position in a contest [Lynn *placed* sixth in the race.] —**placed, plac′ing**

plan (plan) *n.* **1** a method or way of doing something that has been thought out ahead of time [vacation *plans*]. **2** a drawing that shows how the parts of a building or piece of ground are arranged [floor *plans* of a house; a *plan* of the battlefield]. ◆*v.* **1** to think out a way of making or doing something [They *planned* their escape carefully.] **2** to make a drawing or diagram of beforehand [An architect is *planning* our new school.] **3** to have in mind; intend [I *plan* to visit Hawaii soon.] —**planned, plan′ning**

plane (plān) *n.* *a short form of* **airplane.**

plant (plant) *n.* **1** any living thing that cannot move about by itself, has no sense organs, and usually makes its own food by photosynthesis [Trees, shrubs, and vegetables are *plants*.] **2** the machinery, buildings, etc., of a factory or business. ◆*v.* to put into the ground so that it will grow [to *plant* corn].

play (plā) *v.* **1** to have fun; amuse oneself [children *playing* in the sand]. **2** to do in fun [to *play* a joke on a friend]. **3** to take part in a game or sport [to *play* golf]. **4** to perform music on [He *plays* the piano.] **5** to give out sounds: said of a phonograph, tape recorder, etc. ◆*n.* **1** something done just for fun or to amuse oneself; recreation [She has little time for *play*.] **2** fun; joking [Jan said it in *play*.] **3** the playing of a game [Rain halted *play*.] **4** a story that is acted out, as on a stage, on radio or television, etc.; drama.

play·ful (plā′fəl) *adj.* **1** fond of play or fun; lively; frisky [a *playful* puppy]. **2** said or done in fun; joking [She gave her brother a *playful* shove.] —**play′ful·ly** *adv.* —**play′ful·ness** *n.*

please (plēz) *v.* **1** to give pleasure to; satisfy [Few things *please* me more than a good book.] **2** to be kind enough to: *used in asking for something politely* [*Please* pass the salt.] **3** to wish or desire; like [Do as you *please*.] —**pleased, pleas′ing**

plen·ty (plen′tē) *n.* a supply that is large enough; all that is needed [We have *plenty* of help.]

plumb·er (plum′ər) *n.* a person whose work is putting in and repairing the pipes and fixtures of water and gas systems in a building.

point (point) *n.* **1** a position or place; location [the *point* where the roads meet]. **2** a dot in printing or writing [a decimal *point*]. **3** a unit used in measuring or scoring [A touchdown is worth six *points*.] **4** a sharp end [the *point* of a needle]. **5** an important or main idea or fact [the *point* of a joke]. ◆*v.* to aim one's finger [He *pointed* to the book he wanted.]

pol·ish (päl′ish) *v.* to make smooth and bright or shiny, usually by rubbing [to *polish* a car with wax]. ◆*n.* **1** brightness or shine on a surface [a wood floor with a fine *polish*]. **2** a substance used for polishing [shoe *polish*]. —*pl.* **pol′ish·es**

po·lite (pə līt′) *adj.* having or showing good manners; thoughtful of others; courteous [a *polite* note of thanks]. —**po·lite′ly** *adv.* —**po·lite′ness** *n.*

pool¹ (pōol) *n.* **1** a small pond. **2** a puddle. **3** *a shorter form of* **swimming pool**.

pool² (pōol) *n.* a game of billiards played on a table, called a **pool table,** having six pockets into which the balls are knocked.

po·ta·to (pə tāt′ō) *n.* a plant whose tuber, or thick, starchy underground stem, is used as a vegetable. —*pl.* **po·ta′toes**

pound¹ (pound) *n.* a unit of weight, equal to 16 ounces in avoirdupois weight or 12 ounces in troy weight. One pound avoirdupois equals 453.59 grams.

pound² (pound) *v.* **1** to hit with many heavy blows; hit hard [to *pound* on a door]. **2** to beat in a heavy way; throb [Her heart *pounded* from the exercise.] ◆*n.* a hard blow or the sound of it.

pound³ (pound) *n.* a closed-in place for keeping animals, especially stray ones [a dog *pound*].

pow·er (pou′ər) *n.* **1** ability to do or act [Lobsters have the *power* to grow new claws.] **2** strength or force [the *power* of a boxer's blows]. **3** force or energy that can be put to work [electric *power*]. **4** the ability to control others; authority [the *power* of the law]. ◆*adj.* worked by electricity or other kind of power [a *power* saw].

pray (prā) *v.* **1** to talk or recite a set of words to God in worship or in asking for something. **2** to beg or ask for seriously ["*Pray* tell me" means "I beg you to tell me."]

pret·ty (prit′ē) *adj.* pleasant to look at or hear, especially in a delicate, dainty, or graceful way [a *pretty* girl; a *pretty* voice; a *pretty* garden]. —**pret′ti·er, pret′ti·est** ◆*adv.* somewhat; rather [I'm *pretty* tired.] ◆*v.* to make pretty [She *prettied* up her room.] —**pret′tied, pret′ty·ing** —**pret′ti·ly** *adv.* —**pret′ti·ness** *n.*

prize (prīz) *n.* **1** something offered or given to a winner of a contest, lottery, etc. [The first *prize* is a bicycle.] **2** anything worth trying to get [Her friendship would be a great *prize*.]

prom·ise (präm′is) *n.* an agreement to do or not to do something; vow [to make and keep a *promise*]. ◆*v.* to make a promise to [I *promised* them I'd arrive at ten.] —**prom′ised, prom′is·ing**

proud (proud) *adj.* **1** having proper respect for oneself, one's work, one's family, etc. [He is too *proud* to ask for help.] **2** thinking too highly of oneself; conceited; vain or haughty [They are too *proud* to say hello to us.] **3** feeling or causing pride or pleasure [his *proud* mother; a *proud* moment]. —**proud′ly** *adv.*

pud·dle (pud′əl) *n.* a small pool of water or water mixed with earth [*puddles* after the rain; a mud *puddle*].

pup·py (pup′ē) *n.* a young dog. —*pl.* **pup′pies**

push (poosh) *v.* **1** to press against so as to move; shove [to *push* a stalled car; to *push* a stake into the ground]. **2** to urge the use, sale, etc., of [The company is *pushing* its new product.] ◆*n.* the act of pushing; a shove or thrust [One hard *push* opened the door.]

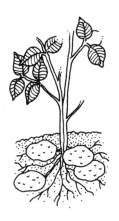

potato

Qq

quite (kwīt) *adv.* **1** completely; entirely [I haven't *quite* finished eating.] **2** really; truly [You are *quite* a musician.] **3** very or somewhat [It's *quite* warm outside.]

a	ask, fat
ā	ape, date
ä	car, lot
e	elf, ten
ē	even, meet
i	is, hit
ī	ice, fire
ō	open, go
ô	law, horn
oi	oil, point
oo	look, pull
ōo	ooze, tool
ou	out, crowd
u	up, cut
u	fur, fern
ə	a in ago
	e in agent
	e in father
	i in unity
	o in collect
	u in focus
ch	chin, arch
ŋ	ring, singer
sh	she, dash
th	thin, truth
th	then, father
zh	s in pleasure

Rr

rac·coon (ra kōōn′) *n.* a furry animal having a long tail with black rings and black face markings that look like a mask.

race (rās) *n.* a contest, as among runners, swimmers, cars, boats, etc., to see who can go fastest. ◆ *v.* **1** to take part in a race [How many planes are *racing*?] **2** to have a race with [I'll *race* you to the corner.] **3** to go very fast [Her eye *raced* over the page.] —**raced, rac′ing**

rain (rān) *n.* **1** water that falls to the earth in drops formed from the moisture in the air. **2** the falling of such drops; a shower [Sunshine followed the *rain*.] ◆ *v.* to fall as rain [It is *raining*.]

raise (rāz) *v.* **1** to cause to rise; lift [*Raise* your hand if you have a question. *Raise* the window.] **2** to make larger, greater, higher, louder, etc. [to *raise* prices; to *raise* one's voice]. **3** to bring up; take care of; support [to *raise* a family]. —**raised, rais′ing** ◆ *n.* a making or becoming larger; especially, an increase in salary or wages.

rash (rash) *n.* a breaking out of red spots on the skin [The measles gave her a *rash*.]

re- *a prefix meaning:* **1** again [To *reappear* is to appear again.] **2** back [To *repay* is to pay back.]

read¹ (rēd) *v.* **1** to get the meaning of something written or printed by understanding its letters, signs, or numbers [I *read* the book. She *read* the gas meter. Can you *read* music?] **2** to speak printed or written words aloud [*Read* the story to me.] —**read** (red), **read′ing**

read² (red) *past tense and past participle of* **read¹**. ◆ *adj.* having knowledge got from reading; informed [They are both well-*read*.]

read·y (red′ē) *adj.* prepared to act or to be used at once [Is everyone *ready* to leave? Your bath is *ready*.] —**read′i·er, read′i·est** ◆ *v.* to prepare [to *ready* the house for guests]. —**read′ied, read′y·ing** —**read′i·ness** *n.*

re·ap·ply (rē ə plī′) *v.* to put or spread on again [*Reapply* glue to that corner.] —**re·ap·plied, re·ap·ply′ing**

re·as·sign (rē ə sīn′) *v.* to give out as a task again [The teacher *reassigned* the same homework.]

re·build (rē bild′) *v.* to build again, especially something that was damaged, ruined, etc. —**re·built′, re·build′ing**

re·do (rē dōō′) *v.* **1** to do again **2** to redecorate, as a room. —**re·did′, re·done′, re·do′ing**

re·fill (rē fil′) *v.* to fill again. ◆ *n.* (re′fil) **1** something to refill a special container [a *refill* for a ballpoint pen]. **2** any extra filling of a prescription for medicine. —**re·fill′a·ble** *adj.*

re·form (rē fôrm′) *v.* **1** to make better by getting rid of faults, wrongs, etc.; improve [to *reform* working conditions in a factory; to *reform* a criminal]. **2** to become better; give up one's bad ways [The outlaw *reformed* and became a better citizen.] ◆ *n.* correction of faults or evils, as in government.

re·fresh (rē fresh′) *v.* to make fresh again; bring back into good condition [A soft rain *refreshed* the wilted plants. She *refreshed* herself with a short nap. *Refresh* my memory by playing the piece again.]

re·lease (rē lēs′) *v.* to set free or relieve [*Release* the bird from the cage.] —**re·leased′, re·leas′ing**

re·mind (rē mīnd′) *v.* to make remember or think of [*Remind* me to pay the gas bill.]

re·name (rē nām') *v.* to give a new or different name to [Ceylon was *renamed* Sri Lanka.]
—**re·named', re·nam'ing**

re·new (rē nōō' *or* rē nyōō') *v.* **1** to make new or fresh again; restore [*Renew* that old table by painting it.] **2** to give or get again for a new period of time [It is time to *renew* your subscription.] —**re·new'al** *n.*

re·pay (rē pā') *v.* **1** to pay back [to *repay* a loan]. **2** to do or give something to someone in return for some favor, service, etc., received [to *repay* a kindness].
—**re·paid', re·pay'ing**
—**re·pay'ment** *n.*

re·place (rē plās') *v.* **1** to put back in the right place [*Replace* the tools on my bench when you are through.] **2** to take the place of [Many workers have been *replaced* by computers.] **3** to put another in the place of one used, lost, broken, etc. [to *replace* a worn tire]. —**re·placed', re·plac'ing**

re·ply (rē plī') *v.* to answer by saying or doing something [to *reply* to a question; to *reply* to the enemy's fire with a counter-attack]. —**re·plied', re·ply'ing** ◆*n.* an answer.
—*pl.* **re·plies'**

re·run (rē run') *v.* to run again.
—**re·ran', re·run'ning** ◆*n.* (rē'run) ☆ a repeat showing of a movie, taped TV program, etc.

ret·i·na (ret'n ə) *n.* the part at the back of the eyeball, made up of special cells that react to light. The image picked up by the lens of the eye is formed on the retina.

re·triev·er (rē trēv'ər) *n.* a dog that is trained to retrieve game in hunting.

re·write (rē rīt') *v.* to write again or in different words; revise [to *rewrite* a story]. —**re·wrote', re·writ'ten, re·writ'ing**

rich (rich) *adj.* **1** having wealth; owning much money or property; wealthy. **2** having much of something; well supplied [Tomatoes are *rich* in vitamin C.] **3** full of fats, or fats and sugar [*rich* foods]. —**rich'ly** *adv.*
—**rich'ness** *n.*

ring¹ (riŋ) *v.* **1** to cause a bell to sound [*Ring* the doorbell.] **2** to make the sound of a bell [The phone *rang.*] —**rang** or rarely **rung, rung, ring'ing** ◆*n.* **1** the sound of a bell. **2** a telephone call [Give me a *ring* soon.]
—**ring'er** *n.*

ring² (riŋ) *n.* **1** a thin band of metal, plastic, etc., shaped like a circle and worn on the finger or used to hold or fasten things [a wedding *ring*; a curtain *ring*]. **2** a line or edge forming a circle [a *ring* around the moon]. **3** an enclosed space for contests, shows, etc. [the *ring* of a circus; a boxing *ring*]. ◆*v.* to make a circle around or form in a ring.
—**ringed, ring'ing** —**ringed** *adj.*
—**ring'er** *n.*

rise (rīz) *v.* **1** to stand up or get up from a lying or sitting position. **2** to become greater, higher, or stronger [The temperature *rose.* Prices are *rising.* Her voice *rose.*] —**rose, ris'en, ris'ing** ◆*n.* **1** a piece of ground higher than that around it [There's a good view of the countryside from the top of the *rise.*] **2** the fact of becoming greater, higher, etc.; increase [a *rise* in prices].

rock¹ (räk) *n.* a large mass of stone.

rock² (räk) *v.* to move or swing back and forth or from side to side [to *rock* a cradle]. ◆*n* a rocking movement.

roof (rōōf *or* roof) *n.* **1** the outside top covering of a building. **2** anything like a roof in the way it is placed or used [the *roof* of the mouth; the *roof* of a car]. —**roof'less** *adj.*

retina

a	ask, fat
ā	ape, date
ä	car, lot
e	elf, ten
ē	even, meet
i	is, hit
ī	ice, fire
ō	open, go
ô	law, horn
oi	oil, point
oo	look, pull
ōo	ooze, tool
ou	out, crowd
u	up, cut
u	fur, fern
ə	a in ago
	e in agent
	e in father
	i in unity
	o in collect
	u in focus
ch	chin, arch
ŋ	ring, singer
sh	she, dash
th	thin, truth
th	then, father
zh	s in pleasure

rough (ruf) *adj.* **1** not smooth or level; uneven [a *rough* road; *rough* fur]. **2** full of noise and wild action; disorderly [*rough* play]. **3** not gentle or mild, as in manners; rude, harsh, etc. [*rough* language]. **4** having little comfort or luxury [the *rough* life of a pioneer].

round (round) *adj.* shaped like a ball, a circle, or a tube; having an outline that forms a circle or curve [The world is *round*. Wheels are *round*. The ship has a *round* smokestack.] ◆*n.* a short song for two or more persons or groups, in which the second starts when the first gets to the second phrase, and so on.

ru·ler (rōōl′ər) *n.* a straight, thin strip of wood, metal, or plastic used in drawing straight lines and measuring.

rush (rush) *v.* **1** to move, send, take, etc., with great speed [I *rushed* from the room. We *rushed* him to a hospital.] **2** to act in haste, without thinking carefully [Don't *rush* into marriage.] ◆*adj.* that must be done or sent in a hurry [a *rush* order].

sail

Ss

said (sed) *past tense and past participle of* **say.** ◆*adj.* named or mentioned before [The *said* contract is no longer in force.]

sail (sāl) *n.* **1** a sheet of heavy cloth such as canvas, used on a ship or boat to move it by catching the wind. **2** a trip in a ship or boat, especially one moved by sails [Let's go for a *sail*.] ◆*v.* **1** to travel on water [This liner *sails* between Miami and New York.] **2** to move smoothly [a hawk *sailing* in the sky].

sale (sāl) *n.* **1** the act of selling, or exchanging something for money [The clerk made ten *sales* today.] **2** a special selling of goods at prices lower than usual [a clearance *sale*].

sam·ple (sam′pəl) *n.* a part or piece that shows what the whole group or thing is like; specimen or example [little pieces of wallpaper for *samples*; a *sample* of his typing]. ◆*adj.* that is a sample [a *sample* page of the book]. ◆*v.* to test by trying a sample [He *sampled* the basket of grapes.] —**sam′pled, sam′pling**

sat·is·fy (sat′is fī′) *v.* to meet the needs or wishes of; to content; to please [Only first prize will *satisfy* him.] —**sat′is·fied′, sat′is·fy′ing**

Sat·ur·day (sat′ər dē) *n.* the seventh and last day of the week.

sau·sage (sô′sij *or* sä′sij) *n.* pork or other meat, chopped up and seasoned and, usually, stuffed into a tube made of thin skin.

save (sāv) *v.* **1** to rescue or keep from harm or danger [He was *saved* from drowning.] **2** to keep or store up for future use [She *saved* her money for a vacation.] —**saved, sav′ing** —**sav′er** *n.*

scale¹ (skāl) *n.* **1** a series of marks along a line, with regular spaces in-between, used for measuring [A Celsius thermometer has a basic *scale* of 100 degrees.] **2** the way that the size of a map, model, or drawing compares with the size of the thing that it stands for [One inch on a map of this *scale* equals 100 miles of real distance.] **3** a series of musical tones arranged in order from the highest to the lowest or from the lowest to the highest. —**on a large scale,** to a large extent.

scale² (skāl) *n.* any of the thin, flat, hard plates that cover and protect certain fish and reptiles.

scale³ (skāl) *n.* **1** either of the shallow pans of a balance. **2** *often* **scales,** *pl.* the balance itself; also, any device or machine for weighing.

scarf (skärf) *n.* a long or broad piece of cloth worn about the head, neck, or shoulders for warmth or decoration. —*pl.* **scarves** (skärvz) or **scarfs**

scent (sent) *n.* **1** a smell; odor [the *scent* of apple blossoms]. **2** the sense of smell [Lions hunt partly by *scent.*]

school¹ (skōōl) *n.* **1** a place, usually a special building, for teaching and learning, as a public school, dancing school, college, etc. **2** the students and teachers of a school [an assembly for the *school*]. ◆*adj.* of or for a school or schools [our *school* band].

school² (skōōl) *n.* a large group of fish or water animals of the same kind swimming together [a *school* of porpoises]. ◆*v.* to swim together in a school.

scold (skōld) *v.* to find fault with someone in an angry way [I *scolded* her for being late.]

scoop (skōōp) *n.* **1** a kitchen tool like a small shovel, used to take up sugar, flour, etc., or one with a small, round bowl for dishing up ice cream, etc. **2** the amount taken up at one time by a scoop [three *scoops* of ice cream]. ◆*v.* to take up as with a scoop [We *scooped* it up with our hands.]

scram·ble (skram'bəl) *v.* to cook eggs while stirring the mixed whites and yolks. —**scram'bled, scram'bling**

scratch (skrach) *v.* **1** to mark or cut the surface of slightly with something sharp [Thorns *scratched* her legs. Our cat *scratched* the chair with its claws.] **2** to rub or scrape, as with the nails, to relieve itching [to *scratch* a mosquito bite]. **3** to cross out by drawing lines through [She *scratched* out what he had written.] ◆*n.* **1** a mark or cut made in a surface by something sharp. **2** a slight wound. **3** a harsh, grating sound [the *scratch* of chalk on a blackboard].

scream (skrēm) *v.* to give a loud, shrill cry, as in fright or pain [They *screamed* as the roller coaster hurtled downward.] ◆*n.* a loud, shrill cry or sound; shriek.

screen (skrēn) *n.* **1** a mesh woven loosely of wires so as to leave small openings between them. Screens are used in windows, doors, etc., to keep insects out. **2** a covered frame or curtain used to hide, separate, or protect. **3** a surface on which movies, television pictures, etc., are shown.

seat (sēt) *n.* **1** a thing to sit on, as a chair, bench, etc. **2** a place to sit or the right to sit [to buy two *seats* for the opera; to win a *seat* in the Senate]. ◆*v.* **1** to cause to sit; put in or on a seat [*Seat* yourself quickly.] **2** to have seats for [This car *seats* six people.]

see (sē) *v.* **1** to be aware of through the eyes; have or use the sense of sight [We *saw* two birds. I don't *see* so well.] **2** to get the meaning of; understand [Do you *see* the point of the joke?] **3** to visit with [We stopped to *see* a friend.] **4** to go to for information or advice; consult [*See* a doctor about your cough.] **5** to think or try to remember [Let me *see*, where did I put that?] —**saw, seen, see'ing**

seek (sēk) *v.* to try to find; search for [to *seek* gold]. —**sought, seek'ing**

seen (sēn) *past participle of* **see**.

sel·fish (sel'fish) *adj.* caring too much about oneself, with little or no thought or care for others. —**self'ish·ly** *adv.* — **self'ish·ness** *n.*

send (send) *v.* **1** to cause to be carried [Food was *sent* by plane.] **2** to cause a message to be transmitted by mail, radio, or other means [I will *send* the letter tomorrow.] **3** to cause or force to go [The teacher *sent* her home.] —**sent, send'ing**

a	ask, fat
ā	ape, date
ä	car, lot
e	elf, ten
ē	even, meet
i	is, hit
ī	ice, fire
ō	open, go
ô	law, horn
oi	oil, point
͏oo	look, pull
o͞o	ooze, tool
ou	out, crowd
u	up, cut
ʉ	fur, fern
ə	a in ago
	e in agent
	e in father
	i in unity
	o in collect
	u in focus
ch	chin, arch
ŋ	ring, singer
sh	she, dash
th	thin, truth
th	then, father
zh	s in pleasure

sent (sent) *past tense and past participle of* **send**.

serve (surv) *v.* **1** to aid; to help [She *served* her country well.] **2** to wait on [The waiter *served* our table first.] —**served, serv′ing**

set (set) *v.* **1** to put in a certain place or position [*Set* the book on the table.] **2** to put in order or in the right condition, position, etc.; arrange; adjust [to *set* a trap; to *set* a thermostat; to *set* a broken bone; to *set* a table for a meal.] **3** to establish or fix, as a time for a meeting, a price, a rule, a limit, etc. **4** to sink below the horizon [The sun *sets* in the west.] —**set, set′ting** ◆*n.* **1** a number of parts put together, as in a cabinet [a TV *set*]. **2** in mathematics, any collection of units, points, numbers, etc.

set·ting (set′iŋ) *n.* the time, place, and circumstances of an event, story, play, etc.

shad·ow (shad′ō) *n.* the darkness or the dark shape cast upon a surface by something cutting off light from it [Her large hat put her face in *shadow*. His hand cast a *shadow* on the wall.]

shape (shāp) *n.* the way a thing looks because of its outline; outer form; figure [The cloud had the *shape* of a lamb.] ◆*v.* to give a certain shape to; form [The potter *shaped* the clay into a bowl.] —**shaped, shap′ing**

share (sher) *n.* a part that each one of a group gets or has [your *share* of the cake; my *share* of the blame]. ◆*v.* to have a share of with others; have or use together [The three of you will *share* the back seat.] —**shared, shar′ing**

sharp (shärp) *adj.* **1** having a thin edge for cutting or a fine point for piercing [a *sharp* knife; a *sharp* needle]. **2** very clever or shrewd [a *sharp* mind]. ◆*adv.* exactly or promptly [She gets up at 6:30 *sharp*.] —**sharp′ly adv.** —**sharp′ness n.**

sheep (shēp) *n.* an animal that chews its cud and is related to the goat. Its body is covered with heavy wool, and its flesh is used as food, called mutton. —*pl.* **sheep**

shelf (shelf) *n.* a thin, flat length of wood, metal, etc., fastened against a wall or built into a frame so as to hold things [the top *shelf* of a bookcase]. —*pl.* **shelves**

shelves (shelvz) *n.* *plural of* **shelf**.

shine (shīn) *v.* **1** to give off light or reflect light; be bright [The sun *shines*. Her hair *shone*.] **2** to make bright by polishing [to *shine* shoes]. —**shone** or **shined, shin′ing** ◆*n.* the act of polishing, as shoes.

shirt (shurt) *n.* **1** the common garment worn by a boy or man on the upper part of the body.

shi·ver (shiv′ər) *v.* to shake or tremble, often from fear or cold [We *shivered* when we heard scary sounds.]

shoot (shoot) *v.* to send a bullet, arrow, etc., from [to *shoot* a gun]. —**shot, shoot′ing** ◆*n.* a new growth; sprout. —**shoot′er n.**

short (shôrt) *adj.* **1** not measuring much from end to end or from beginning to end; not long [a *short* stick; a *short* trip; a *short* novel; a *short* wait]. **2** not tall; low [a *short* tree]. **3** less or having less than what is enough or correct [Our supply of food is *short*. We are *short* ten dollars.] **4** taking a shorter time to say than other sounds [The "e" in "bed" and the "i" in "rib" are *short*.] ◆*adv.* so as to be short [Cut your speech *short*. We fell *short* of our goal.] ◆*v.* to give less than what is needed, usual, etc. [The cashier *shorted* the customer a dollar.]

shadow

shoul·der (shōl′dər) **n.** the part of the body to which an arm or foreleg is connected.

should·n't (shood′nt) should not.

shov·el (shuv′əl) **n.** a tool with a broad scoop and a handle, for lifting and moving loose material. ◆ **v.** to lift and move with a shovel [to *shovel* coal]. —**shov′eled** or **shov′elled, shov′el·ing** or **shov′el·ling**

shy (shī) **adj.** **1** easily frightened; timid [a *shy* animal]. **2** not at ease with other people; bashful [a *shy* child]. —**shi′er** or **shy′er, shi′est** or **shy′est** —**shy′ly adv.** —**shy′ness n.**

side·walk (sīd′wôk) **n.** a path for walking; usually paved, along the side of a street.

sigh (sī) **v.** to let out a long, deep, sounded breath, usually to show that one is sad, tired, relieved, etc. ◆ **n.** the act or sound of sighing [She breathed a *sigh* of relief.]

sight (sīt) **n.** **1** something that is seen; especially, something unusual worth seeing [The Grand Canyon is a *sight* you won't forget.] **2** the ability to see; vision; eyesight [He lost his *sight* in the war.] **3** the distance over which one can see [The airplane passed out of *sight*.] ◆ **v.** to see [The sailor *sighted* land.]

sign (sīn) **n.** **1** a thing or act that stands for something else; symbol [Black is worn as a *sign* of grief. She saluted the flag as a *sign* of respect. The *sign* (+) means "add."] **2** a board, card, etc., put up in a public place, with information, a warning, etc., on it [The *sign* said, "Do not enter."] **3** anything that tells of the existence or coming of something else [Red spots on the face may be a *sign* of measles.] ◆ **v.** to write one's name on [to *sign* a contract to make it legal].

since (sins) **adv.** from then until now [Lynn came Monday and has been here ever *since*.] ◆ **prep.** from or during the time given until now [I've been up *since* dawn.] ◆ **conj.** **1** after the time that [It's been two years *since* I saw you.] **2** because [You may have these tools, *since* I no longer need them.]

sis·ter (sis′tər) **n.** a girl or woman as she is related to the other children of her parents.

sixth (siksth) **adj.** coming after five others; 6th in order. ◆ **n.** one of the six equal parts of something; 1/6.

six·ty (siks′tē) **n.** the cardinal number that is equal to six times ten; 60. —*pl.* **six′ties**

size (sīz) **n.** **1** the amount of space taken up by a thing; how large or how small a thing is [Tell me the *size* of your room. He is strong for his *size*.] **2** any of a series of measures, often numbered, for grading things [She wears a *size* 12 dress. These are jumbo *size* peanuts.] ◆ **v.** to arrange according to size. —**sized, siz′ing**

slight (slīt) **adj.** small in amount or degree; not great, strong, important, etc. [a *slight* change in temperature; a *slight* advantage; a *slight* bruise]. —**slight′ly adv.**

slip (slip) **v.** **1** to go or pass quietly or without being noticed; escape [We *slipped* out the door. It *slipped* my mind. Time *slipped* by.] **2** to move, shift, or drop, as by accident [The plate *slipped* from my hand.] **3** to slide by accident [He *slipped* on the ice.] —**slipped, slip′ping**

slum·ber (slum′bər) **v.** **1** to sleep. **2** to be quiet or inactive [The volcano has *slumbered* for years.] ◆ **n.** sleep.

sly (slī) **adj.** able to fool or trick others; cunning; crafty [the *sly* fox]. —**sli′er** or **sly′er, sli′est** or **sly′est** —**sly′ly** or **sli′ly adv.**

shovel

a	ask, fat
ā	ape, date
ä	car, lot
e	elf, ten
ē	even, meet
i	is, hit
ī	ice, fire
ō	open, go
ô	law, horn
oi	oil, point
͝oo	look, pull
͞oo	ooze, tool
ou	out, crowd
u	up, cut
u	fur, fern
ə	a in ago
	e in agent
	e in father
	i in unity
	o in collect
	u in focus
ch	chin, arch
ŋ	ring, singer
sh	she, dash
th	thin, truth
th	then, father
zh	s in pleasure

smart (smärt) *adj.* **1** intelligent or clever [a *smart* student]. **2** neat, clean, and well-groomed. **3** of the newest fashion; stylish [a *smart* new hat]. ◆*v.* to cause a sharp, stinging pain [A bee sting *smarts*.] —**smart′ly** *adv.* —**smart′ness** *n.*

smile (smīl) *v.* to show that one is pleased, happy, amused, etc., or sarcastic or scornful, by making the corners of the mouth turn up. —**smiled, smil′ing** ◆*n.* the act of smiling or the look on one's face when one smiles.

smog·gy (smôg′ē *or* smäg′ē) *adj.* full of polluted air. —**smog′gi· er, smog′gi·est**

soak (sōk) *v.* **1** to make or become completely wet by keeping or staying in a liquid [She *soaked* her sore hand in hot water. Let the beans *soak* overnight to soften them.] **2** to suck up or absorb [Use a sponge to *soak* up that water.] ◆*n.* the act of soaking.

some (sum) *adj.* **1** being a certain one or ones not named or not known [*Some* people were playing ball.] **2** being of a certain but not a definite number or amount [Have *some* candy.] ◆*pron.* a certain number or amount, but not all [Take *some*.]

somewhat (sum′hwut *or* sum′wut) *adv.* to some degree; rather; a little [They are *somewhat* late.]

soon (sōōn) *adv.* **1** in a short time; before much time has passed [Spring will *soon* be here.] **2** fast or quickly [as *soon* as possible]. **3** ahead of time; early [She left too *soon*.] —**soon′er, soon′est**

soot (soot) *n.* a black powder formed when some things burn. It is mostly carbon and makes smoke gray or black.

soothe (sōō*th*) *v.* **1** to make quiet or calm by being gentle or friendly [The clerk *soothed* the angry customer with helpful answers.] **2** to take away some of the pain or sorrow of; ease [I hope this lotion will *soothe* your sunburn.] —**soothed, sooth′ing** —**sooth′ing·ly** *adv.*

sought (sôt *or* sät) *past tense and past participle of* **seek.**

spare (sper) *v.* to save or free from something [*Spare* us from listening to that story again.] ◆ *adj.* kept for use when needed [a *spare* tire].

speak (spēk) *v.* **1** to say something with the voice; talk [They *spoke* to each other on the phone.] **2** to make a speech [Who *speaks* first on the show?]

spe·cial (spesh′əl) *adj.* **1** not like others; different; distinctive [The cook has a *special* recipe for tacos.] **2** unusual; extraordinary [Your idea has *special* merit.] **3** more than others; chief; main [her *special* friend]. —**spe′cial·ly** *adv.*

spend (spend) *v.* to pay out or give up, as money, time, or effort [He *spent* $50 for food. *Spend* some time with me.] —**spent, spend′ing** —**spend′er** *n.*

spic·y (spī′sē) *adj.* seasoned with spice or spices. —**spic′i·er, spic′i·est**

spied (spīd) *past tense and past participle of* **spy.**

spill (spil) *v.* to let flow over or run out [Who *spilled* water on the floor? Try not to *spill* any sugar.] —**spilled** *or* **spilt, spill′ing** ◆*n.* **1** the act of spilling. **2** a fall or tumble, as from a horse: *used only in everyday talk.*

splash (splash) *v.* **1** to make a liquid scatter and fall in drops [to *splash* water or mud about]. **2** to dash a liquid on, so as to wet or soil [The car *splashed* my coat.] —**splash′y** *adj.*

split (split) **v.** to separate or divide along the length into two or more parts [to *split* a wiener bun]. —**split, split′ting** ◆**n.** a break, crack, or tear [a *split* in the seam of a dress]. ◆**adj.** broken into parts; divided.

spoil (spoil) **v.** **1** to make or become useless, worthless, or rotten; to damage; to ruin [Ink stains *spoiled* the paper.] **2** to cause a person to ask for or expect too much by giving in to all of that person's wishes [to *spoil* a child]. —**spoiled** or **spoilt, spoil′ing**

sprang (spraŋ) *past tense of* **spring**.

spray (sprā) **n.** a mist of tiny drops, as of water thrown off from a waterfall. ◆**v.** to put something on in a spray [to *spray* a car with paint]. —**spray′er n.**

spread (spred) **v.** **1** to open out or stretch out, in space or time [*Spread* out the tablecloth. The eagle *spread* its wings. Our trip *spread* out over two weeks.] **2** to put or cover in a thin layer [to *spread* bread with jelly]. ◆**n.** **1** a cloth cover, as for a table or bed. **2** any soft substance, as jam or butter, that can be spread in a layer. —**spread′er n.**

spring (spriŋ) **v.** **1** to move suddenly and quickly; leap; jump up [I *sprang* to my feet.] **2** to snap back into position or shape, as a rubber band that is stretched and then let go. —**sprang** or **sprung, sprung, spring′ing** ◆**n.** **1** a device, as a coil of wire, that returns to its original shape when pressure on it is released. Springs are used in beds and automobiles to take up shock or in clocks, etc., to make them go. **2** water flowing up from the ground. **3** the season when plants begin to grow, between winter and summer.

spy (spī) **n.** a person who watches others secretly and carefully. —*pl.* **spies** ◆**v.** to watch closely and secretly [She likes to *spy* on her neighbors.] —**spied, spy′ing**

squirm (skwʉrm) **v.** to twist and turn the body as a snake does; wriggle; writhe [The rabbit *squirmed* out of the trap.]

stain (stān) **v.** to spoil with dirt or a patch of color; to soil or spot [The rug was *stained* with ink.] ◆**n.** a dirty or colored spot [grass *stains*].

stand (stand) **v.** **1** to be or get in an upright position on one's feet [*Stand* by your desk.] **2** to be or place in an upright position on its base, bottom, etc. [Our trophy *stands* on the shelf. *Stand* the broom in the corner.] **3** to be placed or situated [Our house *stands* on a hill.] —**stood, stand′ing**

start (stärt) **v.** **1** to begin to go, do, act, be, etc. [We *start* for Toledo today. The show *starts* at 8:30.] **2** to cause to begin; set in motion or action [*Start* the car. Who *started* the fight?] ◆**n.** the act of starting or beginning.

stead·y (sted′ē) **adj.** **1** firm or stable; not shaky [a *steady* chair]. **2** not changing or letting up; regular [a *steady* rain]. —**stead′i·er, stead′i·est**

steel (stēl) **n.** a hard, tough metal made of iron mixed with a little carbon.

stem (stem) **n.** the main part of a plant or tree that grows up from the ground and bears the leaves, flowers, or fruit.

step (step) **n.** **1** the act of moving and placing the foot forward, backward, sideways, up, or down, as in walking, dancing, or climbing. **2** a place to rest the foot in going up or down, as a stair or the rung of a ladder. ◆**v.** to move by taking a step or steps. —**stepped, step′ping**

a	ask, fat
ā	ape, date
ä	car, lot
e	elf, ten
ē	even, meet
i	is, hit
ī	ice, fire
ō	open, go
ô	law, horn
oi	oil, point
oo	look, pull
o͞o	ooze, tool
ou	out, crowd
u	up, cut
ʉ	fur, fern
ə	a in ago
	e in agent
	e in father
	i in unity
	o in collect
	u in focus
ch	chin, arch
ŋ	ring, singer
sh	she, dash
th	thin, truth
th	then, father
zh	s in pleasure

sting (stiŋ) *v.* **1** to hurt by pricking [Wasps can *sting* you.] **2** to cause or feel sharp pain [The cold wind *stung* her cheeks.] —**stung, sting′ing** ◆*n.* the act or power of stinging [The *sting* of a bee may be dangerous.]

stir (stur) *v.* to move or shake slightly [Not a leaf *stirred* in the quiet air.] —**stirred, stir′ring**

stone (stōn) *n.* **1** hard mineral matter that is found in the earth but is not metal; rock [a monument built of *stone*]. **2** a small piece of this [Don't throw *stones*. Rubies are precious *stones*.]

stood (stood) *past tense and past participle of* **stand**.

stop (stäp) *v.* **1** to halt or keep from going on, moving, acting, etc.; bring or come to an end [My watch *stopped*. The noise *stopped*. *Stop* the car. They *stopped* us from talking.] **2** to clog or block [The drain in the sink is *stopped* up.] **3** to stay or visit [We *stopped* there overnight.] —**stopped, stop′ping** ◆*n.* **1** a place stopped at [a *stop* on a bus route]. **2** the act or fact of stopping; finish; end [Put a *stop* to this argument.]

stran·ger (strān′jər) *n.* **1** a person who is new to a place; outsider or foreigner. **2** a person not known to one [Don't speak to *strangers*.]

straw·ber·ry (strô′ber′ē) *n.* the small, red, juicy fruit of a low plant of the rose family. —*pl.* **straw′ber′ries**

stream (strēm) *n.* a flow of water; especially, a small river. ◆*v.* **1** to flow in a stream. **2** to pour out or flow [eyes *streaming* with tears].

street (strēt) *n.* a road in a city or town; also, such a road with its sidewalks and buildings.

strike (strīk) *v.* **1** to hit by giving a blow, coming against with force, etc. [Nina *struck* him in anger. The car *struck* the curb.] **2** to make a sound by hitting some part [The clock *struck* one. *Strike* middle C on the piano.] **3** to set on fire as by rubbing [to *strike* a match]. **4** to stop working until certain demands have been met [The workers are *striking* for shorter hours.] —**struck, struck** or **strick′en, strik′ing**

string (striŋ) *n.* **1** a thick thread or thin strip of cloth, leather, etc., used for tying or pulling; cord. **2** a number of things in a row [a *string* of lights]. ◆*v.* **1** to put on a string [to *string* beads]. **2** to stretch like a string; extend [to *string* telephone wires on poles; to *string* out a speech]. —**strung, string′ing**

strong (strôŋ) *adj.* **1** having great force or power; not weak; powerful [a *strong* person; *strong* winds]. **2** having a powerful effect on the senses or mind; not mild [a *strong* taste, smell, light, sound, liking, etc.]. —**strong′ly** *adv.* —**strong′ness** *n.*

struck (struk) *past tense and a past participle of* **strike**.

stud·y (stud′ē) *v.* **1** to try to learn by reading, thinking, etc. [to *study* law]. **2** to look at or into carefully; examine or investigate [We must *study* the problem of crime.] **3** to read so as to understand and remember [to *study* a lesson]. —**stud′ied, stud′y·ing** ◆*n.* **1** a branch of learning; subject [the *study* of medicine]. **2** a room used for studying, reading, etc. —*pl.* **stud′ies**

sug·ar (shoog′ər) *n.* any of certain sweet substances in the form of crystals that dissolve in water. Glucose, lactose, and sucrose are different kinds of sugar. Sucrose is the common sugar used to sweeten food.

sweat·er (swet′ər) **n.** a knitted outer garment for the upper part of the body.

swim (swim) **v.** to move in water by working the arms, legs, fins, etc. —**swam, swum, swim′ming** ◆ **n.** an act, time, or distance of swimming. —**swim′mer n.**

take (tāk) **v.** **1** to get hold of; grasp [*Take* my hand as we cross the street.] **2** to write down; copy [*Take* notes on the lecture.] **3** to carry [*Take* your skis with you.] **4** to lead or bring [I *took* Lee to the movie. This road *takes* us to the park.] —**took, tak′en, tak′ing**

tax (taks) **n.** money that one must pay to help support a government. It is usually a percentage of one's income or of the value of something bought or owned. —*pl.* **tax′es** —**tax′a·ble adj.**

teach·er (tēch′ər) **n.** a person who teaches, especially in a school or college.

team (tēm) **n.** **1** two or more horses, oxen, etc., harnessed together as for pulling a plow or wagon. **2** a group of people working together or playing together in a contest against another such group [a *team* of scientists; a baseball *team*]. ◆ **v.** to join together in a team [Let's *team* up with them.]

teeth (tēth) **n.** *plural of* **tooth.**

ten·der (ten′dər) **adj.** **1** soft or delicate and easily chewed or cut [a *tender* piece of meat]. **2** feeling pain or hurting easily; sensitive [My sprained ankle still feels *tender.*] **3** warm and gentle; loving [a *tender* smile].

Tex·as (teks′əs) a state in the south central part of the U.S.: abbreviated **Tex., TX** —**Tex′an adj., n.**

than (than *or* thən) **conj.** compared to. *Than* is used before the second part of a comparison [I am taller *than* you.]

thank (thaŋk) **v.** to say that one is grateful to another for a kindness [We *thanked* her for her help.]

that (that *or* thət) **pron.** **1** the person or thing mentioned [*That* is José.] **2** who, whom, or which [She's the one *that* I saw. Here's the book *that* I borrowed.] —*pl.* **those**

that's (thats *or* thəts) that is.

thaw (thô) **v.** **1** to melt [The snow *thawed.*] **2** to become unfrozen: said of frozen foods. ◆ **n.** weather that is warm enough to melt snow and ice.

them (them) **pron.** the form of **they** that is used as the object of a verb or preposition [I met *them* at the airport. Give the flowers to *them.*]

there's (therz) there is.

they'll (thāl) **1** they will. **2** they shall.

they're (ther) they are.

thief (thēf) **n.** a person who steals, especially one who steals secretly. —*pl.* **thieves** (thēvz)

think (thiŋk) **v.** **1** to use the mind; reason [*Think* before you act.] **2** to form or have in the mind [She was *thinking* happy thoughts.] —**thought, think′ing**

third (thurd) **adj.** coming after two others; 3rd in order. ◆ **n.** one of three equal parts of something; 1/3.

thir·teen (thur′tēn′) **n., adj.** three more than ten; the number 13.

thir·ty (thur′tē) **n., adj.** three times ten; the number 30. —*pl.* **thir′ties**

thought¹ (thôt) **n.** **1** the act or process of thinking [When deep in *thought*, he doesn't hear.] **2** what one thinks; idea, opinion, plan, etc. [a penny for your *thoughts*].

thread

a	ask, fat
ā	ape, date
ä	car, lot
e	elf, ten
ē	even, meet
i	is, hit
ī	ice, fire
ō	open, go
ô	law, horn
oi	oil, point
o͝o	look, pull
o͞o	ooze, tool
ou	out, crowd
u	up, cut
u	fur, fern
ə	a in ago
	e in agent
	e in father
	i in unity
	o in collect
	u in focus
ch	chin, arch
ŋ	ring, singer
sh	she, dash
th	thin, truth
th	then, father
zh	s in pleasure

187

thought² (thôt) *past tense and past participle of* **think**.

thread (thred) *n.* a very thin cord used in sewing and made of strands of spun cotton, silk, etc., twisted together. ◆*v.* to put a thread through the eye of [to *thread* a needle]. —**thread′like** *adj.*

thrill (thril) *v.* to feel or make greatly excited; shiver or tingle with strong feeling [She *thrilled* at the praise. That movie *thrilled* us.] ◆*n.* a strong feeling of excitement that makes one shiver [Seeing a lion gave me a *thrill.*]

throat (thrōt) *n.* **1** the front part of the neck. **2** the upper part of the passage from the mouth to the stomach or lungs [I have a sore *throat.*]

throne (thrōn) *n.* the raised chair on which a king or other important person sits during ceremonies.

through (thrōō) *prep.* **1** in one side and out the other side of; from end to end of [The nail went *through* the board. We drove *through* the tunnel.] **2** from the beginning to the end of [We stayed in Maine *through* the summer.] ◆*adv.* in a complete and thorough way; entirely [We were soaked *through* by the rain.] ◆*adj.* finished [Are you *through* with your homework?]

throw (thrō) *v.* to send through the air by a fast motion of the arm; hurl, toss, etc. [to *throw* a ball]. —**threw, thrown, throw′ing** ◆*n.* the act of throwing [The fast *throw* put the runner out at first base.]

thumb (thum) *n.* the short, thick finger nearest the wrist. ◆*v.* to handle, turn, soil, etc., with the thumb [to *thumb* the pages of a book].

tide (tīd) *n.* the regular rise and fall of the ocean's surface, about every twelve hours, caused by the attraction of the moon and sun.

◆*v.* to help in overcoming a time of trouble [Will ten dollars *tide* you over till Monday?] —**tid′ed, tid′ing**

tie (tī) *v.* **1** to bind together or fasten with string, rope, cord, etc. [They *tied* his hands together. *Tie* the boat to the pier.] **2** to equal, as in a score [Pablo *tied* with Carmela for first place.] —**tied, ty′ing** ◆*n.* **1** *a shorter word for* **necktie**. **2** the fact of being equal, as in a score; also, a contest in which scores are equal. —*pl.* **ties**

to (tōō *or* too *or* tə) *prep.* **1** in the direction of [Turn *to* the right.] **2** on, onto, against, etc. [Put your hand *to* your mouth. Apply the lotion *to* the skin.]

too (tōō) *adv.* **1** in addition; besides; also [You come, *too.*] **2** more than enough [This hat is *too* big.] **3** very [You are *too* kind.]

toss (tôs *or* täs) *v.* to throw from the hand in a light way [to *toss* a ball]

tough (tuf) *adj.* **1** able to bend or twist without tearing or breaking [*tough* rubber]. **2** rough or brutal [Don't get *tough* with me.]

town (toun) *n.* a place where there are a large number of houses and other buildings, larger than a village but smaller than a city.

toy (toi) *n.* a thing to play with; especially, a plaything for children. ◆*adj.* **1** like a toy in size or use [a *toy* dog]. **2** made for use as a toy; especially, made as a small model [a *toy* train].

track (trak) *n.* **1** a mark left in passing, as a footprint or wheel rut. **2** a path or trail. ◆*v.* **1** to follow the tracks of [We *tracked* the fox to its den.] **2** to make tracks or dirty marks [The children *tracked* up the clean floor.]

toy

treas·ure (trezh′ər) **n.** money or jewels collected and stored up.

trip (trip) **v.** to stumble or make stumble [She *tripped* over the rug. Bill put out his foot and *tripped* me.] —**tripped, trip′ping** ◆**n.** a traveling from one place to another and returning; journey, especially a short one.

tur·key (tur′kē) **n.** ☆**1** a large, wild or tame bird, originally of North America, with a small head and spreading tail. ☆**2** its flesh, used as food. —*pl.* **tur′keys** or **tur′key**

twen·ty (twen′tē) **n., adj.** two times ten; the number 20 —*pl.* **twen′ties**

two (to̅o̅) **n., adj.** one more than one; the number 2. —**in two,** in two parts.

un- **1** *a prefix meaning* not *or the* opposite of [An *unhappy* person is one who is not happy, but sad.] **2** *a prefix meaning* to reverse *or* undo the action of [To *untie* a shoelace is to reverse the action of tying it.]

un·a·ble (un ā′bəl) **adj.** not able; not having the means or power to do something.

un·but·ton (un but′n) **v.** to unfasten the button or buttons of.

un·clean (un klēn′) **adj.** dirty; filthy.

un·der (un′dər) **prep.** in or to a place, position, amount, value, etc., lower than; below [He sang *under* her window. It rolled *under* the table. It weighs *under* a pound.] ◆**adv.** less in amount, value, etc. [It cost two dollars or *under*.]

un·eas·y (un ē′zē) **adj.** **1** having or giving no ease; not comfortable [an *uneasy* conscience]. **2** worried; anxious [Dad felt *uneasy* when I was late.] —**un·eas′i·er, un·eas′i·est**

un·e·ven (un ē′vən) **adj.** not even, level, or smooth; irregular [*uneven* ground]. —**un·e′ven·ly adv.** —**un·e′ven·ness n.**

un·load (un lōd′) **v.** to take a load or cargo from a truck, ship, etc.

un·luck·y (un luk′ē) **adj.** having or bringing bad luck; not lucky; unfortunate [There is a superstition that breaking a mirror is *unlucky*.] —**un·luck′i·er, un·luck′i·est** —**un·luck′i·ly adv.**

un·paid (un pād′) **adj.** not receiving pay [an *unpaid* helper].

un·pre·pared (un′prē perd′) **adj.** not prepared or ready [We are still *unprepared* for the visitors.]

un·true (un tro̅o̅′) **adj.** **1** not correct; false. **2** not faithful or loyal. —**un·tru′ly adv.**

u·su·al (yo̅o̅′zho̅o̅ əl) **adj.** such as is most often seen, heard, or used; common; normal [the *usual* time].—**u′su·al·ly adv.**

un·wrap (un rap′) **v.** to open by taking off the wrapping; also, to become opened in this way. —**un·wrapped′, un·wrap′ping**

use (yo̅o̅z) **v.** **1** to put or bring into service or action [*Use* the vacuum cleaner on the rugs. What kind of toothpaste do you *use*?] **2** to do away with by using; consume [She *used* up all the soap. Don't *use* up your energy.] —**used, us′ing**

used (yo̅o̅zd) **adj.** that has been used; not new; secondhand [*used* cars].

ver·y (ver′ē) **adv.** in a high degree; to a great extent; extremely [*very* cold; *very* funny; *very* sad].

a	ask, fat
ā	ape, date
ä	car, lot
e	elf, ten
ē	even, meet
i	is, hit
ī	ice, fire
ō	open, go
ô	law, horn
oi	oil, point
o͞o	look, pull
o̅o̅	ooze, tool
ou	out, crowd
u	up, cut
u	fur, fern
ə	a in ago
	e in agent
	e in father
	i in unity
	o in collect
	u in focus
ch	chin, arch
ŋ	ring, singer
sh	she, dash
th	thin, truth
th	then, father
zh	s in pleasure

189

wagon

whale

wag·on (wag′ən) **n.** a vehicle with four wheels, especially for carrying heavy loads.

wal·let (wôl′ət *or* wäl′ət) **n.** ☆a thin, flat case for carrying money, cards, etc., in the pocket.

was (wuz *or* wäz) *the form of* **be** *showing the past time with singular nouns and with* I, he, she, *or* it.

was·n't (wuz′ənt *or* wäz′ənt) was not.

watch (wäch *or* wôch) **v.** **1** to keep one's sight on; look at [We *watched* the parade.] **2** to take care of; look after; guard [The shepherd *watched* his flock.] ◆**n.** **1** the act of watching or guarding [The dog keeps *watch* over the house.] **2** a device for telling time that is like a clock but small enough to be worn, as on the wrist, or carried in the pocket. —*pl.* **watch′es**

wa·ter (wôt′ər) **n.** the colorless liquid that falls as rain, is found in springs, rivers, lakes, and oceans, and forms a large part of the cells of all living things. It is made up of hydrogen and oxygen, with the chemical formula H_2O. ◆**v.** **1** to give water to [to *water* a horse]. **2** to supply with water, as by sprinkling [to *water* a lawn].

wax (waks) **n.** **1** a yellow substance that bees make and use for building honeycombs; beeswax. **2** any substance like this, as paraffin. Wax is used to make candles, polishes, etc. ◆**v.** to put wax or polish on.

weak (wēk) **adj.** having little strength, force, or power; not strong or firm [*weak* from illness].

wear (wer) **v.** **1** to have or carry on the body [*Wear* your coat. Do you *wear* glasses?] **2** to have or show in the way one appears [She *wore* a frown. He *wears* his hair long.] **3** to make or become damaged, used up, etc. by use or friction [She *wore* her jeans to rags. The water is *wearing* away the river bank.] —**wore, worn, wear′ing**

weight (wāt) **n.** **1** heaviness, the quality a thing has because of the pull of gravity on it. **2** amount of heaviness [What is your *weight*?] **3** any solid mass used for its heaviness [to lift *weights* for exercise; a paper *weight*.]

we'll (wēl) **1** we shall. **2** we will.

wet (wet) **adj.** covered or soaked with water or some other liquid [Wipe it off with a *wet* rag.] —**wet′ter, wet′test**

whack (hwak) **v.** to hit or slap with a sharp sound. ◆**n.** a blow that makes a sharp sound; also, this sound.

whale (hwāl) **n.** a very large mammal that lives in the sea and looks like a fish.

wheel (hwēl) **n.** a round disk or frame that turns on an axle fixed at its center [a wagon *wheel*]. ◆**v.** to move on wheels or in a vehicle with wheels [to *wheel* a grocery cart].

where's (hwerz *or* werz) **1** where is. **2** where has.

wheth·er (hwe*th*′ər) **conj.** **1** if it is true or likely that [I don't know *whether* I can go.] **2** in either case that [It makes no difference *whether* he comes or not.]

which (hwich) **pron.** what one or what ones of those being talked about or suggested [*Which* will you choose?]

while (hwīl) **n.** a period of time [I waited a short *while*.] ◆**conj.** during the time that [I read a book *while* I waited.]

whine (hwīn *or* wīn) **v.** to make a long, high sound or cry [The injured dog *whined*.] —**whined, whin′ing**

whirl (hwurl *or* wurl) **v.** to turn rapidly around and around; spin fast [The dancers *whirled* around the room.]

whisk (hwisk) **v.** to move, brush, etc., with a quick, sweeping motion [He *whisked* the lint from his coat with a brush.] ◆**n.** **1** a small broom with a short handle, for brushing clothes: *the full name is* **whisk broom**. **2** a kitchen tool made up of wire loops fixed in a handle, for whipping eggs, etc.

whisper (hwis′pər) **v.** to speak or say in a low, soft voice, especially without vibrating the vocal cords. ◆**n.** soft, low tone of voice [to speak in a *whisper*].

who (hо̄о) **pron.** what person or persons? [*Who* helped you?]

whole (hōl) **adj.** **1** not divided or cut up; in one piece [Put *whole* carrots in the stew.] **2** having all its parts, complete [The *whole* opera is on two records.] ◆**n.** the total amount [He saved the *whole* of his allowance.] —**whole′ness n.**

wife (wīf) **n.** the woman to whom a man is married; married woman. —*pl.* **wives**

win·ner (win′ər) **n.** **1** one that wins. **2** a person who seems very likely to win or be successful: *used only in everyday talk.*

witch (wich) **n.** a person, now especially a woman, who is believed to have magic power with the help of the devil. —*pl.* **witch′es**

wives (wīvz) **n.** *plural of* **wife.**

wolf (woolf) **n.** **1** a wild animal that looks like a dog. It kills other animals for food. **2** a person who is fierce, cruel, greedy, etc. —*pl.* **wolves**

wolves (woolvz) **n.** *plural of* **wolf.**

wom·an (woom′ən) **n.** **1** an adult, female human being. **2** women as a group —*pl.* **wom′en**

wom·en (wim′ən) **n.** *plural of* **woman.**

won't (wōnt) will not.

wood·en (wood′n) **adj.** made of wood.

wool (wool) **n.** **1** the soft, curly hair of sheep or the hair of some other animals, as the goat or llama. **2** yarn, cloth, or clothing made from such hair.

wore (wôr) *past tense of* **wear.**

work·book (wurk′book) **n.** ☆a book that has questions and exercises to be worked out by students.

wor·ry (wur′ē) **v.** to be or make troubled in mind; feel or make uneasy or anxious [Don't *worry*. Her absence *worried* us.] —**wor′ried, wor′ry·ing** ◆**n.** a troubled feeling; anxiety; care [sick with *worry*]. —*pl.* **wor′ries**

would (wood) *the past tense of* **will** [He promised that he *would* return.]

would·n't (wood′nt) would not.

would've (wood′uv) would have.

wrap (rap) **v.** **1** to wind or fold around something [She *wrapped* a scarf around her head.] **2** to cover in this way [They *wrapped* the baby in a blanket.] **3** to cover with paper, etc. [to *wrap* a present]. —**wrapped** or **wrapt** (rapt), **wrap′ping** ◆**n.** an outer covering or outer garment [Put your *wraps* in the closet.]

wreck (rek) **n.** the remains of something that has been destroyed or badly damaged [an old *wreck* stranded on the reef]. ◆**v.** to destroy or damage badly; ruin [to *wreck* a car in an accident; to *wreck* one's plans for a picnic].

wren (ren) **n.** a small songbird with a long bill and a stubby tail that tilts up.

wrin·kle (riŋ′kəl) **n.** a small or uneven crease or fold [*wrinkles* in a coat]. ◆**v.** **1** to make wrinkles in [a brow that is *wrinkled* with care]. **2** to form wrinkles [This cloth *wrinkles* easily.] — **wrin′kled, wrin′kling**

wolf

a	ask, fat
ā	ape, date
ä	car, lot
e	elf, ten
ē	even, meet
i	is, hit
ī	ice, fire
ō	open, go
ô	law, horn
oi	oil, point
oo	look, pull
o͞o	ooze, tool
ou	out, crowd
u	up, cut
u	fur, fern
ə	a in ago
	e in agent
	e in father
	i in unity
	o in collect
	u in focus
ch	chin, arch
ŋ	ring, singer
sh	she, dash
th	thin, truth
th	then, father
zh	s in pleasure

write (rīt) **v.** **1** to form words, letters, etc., as with a pen or pencil. **2** to form the words, letters, etc., of [*Write* your address here.] **3** to be the author or composer of [Dickens *wrote* novels. Mozart *wrote* symphonies.] **4** to fill in or cover with writing [to *write* a check; to *write* ten pages]. **5** to send a message in writing; write a letter [*Write* me every week. He *wrote* that he was ill.]—**wrote, writ′ten, writ′ing**

writ·er (rīt′ər) **n.** a person who writes, especially one whose work is writing books, essays, articles, etc.; author.

wrong (rôŋ) **adj.** **1** not right, just, or good; unlawful, wicked, or bad [It is *wrong* to steal.] **2** not the one that is true, correct, wanted, etc. [the *wrong* answer]. **3** in error; mistaken [He's not *wrong.*] ◆**n.** something wrong; especially, a wicked or unjust act [Does she know right from *wrong*?] ◆**adv.** in a wrong way, direction, etc.; incorrectly [You did it *wrong.*] —**wrong′ly adv.** —**wrong′ness n.**

wrote (rōt) *past tense of* **write.**

year (yir) **n.** **1** a period of 365 days, or, in leap year, 366, divided into 12 months and beginning January 1. It is based on the time taken by the earth to go completely around the sun, about 365 1/4 days. **2** any period of twelve months starting at any time [She was six *years* old in July.]

yell (yel) **v.** to cry out loudly; scream. ◆**n.** **1** a loud shout. **2** a cheer by a crowd, usually in rhythm, as at a football game.

your (yoor) **pron.** of you or done by you. *This possessive form of* **you** *is used before a noun and thought of as an adjective* [*your* book; *your* work]. *See also* **yours.**

you're (yoor *or* yōōr) you are.

yours (yoorz) **pron.** the one or the ones that belong to you. *This form of* **your** *is used when it is not followed by a noun* [Is this pen *yours? Yours* cost more than ours.] *Yours is used as a polite closing of a letter, often with truly, sincerely, etc.*

you've (yōōv) you have.

Level C Student Record Chart

Name _____

		Pretest	Final Test
Lesson 1	Consonants		
Lesson 2	Consonants		
Lesson 3	Hard and Soft **c** and **g**		
Lesson 4	Short-Vowel Sounds		
Lesson 5	Long-Vowel Sounds		
Lesson 6	Instant Replay	■■■■■■	
Lesson 7	Long-Vowel Sounds		
Lesson 8	Consonant Blends		
Lesson 9	Consonant Blends		
Lesson 10	**y** as a Vowel		
Lesson 11	**y** as a Vowel		
Lesson 12	Instant Replay	■■■■■■	
Lesson 13	Vowels with **r**		
Lesson 14	Vowels with **r**		
Lesson 15	Suffixes Added to Root Words		
Lesson 16	Suffixes Added to Root Words		
Lesson 17	Suffixes Added to Root Words		
Lesson 18	Instant Replay	■■■■■■	
Lesson 19	Regular Plurals: Adding **s** or **es**		
Lesson 20	Irregular Plurals		
Lesson 21	Vowel Pairs		
Lesson 22	Double **o**		
Lesson 23	Silent Consonants		
Lesson 24	Instant Replay	■■■■■■	
Lesson 25	/ô/		
Lesson 26	/oi/ or /ou/		
Lesson 27	/sh/, /th/, or /*th*/		
Lesson 28	/ch/, /hw/, or /h/		
Lesson 29	Consonant Clusters		
Lesson 30	Instant Replay	■■■■■■	
Lesson 31	Consonant Digraphs		
Lesson 32	Prefixes **un, dis**		
Lesson 33	Prefix **re**		
Lesson 34	Contractions		
Lesson 35	Homonyms		
Lesson 36	Instant Replay	■■■■■■	

Lesson	6	12	18	24	30	36
Standardized Instant Replay Test						

158

Instant Replay Test

ANSWER KEY

Lesson 6

1.	a	11.	a
2.	b	12.	d
3.	c	13.	c
4.	d	14.	d
5.	d	15.	b
6.	a	16.	a
7.	b	17.	d
8.	c	18.	a
9.	a	19.	d
10.	c	20.	b

Lesson 12

1.	b	11.	d
2.	d	12.	a
3.	a	13.	c
4.	c	14.	a
5.	d	15.	b
6.	a	16.	c
7.	a	17.	a
8.	c	18.	b
9.	b	19.	c
10.	b	20.	d

Lesson 18

1.	d	11.	b
2.	a	12.	a
3.	a	13.	d
4.	d	14.	c
5.	a	15.	c
6.	d		
7.	c		
8.	b		
9.	c		
10.	b		

Lesson 24

1.	c	11.	b
2.	a	12.	c
3.	b	13.	b
4.	c	14.	d
5.	b	15.	d
6.	d	16.	a
7.	a	17.	c
8.	d	18.	a
9.	c	19.	b
10.	c	20.	a

Lesson 30

1.	c	11.	d
2.	b	12.	b
3.	c	13.	a
4.	a	14.	d
5.	a	15.	b
6.	d	16.	d
7.	b	17.	c
8.	b	18.	a
9.	d	19.	b
10.	c	20.	c

Lesson 36

1.	d	11.	d
2.	d	12.	c
3.	a	13.	a
4.	c	14.	b
5.	a	15.	b
6.	a	16.	d
7.	c	17.	c
8.	d	18.	a
9.	b	19.	c
10.	b	20.	b

List Words

Word	Lesson	Word	Lesson	Word	Lesson	Word	Lesson
about	26	brushes	19	crowd	26	fifth	27
across	25	bunches	19	crown	26	fight	23
acted	15	bushes	19	cutting	16	finish	27
admitted	16	buy	11	dancing	17	first	14
afternoon	22	cage	3	danger	3	fish	20
again	21	calf	23	dash	27	flaw	25
age	3	camping	15	dead	4	flexing	16
alive	7	candy	11	deer	20	float	8
allow	26	cannot	1	desks	19	floors	9
all right	25	care	13	didn't	34	flowers	9
almost	25	carry	10	disappear	32	flying	15
already	25	case	3	discover	32	foggy	16
always	10	catch	28	dishes	19	foil	26
angry	10	cattle	20	dislike	32	forest	1
any	10	caught	25	disobey	32	fork	13
anyone	11	chair	13	disorder	32	fought	23
anyway	10	chalk	25	displease	32	four	2
appear	13	chapter	28	distrust	32	fourth	27
army	11	chart	28	ditch	29	framed	17
August	25	chased	17	does	4	free	8
awful	25	cheap	21	doesn't	34	fresh	9
babies	19	check	28	don't	34	Friday	9
because	25	cheer	13	dressing	15	friends	8
before	13	chewy	28	drive	5	fright	23
beginning	16	children	20	drove	9	frowning	8
belong	25	chimney	11	dry	11	frozen	9
below	21	choice	26	dug	4	fumes	5
bench	28	choose	22	each	28	garden	13
berries	19	classes	19	eager	21	geese	20
beside	1	cleaning	15	early	14	giant	3
best	8	clear	13	earth	14	give	3
better	14	climb	3	east	7	glue	8
biggest	16	closely	17	egg	1	gobble	4
bird	1	clown	26	eight	23	gone	3
blame	5	clue	21	elephant	31	goodbye	22
blaze	9	coin	26	else	2	goodness	22
blind	8	collar	4	empty	10	goose	22
blood	22	compare	13	enjoy	26	graph	31
blouse	26	cones	19	every	11	grate	35
body	11	contain	21	everywhere	28	great	35
bottom	4	cookie	22	eye	11	grind	7
bought	25	cooler	22	faces	3	ground	2
branches	19	copying	15	fail	21	group	21
break	7	cost	25	family	10	half	23
bright	23	cough	31	farmer	14	haul	25
bring	8	couldn't	34	fast	1	haven't	34
broken	9	crawl	25	feast	21	hear	35
brook	22	crazy	7	feel	21	heavy	10
broom	22	creek	8	felt	4	hello	5

List Words

Word	Lesson
helped	15
here	35
heroes	20
he's	34
highway	23
honey	11
honor	14
hoped	17
hour	35
huge	5
human	7
hungry	10
hunters	19
hurried	15
hurt	14
ice	3
icy	17
I'd	34
I'll	34
inches	19
inside	7
into	2
isn't	34
itch	29
its	4
I've	34
jogger	16
join	26
joke	7
kept	2
kill	1
kind	9
knee	31
knew	31
knife	31
knight	23
knives	20
knock	31
knots	31
know	5
lady	10
large	13
lately	17
laugh	31
lawn	25
laws	25
learn	14
least	21
leaves	20

Word	Lesson
left	2
level	4
lie	21
life	1
light	23
lines	5
little	4
lives	20
living	17
load	7
loaves	20
long	25
loose	22
lost	25
loud	26
lovely	17
loyal	26
made	35
magic	3
maid	35
mail	5
making	17
mark	1
married	15
maybe	10
melting	9
men	20
mice	20
might	23
money	11
moonlight	23
morning	13
mostly	2
music	7
mustn't	34
needle	21
next	4
nicely	17
night	23
nine	1
noisy	17
nurse	14
once	3
only	5
order	13
our	35
oxen	20
page	7
pair	35

Word	Lesson
paper	14
pare	35
party	13
past	4
patch	29
pear	35
people	5
perhaps	2
person	1
phone	31
pick	3
pinch	28
pitch	29
places	3
plan	9
plant	8
playful	10
please	9
plenty	10
point	26
pool	22
potatoes	20
pound	26
power	26
prayed	15
pretty	10
prize	2
proud	26
puppies	19
push	27
quite	1
racing	17
rained	15
raise	5
read	7
ready	21
rebuild	33
recopy	33
redo	33
refill	33
reform	33
refresh	33
regroup	33
reload	33
remind	33
rename	33
renew	33
repay	33
replace	33

Word	Lesson
replant	33
replay	33
replied	15
rerun	33
retell	33
rethink	33
rework	33
rewrite	33
rich	28
rise	2
rock	4
roof	22
rough	31
round	26
rush	27
said	21
sail	35
sale	35
Saturday	14
school	31
scoop	22
scratch	29
scream	29
screen	29
seat	5
seen	7
setting	16
shadow	27
shape	27
shared	17
sharp	27
sheep	20
shelves	20
shine	27
shoot	22
short	27
shouldn't	34
shovel	27
shy	11
sigh	23
sight	23
sign	31
since	1
sister	1
sixth	27
size	2
slight	23
slipped	16
slumber	8

List Words

Word	Lesson	Word	Lesson	Word	Lesson	Word	Lesson
sly	11	swimmer	16	trip	9	wheel	28
smart	8	taking	17	turkey	11	whether	28
smile	8	taxes	19	twenty	11	which	28
soak	21	teacher	21	two	35	while	28
some	2	team	7	unable	32	whisk	28
sooner	21	teeth	20	unbutton	32	whisper	28
soot	22	than	27	unchanged	32	who	28
soothe	22	thanked	15	unclean	32	whole	28
speak	21	that	27	under	4	winner	16
special	9	that's	34	uneven	32	wives	20
spend	8	thaw	27	unload	32	wolves	20
spill	9	them	4	unlucky	32	women	20
splash	29	there's	34	unpaid	32	won't	34
split	29	they're	34	unseen	32	wooden	22
spray	29	thinking	27	unsure	32	wool	22
spread	29	third	14	untouched	32	wore	2
spring	29	thirteen	27	untrue	32	workbook	14
start	13	thirty	27	unwrap	32	worried	15
steel	5	thought	23	used	5	worry	14
stepping	16	thread	29	very	10	would	23
sting	8	thrills	29	wagon	3	wouldn't	34
stone	7	throat	21	wallet	25	wrap	31
stood	22	through	23	was	2	wreck	31
stopped	16	throw	29	wasn't	34	wren	31
strawberry	29	thumb	27	watches	19	writer	31
stream	29	tide	35	water	1	wrong	31
street	5	tied	35	waxed	16	wrote	31
string	29	to	35	weight	23	year	13
strong	29	too	35	we'll	34	yell	2
struck	29	town	26	wetter	16	your	35
studied	15	toys	26	whack	28	you're	35
sugar	14	track	31	whale	28	you've	34

All-Star Words

Word	Lesson	Word	Lesson	Word	Lesson	Word	Lesson
afford	14	dessert	14	humble	4	sixty	10
airport	13	destroy	26	instead	4	smoggy	16
although	23	device	5	knit	31	somewhat	28
altogether	25	dimmer	16	lack	4	sought	23
anchor	31	disrespect	32	losing	17	spare	9
anyhow	11	distaste	32	maddest	16	spicy	17
ashes	2	doubt	26	mile	1	spied	15
avoid	26	drain	5	mixes	19	spoil	26
awkward	25	drown	26	Monday	10	sprang	29
aye	11	earn	14	mood	21	spy	11
bamboo	22	easy	10	moth	25	squirm	14
behalf	23	erase	7	pack	3	stain	21
beneath	21	everybody	11	pirate	7	steady	21
bison	20	exercise	3	plane	9	stem	8
blast	8	fear	13	polishes	19	stirred	16
blew	35	flight	23	politely	17	stranger	29
blue	35	flood	22	promise	2	sweaters	19
bouquet	21	fold	5	raccoon	22	tender	4
breathe	27	forward	13	reappear	33	they'll	34
brought	25	freeze	8	reapply	33	thief	27
buffaloes	20	freight	23	reassign	33	thieves	20
businesses	19	frost	9	release	7	throne	29
butterflies	19	frying	15	reorder	33	tossed	15
canvas	1	garage	3	rewire	33	tough	31
cargo	3	gaze	2	ruler	7	treasure	9
carpet	1	gazed	17	satisfied	15	uneasy	32
cent	35	glide	8	sausage	25	unprepared	32
champion	28	glisten	3	scarves	20	unusual	32
chop	4	gloomy	22	scent	35	usually	5
churn	14	grind	2	scolding	15	weak	5
clapping	16	halves	20	scramble	29	where's	34
coach	7	harm	13	selfish	27	whine	28
country	10	hasn't	34	sent	35	whirl	28
crack	8	hatch	29	serving	17	witch	28
cricket	31	hockey	11	shirt	1	would've	34
crooked	22	holiday	10	shiver	27	wrinkle	31
darkness	13	honest	2	shoulder	27		
depend	9	how's	34	sidewalk	1		

Spelling Enrichment

Bulletin-Board Suggestion

Slices of Spelling Success   Display uncovered pizza slices made of brown construction paper for each member of the class. The names of students should appear on the slices. Using brightly colored construction paper, prepare circles, triangles, and squiggles that represent toppings for a pizza. Each time a student seeks help spelling a word, have the student use a dictionary to write the correct spelling of the word onto a shape. Then allow students to add each topping to their own slice of pizza. The slices will form personal spelling lists.

Group Practice

Fill-In   Write spelling words on the board. Omit some of the letters and replace them with dashes. Have the first student in Row One come to the board to fill in any of the missing letters in any of the words. Then have the first student in Row Two continue the procedure. Continue having students in each row take turns coming up to the board to fill in letters until all the words are completed. Any student who is able to correctly fill in a word earns a point for his or her row. The row with the most points at the end of the game wins.

Erase   Write List Words on the board. Then ask the class to put their heads down while you call on a student to come to the board and erase one of the words. This student then calls on a class member to identify the erased word. The identified word is then restored and the student who correctly identified the erasure can be the person who erases next.

Crossword Relay   First draw a large grid on the board. Then, divide the class into several teams. Teams compete against each other to form separate crossword puzzles on the board. Individuals on each team take turns racing against members of the other teams to join List Words until all possibilities have been exhausted. A List Word may appear on each crossword puzzle only once. The winning team is the team whose crossword puzzle contains the greatest number of correctly spelled List Words or the team who finishes first.

Scramble   Prepare letter cards sufficient to spell all the List Words. Distribute letter cards to all students. Some students may be given more than one letter card. The teacher then calls out a List Word. Students holding the letters contained in the word race to the front of the class to form the word by standing in the appropriate sequence with their letter cards.

Proofreading Relay   Write two columns of misspelled List Words on the board. Although the errors can differ, be sure that each list has the same number of errors. Divide the class into two teams and assign each team to a different column. Teams then compete against each other to correct their assigned lists by team members taking turns erasing and replacing an appropriate letter. Each member may correct only one letter per turn. The team that corrects its entire word list first wins.

Detective   Call on a student to be a detective. The detective must choose a spelling word from the list and think of a structural clue, definition, or synonym that will help classmates identify it. The detective then states the clue using the format, "I spy a word that . . . ." Students are called on to guess and spell the mystery word. Whoever answers correctly gets to take a turn being the detective.

Spelling Tic-Tac-Toe   Draw a tic-tac-toe square on the board. Divide the class into X and O teams. Take turns dictating spelling words to members of each team. If the word is spelled correctly, allow the team member to place an X or O on the square. The first team to place three X's or O's in a row wins.

Words of Fortune   Have students put their heads down while you write a spelling word on the board in large letters. Then cover each letter with a sheet of sturdy paper. The paper can be fastened to the board with magnets. Call on a student to guess any letter of the alphabet they think may be hidden. If that particular letter is hidden, then reveal the letter in every place where it appears in the word by removing the paper.

The student continues to guess letters until an incorrect guess is made or the word is revealed. In the event that an incorrect guess is made, a different student continues the game. Continue the game until every List Word has been hidden and then revealed.

Dictionary Activities

Around the World   Designate the first person in the first row to be the traveler. The traveler must stand next to the student seated behind him or her. Then dictate any letter of the alphabet at random. Instruct the two students to quickly name the letter of the alphabet that precedes the given letter. The student who is first to respond with the correct answer

becomes the traveler while the other student sits at that desk. The traveler then moves to compete with the next person in the row. The game continues with the traveler moving up and down the rows as the teacher dictates various alphabet letters. See who can be the traveler who has moved the farthest around the classroom. For variety, you may want to require students to state the letter that follows the given letter. You may also want to dictate pairs of List Words and have students name which word comes first.

Stand-Up   While the teacher pronounces a word from the spelling dictionary, students look up the entry word and point to it. Tell students to stand up when they have located the entry. See who is the first student to stand up.

This game can be played using the following variations:

1. Have students stand when they have located the guide words for a given word.

2. Have students stand when they are able to tell on what page a given List Word appears in the dictionary.

Guide Word Scramble   Prepare tagboard cards with spelling words written on them in large letters. Distribute the cards to students. Call on two students to come to the front of the room to serve as guide words. Then call one student at a time to hold their word card either in front of, in between, or behind the guide words so that the three words are in alphabetical order. You may want to vary the guide words occasionally.

Cut-Off   Distribute a strip of paper to each student. Instruct students to write any four spelling words on the strip. All but one of the words should be in alphabetical order. Then have students exchange their strip with a partner. Students use scissors to cut off the word that is not in alphabetical sequence and tape the remaining word strips together. If students find this activity too difficult, you might have them cut all four words off the strip and arrange them alphabetically on their desks.

Applied Spelling

Journal   Allow time each day for students to write in a journal. A spiral bound notebook can be used for this purpose. Encourage students to express their feelings about events that are happening in their lives at home or at school. Or they could write about what their plans are for the day. To get them started, you may have to

provide starter phrases. Allow them to use "invented" spelling for words they can't spell.

Collect the journals periodically to write comments that echo what the student has written. For example, a student's entry might read, "I'm hape I gt to plae bazball todae" The teacher's response could be "Baseball is my favorite game, too. I'd be happy to watch you play baseball today at recess." This method allows students to learn correct spelling and sentence structure without emphasizing their errors in a negative way.

Letter to the Teacher   On a regular basis, invite students to write a note to you. At first you may have to suggest topics or provide a starter sentence. It may be possible to suggest a topic that includes words from the spelling list. Write a response at the bottom of each letter that provides the student with a model of any spelling or sentence structure that apparently needs improvement.

Daily Edit   Each day, provide a brief writing sample on the board that contains errors in spelling, capitalization, or punctuation. Have students rewrite the sample correctly. Provide time later in the day to have the class correct the errors on the board. Discuss why the spelling is as it is while students self-correct their work.

Acrostic Poems   Have students write a word from the spelling list vertically. Then instruct them to join a word horizontally to each letter of the List Word. The horizontal words must begin with the letters in the List Word. They also should be words that describe or relate feelings about the List Word. Encourage students to refer to a dictionary for help in finding appropriate words. Here is a sample acrostic poem:

Zebras
Otters
Ostriches

Words-in-a-Row   Distribute strips of writing paper to each student. Ask students to write three spelling words in a row. Tell them to misspell two of the words. Then have students take turns writing their row of words on the board. They can call on a classmate to identify and underline the correctly spelled word in the row. Continue until all students have had a chance to write their row of words.

Spelling Enrichment

Partner Spelling Assign spelling buddies. Allow partners to alternate dictating or writing sentences that contain words from the spelling list. The sentences can be provided by the teacher or generated by students. Have students check their own work as their partner provides the correct spelling for each sentence.

Scrap Words Provide each student with several sheets of tagboard, scraps of fabric or wallpaper, and some glue. Ask students to cut letters out of the scrap materials and glue them to the tagboard to form words from the spelling list. Display the colorful scrap words around the classroom.

Punch Words Set up a work center in the classroom with a supply of construction paper strips, a hole puncher, sheets of thin paper, and crayons. Demonstrate to students how the hole puncher can be used to create spelling words out of the construction paper. Permit students to take turns working at the center in their free time. Students may also enjoy placing a thin sheet of paper over the punch words and rubbing them with a crayon to make colorful word designs. You can then display their punch word and crayon creations.

Word Cut-Outs Distribute scissors, glue, a sheet of dark-colored construction paper, and a supply of old newspapers and magazines to the class. Have students look through the papers and magazines for List Words. Tell them to cut out any List Words they find and glue them on the sheet of construction paper. See who can find the most List Words. This technique may also be used to have students construct sentences or cut out individual letters to form words.

Word Sorts Invite students to write each List Word on a separate card. Then ask them how many different ways the words can be organized (e.g., animate vs. inanimate, past-tense or vowel patterns, similarity or contrast in meaning). As students sort the words into each category, have them put words that don't belong in a category into an exception pile.

Word Locker

Definitions and Rules

The alphabet has two kinds of letters. The **vowels** are **a, e, i, o,** and **u** (and sometimes **y** and **w**). All the rest of the letters are **consonants.**

Each **syllable** in a word must have a vowel sound. If a word or syllable has only one vowel and it comes at the beginning or between two consonants, the vowel usually stands for a **short** sound.

cat sit cup

A **long-vowel** sound usually has the same sound as its letter name.

When **y** comes at the end of a word with one syllable, the **y** at the end spells /ī/, as in dry and try. When **y** comes at the end of a word with more than one syllable, it usually has the sound of /ē/, as in city and funny.

When two or more **consonants** come together in a word, their sounds may blend together. In a **consonant blend,** you can hear the sound of each letter.

smile slide friend

A **consonant digraph** consists of two consonants that go together to make one sound.

sharp fourth each

A **consonant cluster** is three consonants together in one syllable.

thrills patch splash

A **suffix** is an addition made at the **end** of a **root word.**

rained helped

A **prefix** is a word part that is added to the beginning of another word called a **root word.** A prefix changes the meaning of the root.

unhappy distrust

When you write words in **alphabetical order,** use these rules:

1. If the <u>first letter</u> of two words is the same, use the second letter.

2. If the <u>first two letters</u> are the same, use the third letter.

There are two **guide words** at the top of each page in the dictionary. The word on the left tells you the first word on the page. The word on the right tells you the last word on the page. All the words in between are in **alphabetical order.**

The dictionary puts an **accent mark** (´) after the syllable with the strong sound.

per´son

There is a vowel sound that can be spelled by any of the vowels. It is often found in a syllable that is *not accented,* or stressed, in a word. This vowel sound has the sound-symbol /ə/. It is called the **schwa.**

The word <u>I</u> is always a **capital** letter.

A **contraction** is a short way of writing two words. It is formed by writing two words together and leaving out one or more letters. Use an **apostrophe** (') to show where something is left out.

it is = it's we will = we'll

A **compound word** is a word made by joining two or more words.

cannot anyway maybe